TANGLED UP IN TEXT

TEFILLIN AND THE ANCIENT WORLD

Yehudah B. Cohn

Brown Judaic Studies
Providence, Rhode Island

Library of Congress Cataloging-in-Publication Data

Cohn, Yehudah, 1951-
   Tangled up in text : tefillin and the ancient world / by Yehudah B. Cohn.
      p. cm. — (Brown Judaic studies ; no. 351)
   Includes bibliographical references and indexes.
   ISBN 978-1-930675-56-8 (cloth binding : alk. paper)
   1. Tefillin—History. I. Title. II. Series.

BM657.P5C64 2008
296.4′612—dc22

2008039485

Printed in the United States of America
on acid-free paper

Contents

Preface

Hearing the topic of my research, a professor at Jerusalem's Hebrew University encouraged me by remarking that while many people "do" *tefillin*, no one thinks about them. He was exaggerating for effect, and the remark has stayed with me. I hope it will be clear to the reader that I have thought about *tefillin* a great deal.

The people I spoke to about this project are too numerous to mention, and I am grateful to all for their input, friends and scholars alike (and many who are both), and to Stephanie—who has been my muse. I particularly enjoyed the libraries where I worked, which I salute in appreciation for the resources and companionship they provided.

Professor Martin Goodman of Oxford University merits special acknowledgment for his influence, encouragement, and gentle interventions. My thanks go to the two readers for Brown University, and to my editor, Professor Michael Satlow, whose astute suggestions have made all the difference. I am also grateful to Paul Kobelski, whose skillful copyediting has contributed to a much improved final product.

I dedicate this book to the memories of my father, Leo Cohn, who sparked my interest in academic Jewish studies, and my mother, Ruth Cohn.

September 2008/Elul 5768

Abbreviations

Abbreviations used for references to rabbinic literature:

B.   Talmud Bavli (pagination of Vilna ed., 1880–86).

E-M   *Mekhilta Derabbi Shimon bar Yohai,* Epstein-Melamed edition. Jerusalem: Meqitse Nirdamim, 1955.

F   *Sifre Deuteronomy,* Finkelstein edition. New York: Jewish Theological Seminary, 1969.

H-R   *Mekhilta Derabbi Yishma'el,* Horovitz-Rabin edition. Jerusalem: Bamberger and Wahrman, 1960.

M.   Mishnah.

T.   Tosefta (numbering of Lieberman ed. where available, New York and Jerusalem: Jewish Theological Seminary, 1992–95; otherwise of Zuckermandel ed., Jerusalem: Wahrmann, 1970).

Y.   Talmud Yerushalmi (pagination of Venice ed., *editio princeps,* Venice, 1523, as well as standard Halakah numbering).

1

Introduction

The Topic

The Hebrew/Aramaic word *tefillin* designates a pair of small leather cases, whose parchment contents are inscribed, according to rabbinic convention, with four passages from the Torah (Exod 13:1–10; 13:11–16; Deut 6:4–9; 11:13–21). Each passage includes one verse that has traditionally been understood by Jews as exhorting adherence to the practice of wearing one of these cases strapped to the head and the other to the left arm.[1] While arm *tefillin* and head *tefillin* contain identical passages, the former include the entire text on a single parchment roll, whereas the latter hold four separate pieces of parchment (in discrete compartments inside their case). Modern-day practitioners wear *tefillin* for weekday morning prayers,[2] but not on Shabbat or festivals. Women (almost without exception) do not wear them; nor do young children. *Tefillin* are associated with Bar-Mitzvah rites of passage, and the first time that a boy puts them on is frequently a celebrated occasion—particularly in contemporary Israel. The present-day Chabad-Lubavitch movement actively campaigns for Jewish men and boys to don them, at stations set up for the purpose in public places. Its Hasidim are known to associate correct *tefillin* practice with healing, as well as relief from other misfortunes, while linking defective *tefillin* practice to a risk of illness or other distress.[3] The word *phylakterion*, literally, "means of protection," has given rise to a term for *tefillin* in modern European languages—in English: phylacteries—but it seems fair to say that its use is generally divorced from the original Greek meaning.

---

1. Or the right arm for left-handers.
2. On the ninth of *Ab* fast day they are, instead, worn for afternoon prayers.
3. Simon Dein, *Religion and Healing among the Lubavitch Community in Stamford Hill, North London* (Lewiston: Edwin Mellen, 2004), 90, 92, 130, 46, 91.

This book will investigate the evolution of the practice, focusing on the roughly six-hundred-year period that begins with Alexander the Great's conquest of the Near East and ends in the third century c.e. In order to set the stage, the above-mentioned biblical verses will also be discussed, together with the early history of their reception. An attempt will be made to locate *tefillin* practice within a cultural matrix that included the reception of canonized Scripture, other aspects of Second Temple Judaism and rabbinic Judaism, and the Jewish interaction with the wider world in which the practice took place. The book investigates how *tefillin* practice came into being, how it developed, and why it developed in that way, and explores what the practice meant.

I will argue that

- There were several ways in which the biblical verses traditionally taken to refer to *tefillin* might have been apprehended, so that the singular form taken by the practice is worthy of exploration.
- Prior to the Hellenistic period, it is unlikely that these verses were understood as referring to a ritual practice.
- *Tefillin* were an "invented tradition" of the late–Second Temple era, initially informed by knowledge of parallel Greek practices, and functioning as a popular amulet for achieving length of days.
- The word *tefillin* originally described the function of the amulet that it signified, as a prayer for long life, much as the Greek word *phylakterion* described a protective function of the amulet it signified.
- The practice was widespread by the tanna'itic era; those who wore *tefillin* did so throughout the day, and women may have had alternative practices.
- The magical function of *tefillin* remained significant, explaining aspects of attendant halakah; *tefillin* were particularly associated with circumstances in which the related practice of *mezuzah* did not provide adequate protection.
- The magic of both these ritual objects came to revolve around the names of God that they contained, thus providing a bridge to other Jewish amuletic practices of late antiquity.

Although all sources of evidence will be considered, the main thrust of this book will be to explore the reception history of the biblical verses taken to refer to *tefillin*, to evaluate the evidence of the Dead Sea Scrolls for the early nature of the practice, and to analyze tanna'itic literature on the subject. No such detailed study, which builds on the evidence of the Dead Sea texts, has been made on the above questions since these discoveries were made.

Prior Scholarship—Its Concerns and Limitations

The Early Stratum of Critical Scholarship
(mid-nineteenth to mid-twentieth century)

Prior to the discovery of the Dead Sea Scrolls in the twentieth century, there was little evidence outside rabbinic literature for *tefillin* practice. The earliest critical treatment to include detailed consideration of this literature was written by the *maskil* Y. H. Schorr, whose interest was to enlighten his traditionally educated coreligionists as to the true historical import of the *tefillin* obligation.[4] In a fiercely polemical style, Schorr sought to demonstrate that the Torah had not commanded the practice, which had originated in the Second Temple period and, for long after, had few adherents beyond the most pious.[5] In his view the ritual was initiated by the Essenes, whose extreme pietistic practices included external symbols such as *tefillin, mezuzah,* and *tsitsit.* According to Schorr, the Pharisees came to embrace such practices, which became associated with Mosaic law, and in ensuing generations rabbis (particularly those in Babylonia) managed to institute *tefillin* performance throughout the Jewish world.

While Schorr's views on Essene origins seem little more than speculation, he exhibited enormous erudition with respect to the rabbinic material. Of particular relevance here is his claim that the practice of *tefillin* had initially been limited to the extremely devout. Schorr's evidence for this position was largely culled from relatively late amora'ic works, and was anyway inconclusive.

Michael Rodkinson, whose work was similarly a product of the *Haskalah* milieu, took issue with Schorr on several fronts.[6] An important distinction between the two scholars, for the period covered by this book, is Rodkinson's contention that R. Yohanan ben Zakkai and his followers initiated the *tefillin* practice known from rabbinic literature after the destruction of the Temple. This position has been decisively overturned by archaeological discoveries, which will be discussed in detail in chapter 3. Rodkinson also asserted that the biblical *totafot* referred to an earlier

---

4. Y. H. Schorr, "Tefillin," *Hehaluts* 5 (1860, in Hebrew). *Maskil* is a description accorded to the personalities of the Jewish enlightenment (*haskalah*) of the eighteenth and nineteenth centuries; see Azriel Shochat, "Haskalah," in *Encyclopaedia Judaica* (Jerusalem: Keter, 1972).

5. For Schorr's polemical tendencies, see D. Halivni, "Reflections on Classical Jewish Hermeneutics," *Proceedings of the American Academy for Jewish Research* 62 (1996): 51 n. 47.

6. Michael L. Rodkinson, *Tefillah Lemosheh* (Pressburg, 1883, in Hebrew); Michael L. Rodkinson, *History of Amulets, Charms and Talismans* (New York, 1893). The English booklet was designed to revise and abridge the earlier work, in part by omitting polemical material. See Rodkinson, *History of Amulets,* vii.

custom, which *tefillin* superseded.[7] According to this conception *tefillin* are to be *contrasted* with *totafot*.[8] In general, as Jacob Mann observed, Rodkinson's work "suffers from lack of method and historical judgement,"[9] and his ideas had little influence. In particular, succeeding scholars largely ignored the focus he introduced on an amuletic nature to the ritual.

Another *Haskalah* writer to deal with *tefillin* was Abraham Krochmal, who agreed with Schorr's claim that the ritual had been initiated by pietists in the late–Second Temple era, although he did not associate these with the Essenes. Krochmal argued for *tefillin* as an external symbol, which had been instituted with the common folk in mind. *Tefillin*-wearing, albeit limited to an elite, was designed to influence its *viewers* against the attractions of Hellenism and reinforce in their place the importance of embracing God and the eternal life that awaited those who did. The word *tefillin*, according to Krochmal, derived from *theophilos*, because those who wore them were identified as God's beloved.[10] No other scholars have embraced his ideas.

In his classic work on ancient Jewish magic, Ludwig Blau noted that amulets and *tefillin* were frequently mentioned in the same context in rabbinic sources because they were similar in form, and accordingly subject to similar rules.[11] In a subsequent article, Blau started out by arguing that since the word phylacteries was not used in truly Jewish circles, no historical conclusions regarding the function of *tefillin* could be drawn from their earliest depiction as such protective objects, in the Gospel of Matthew.[12] Blau saw *tefillin* as having evolved naturally from biblical verses that commanded the practice, which had taken hold at the latest by the third century B.C.E. While these verses may *reflect* an ancient notion that objects worn in similar fashion were considered protective, and a physical correspondence between *tefillin* and amulets persisted—". . . yet there is not a single passage in the old literature to show that they were identified with magic. Their power of protecting is similar to that of the Torah and the Commandments. . . ."[13] Blau asserted that the practice was reasonably popular by the rabbinic era, although not observed in the Diaspora outside Babylon. He further observed that *tefillin* would have been worn throughout the day, and that their customary restriction to prayer time was a rela-

---

7. See chapter 2 for the biblical verses where this word appears, and their connection to *tefillin*.

8. Rodkinson, *Tefillah Lemosheh*, 7–39.

9. Jacob Mann, "Changes in the Divine Service of the Synagogue Due to Religious Persecutions," *Hebrew Union College Annual* 4 (1927): 289 n. 96a.

10. Abraham Krochmal, *Iyyun Tefillah* (Lemberg, 1885, in Hebrew), 25–26.

11. Ludwig Blau, *Das altjüdische Zauberwesen* (Budapest, 1898), 87–88.

12. Ludwig Blau, "Phylacteries—Historical View," in *The Jewish Encyclopedia* (New York and London: Funk & Wagnalls, 1905), 10: 26–28.

13. Ibid., 27.

tively late innovation. Blau's article, in marked contrast to Schorr's, was uncritical in its understanding of rabbinic sources.[14]

In the view of Emil Schürer, the great turn of the century Christian scholar of Jewish history, *tefillin* and *mezuzah* were external reminders of duties to God, as probably intended by Deuteronomy 6 and 11 (alongside *tsitsit*, in Numbers 15 and Deuteronomy 22).[15] All male Israelites faithful to the law would have observed these practices, although many of the detailed rabbinic rules for their observance were to be associated with what Schürer viewed as degenerate *Spätjudentum*. The word *tefillin* was rabbinic Hebrew, derived from the word *tefillah* (prayer), and practitioners would have worn them for morning prayers, except on Shabbat and festivals. Unlike Blau, Schürer ascribed significance to the word *phylakterion*. The Greek designation demonstrated that in the first instance *tefillin* were seen as keeping away evil spirits during prayer (while *mezuzah* would have been used to deny them entry to the home); Schürer pointed to the known use of biblical texts to ward off such spirits in early Christian circles.

The idea that the Greek usage reflected some magical element in *tefillin* practice has been neglected by virtually all scholars of Judaism apart from Schürer, with many others not even bothering to contest it, as Blau had done. Moses Gaster addressed the issue in passing, citing the second-century C.E. figure Justin Martyr, who viewed the *phylakteria* as commanded to Jews by God, as evidence that *tefillin* were not yet viewed as amulets by his time—an assertion that seems contradicted by Justin himself.[16]

While Krochmal had been the first to speculate that some practitioners might have included the Decalogue as a *tefillin* text (contrary to later prescriptions),[17] the idea was developed by Mann, who also embraced the view that *tefillin* had originally been associated with prayer service.[18] The symbolism of *tefillin* was "meant primarily to emphasize the acceptance of the yoke of the kingdom of heaven," just like the rabbinic conception of the first paragraph of the *Shema* prayer[19]—itself found in *tefillin* parchments. In Mann's view, the Decalogue was dropped from *tefillin* at the same time as it was eliminated from the morning prayer service, leaving

---

14. See Mann, "Changes in the Divine Service of the Synagogue," 289 n.96a.

15. Emil Schürer, *Geschichte des jüdischen Volkes im Zeitalter Jesu Christi*, 4th ed. (Leipzig, 1901–1909), 2:566–69. The previous edition had been published in 1886–1890, and cited by Blau. Its discussion of *tefillin* was in large measure identical to the fourth edition's.

16. Moses Gaster, "Charms and Amulets (Jewish)," in *Encyclopaedia of Religion and Ethics*, ed. James Hastings (Edinburgh: T. & T. Clark, 1908), 454. Justin's reference to *tefillin* will be discussed in chapter 4.

17. Krochmal, *Iyyun Tefillah*, 35.

18. Mann, "Changes in the Divine Service of the Synagogue."

19. Ibid., 297. For the rabbinic idea as to the significance of reciting this paragraph (Deut 6:4–9), see, for example, *M. Berakhot* 2:2.

the *Shema* as the centerpiece of both. Only later did the rabbis and their disciples take on a custom of wearing *tefillin* for the entire day. Mann notes the inconvenience this would have entailed, and wonders whether ordinary people would even have worn them for prayer, whether in Palestine or Babylonia. The Palestinian rabbis' piety, in wearing them throughout the day, would also have constituted a political demonstration against the yoke of Roman rule, which was to be contrasted with the "kingdom of heaven." Mann connected this idea to rabbinic reports of Roman suppression of *tefillin* practice and the consequent decline in observance of the ritual. By the first half of the third century, Jews (excluding the most devout) would have been *discouraged* by their leaders from wearing them at any time except for prayer service. Both Schürer and Mann thus imagined a link between *tefillin* and prayer service (*tefillah*), with the word related to a practice of wearing such objects while at prayer. The lexicographer Jacob Levy had earlier denied that derivation, on the grounds that *tefillin* had originally been worn throughout the day, but did not suggest an alternative.[20]

The Strack-Billerbeck excursus on *tefillin*, a detailed study of the rabbinic material on the subject, was published in 1928 (six years after Strack's death).[21] It was part of their *Kommentar zum neuen Testament*, whose interest was to illuminate the New Testament by consideration of Talmud and Midrash. Although there is only one NT verse that mentions *phylakteria*— Matthew 23:5—the article on *tefillin* characteristically cited an enormous range of rabbinic sources, largely in full translation. The approach to the entire body of rabbinic literature was essentially synchronic, although dates were provided for the individual rabbis mentioned. Rabbinic dicta were principally taken at face value, and the rabbis were viewed as later Pharisees.

Strack-Billerbeck's study began with brief discussions of the words *phylakteria*, *tefillin*, and *totafot*, and of the antiquity of the practice. The ensuing sections presented the rabbinic evidence for the physical makeup of *tefillin*, how and when they were worn, and who would have worn them. The presentation was more systematic than anything previously undertaken on the subject, but to the extent that the argument was innovative it was also extremely questionable. Thus Strack-Billerbeck not only claimed, along lines similar to earlier scholars, that the ordinary people had not worn *tefillin*, but also that *tefillin* had been a Pharisaic privilege.[22] This, of course, would have implied that Jesus, as well as his followers and

---

20. Jacob Levy, *Chaldäisches Wörterbuch* (Leipzig, 1881), 551.
21. Hermann L. Strack and Paul Billerbeck, "Die Tephillin (Gebetsriemen)," in *Kommentar zum neuen Testament aus Talmud und Midrasch*, vol. 4, part 1 (Munich: C. H. Beck'sche, 1928), 250–76.
22. Ibid., 264.

the common folk that he encountered, had not worn *tefillin*, and is likely to have been of particular interest to readers of the work.[23]

The study ended with a section on the meaning of *tefillin*, and the manifold blessings/rewards received for wearing them, largely adduced from sources that are amorai'c or even later.[24] According to Strack-Billerbeck *tefillin* were performed in observance of biblical verses, and their meaning to practitioners rested on the idea that in observing these one would be considered appropriately mindful of the Torah, or would symbolically show one's readiness to be subject to God's rule. In addition, however, those who observed the commandment of *tefillin* would have seen themselves as receiving an earthly reward for doing so. Several of the "blessings" adduced by Strack-Billerbeck as rewards for *tefillin* practice are protective in nature, including the attainment of long life, and defense against demons.

It is noteworthy that there is no explicit mention of a reward in any of the sources cited. Strack-Billerbeck's understanding of these features of the practice, as being rewards for its fulfillment, was naturally colored by overarching views on the religious ideas of those believed to have worn *tefillin* (and such belief may itself have been colored by the idea that Jesus could not have done so). While a critique of the *Kommentar* is far beyond the scope of this book, it has been provided by Sanders, who has observed that the entire work is selective in its use of rabbinic material and perverse in its understanding of Judaism as a religion of "legalistic works-righteousness."[25]

Two psychoanalytic studies of *tefillin* appeared in 1930 in *Imago,* a journal published by Sigmund Freud.[26] One was by Theodor Reik,[27] who argued that *tefillin* had its origins as a "substitute for those portions of

---

23. Cf. the explicit statement that Jesus would not have worn *tefillin* in A. R. S. Kennedy, "Phylacteries," in *A Dictionary of the Bible*, ed. James Hastings (New York/Edinburgh: Charles Scribner's Sons/T. & T. Clark, 1903), 873.

24. Strack and Billerbeck, "Die Tephillin," 273–76.

25. E. P. Sanders, *Paul and Palestinian Judaism* (Philadelphia: Fortress, 1977), 42, 58–59, 234–35. (In addition, however, see two reviews of Sanders's work, with respect to his somewhat problematic approach to legalism: P. S. Alexander, "Review of: *Jesus and Judaism*, by E. P. Sanders," *Journal of Jewish Studies* 37 [1986]; Jacob Neusner, "Mr Sanders' Pharisees and Mine: A Response to E. P. Sanders, *Jewish Law from Jesus to the Mishnah*," *Scottish Journal of Theology* [1991].) Geza Vermes, with particular reference to the *tefillin* article in the Strack-Billerbeck *Kommentar*, described it as especially misleading. See Vermes, "Pre-Mishnaic Jewish Worship and the Phylacteries from the Dead Sea," *Vetus Testamentum* 9 (1959): 65 n. 2.

26. My thanks to the artist David Moss, whose work is based on Jewish ritual, for bringing these little-known studies to my attention.

27. Theodor Reik, "Gebetmantel und Gebetriemen der Juden," *Imago* 16, nos. 3–4 (1930): 389–434. The article was reprinted in English translation as "Prayer Shawls and Phylacteries," in *Pagan Rites in Judaism*, ed. Theodor Reik (New York: Farrar, Straus, 1964).

the totemic pelt the ancient Israelites wore in order to identify themselves with their totemic god."[28] At a later time, and mediated by intervening changes from Israelite totemism to the worship of YHWH, *tefillin* ultimately "assumed the indifferent character of religious amulets."[29] Although it cannot of course be disproven, Reik's claim for the existence of a prior ritual was speculative, and the process of its transformation into *tefillin* was not worked out. In particular, some of the evidence asserted for continuity with an earlier practice now seems highly dubious. Thus, for example, significance was accorded to *tefillin* resembling animal horns when worn,[30] but the tiny flattish *tefillin* cases found in the Judean Desert—the earliest ones known—can hardly be said to have done that.[31]

The same issue of *Imago* saw an article on *tefillin* by Georg Langer,[32] who had previously published one on *mezuzah*.[33] Here he began by remarking, in the first footnote, that the article was to form a chapter of a larger work on "Phallic Rudiments in Jewish Rites." The piece on *tefillin* developed along similarly psychoanalytic lines, based initially on modes of wearing *tefillin* and their physical form. Langer then proceeded to buttress his position by mining a vast range of rabbinic, kabbalistic, and other sources for any possible association of *tefillin* with sexual symbolism. Subsequent Judean Desert discoveries, together with a focus on the early stratum of rabbinic literature, cast serious doubt on his ideas as to initial development. Langer did not pay attention to the contents of *tefillin*, preferring to restrict his analysis of the objects to their outer form and how they were worn. Consideration of archaeological data (which was of course not available to Langer or Reik) allows for far simpler explanations of the origins of the practice, as will be demonstrated. It is beyond my scope to investigate whether subsequent development into the Middle Ages can be well explained by reference to psychoanalytic concepts, as suggested by Langer's work.

More frequently cited than these articles is one published by A. M. Habermann some twenty-five years later.[34] He was already aware, from Israeli press reports, of the discovery of the Decalogue in as-yet-unpublished Judean Desert *tefillin*, and suggested an early set of *tefillin* contents

28. "Prayer Shawls and Phylacteries," 145.

29. Ibid.

30. Ibid., 144, 48, 50, 52.

31. See chapter 3 below.

32. Georg Langer, "Die jüdischen Gebetriemen (Phylakterien)," *Imago* 16, nos. 3–4 (1930): 435–85.

33. Georg Langer, "Zur Funktion der jüdischen Türpfostenrolle," *Imago* 14 (1928): 457–68.

34. A. M. Habermann, "The Phylacteries in Antiquity," *Eretz Israel* 3 (1954): 174–77 (in Hebrew).

that had preceded the one known from rabbinic literature. His idea, based on the presumed absence of Exodus verses from early *tefillin*, was not borne out by the publication of the findings themselves. So too with his claim that *tefillin* cases were a relatively late innovation and that parchments had earlier been tied directly to the body. Haberman took some references to *tefillin* by Jerome (fourth/early fifth century) as evidence for the earliest form of *tefillin* practice, and here his methodology is problematic. Similarly, he cited Geonic and other late sources as evidence for a general absence of *tefillin* observance, other than among the most pious.

The Publication of the Dead Sea Scrolls, and Subsequent Scholarship

The Judean Desert discoveries (some found *in situ* and others purchased) provided archaeological evidence of *tefillin* practice, where previously available ancient evidence had been entirely literary. There were preliminary publications of Judean Desert *tefillin* findings from Murabba'at in 1953,[35] and of others from Qumran Cave 4 in 1957,[36] both of which were superseded by fuller treatments in the series entitled Discoveries in the Judaean Desert. The latter had a *tefillin* publication (from Qumran Cave 1) in its first volume, published in 1955,[37] but the series did not provide much analysis of *tefillin*, other than of a textual nature, until DJD 6 (in 1977). It was in that volume that Josef Milik published the vast majority of the Dead Sea *tefillin*.[38]

Scholars had already begun to grapple with the implications of these finds in the 1950s. K. G. Kuhn, in his 1957 publication, had devoted a section to comparing the known Qumran *tefillin* to "rabbinic-orthodox rules."[39] In particular he noted the expanded text of Qumran *tefillin*, when compared to rabbinic ones. Although subsequent finds invalidate some of the textual limits that he hypothesized, his idea that the larger passages were considered the context for certain verses that they contained is an important one, and will be revisited in chapter 3. Kuhn also suggested that the Nash Papy-

---

35. R. De Vaux, "Quelques textes hébreux de Murabba'at: une pièce du phylactère," *Revue Biblique* 60 (1953).

36. K. G. Kuhn, *Phylakterien aus Höhle 4 von Qumran* (Heidelberg: Abhandlungen der heidelberger Akademie der Wissenschaften, Phil.-Hist. Klasse 1, 1957).

37. D. Barthélemy, "Textes bibliques, Phylactère," in *Discoveries in the Judaean Desert*, vol. 1 (Oxford: Oxford University Press, 1955).

38. J. T. Milik, "Tefillin, Mezuzot et Targums," in *Discoveries in the Judaean Desert* (Oxford: Oxford University Press, 1977). 6:33–85.

39. Kuhn, *Phylakterien aus Höhle 4 von Qumran*, 24–31.

rus from Egypt, initially published in 1903,[40] was likely to have been a *tefillin* or *mezuzah* text, basing his judgment on the similarity of its contents to the Qumran *tefillin* (as well as its traces of original folds). He further noted that comparisons *within* the Qumran *tefillin* corpus might be taken to imply that *tefillin* contents had simply not yet been fixed by the first century c.e., although he found this unlikely. Finally, he contrasted the Qumran *tefillin* with the Murabba'at *tefillin*, and correlated the latter with the dominance of rabbinic regulation in the late first century. Kuhn also paid attention to how the fragments were folded and the order of the texts they contained. Kuhn's work, which paid attention to how the fragments were folded and the order of the texts they contained, was remarkably thorough, although subsequent Qumran publications have inevitably rendered it outdated.

In a 1959 article, Geza Vermes investigated whether *tefillin* with the textual contents exhibited at Qumran were likely to have reflected unexceptional pre-Mishnaic practices, rather than have been limited to the Qumran community.[41] He connected the occurrence of the Decalogue in Qumran *tefillin* to rabbinic reports of its presence in early Jewish liturgy, and argued that these *tefillin* findings confirmed Mann's above-mentioned ideas on the common presence of the Decalogue in early *tefillin*.

Yigael Yadin, the Israeli archaeologist, general, and politician, purchased a set of *tefillin* parchments that were still inside a case, shortly after the Six-day War, and published these in 1969.[42] Prior to this time little attention had been paid to *tefillin* cases, perhaps because none of the fragments published had been found inside one. Yadin dealt with the construction of the case, and also paid particular interest to the order of texts and the way parchments had been folded, as well as to the types of material used for both case and parchment. His exhaustive work was devoted in large measure to harmonizing the find with later rabbinic literature in considerable detail, and in the process he accentuated similarities and minimized differences.

The sixth volume of the DJD series, mentioned above, largely consisted of Milik's editions of *tefillin* and *mezuzot*, and almost completed the publication of the Judean Desert *tefillin* (there has been only one publication since, and Milik had already cited the *tefillin* concerned[43]). As had been the case in earlier DJD publications, the major focus was on the contained

---

40. Stanley A. Cook, "A Pre-Masoretic Biblical Papyrus," *Proceedings of the Society of Biblical Archaeology* 25 (1903): 134–56.

41. Vermes, "Pre-Mishnaic Jewish Worship."

42. Yigael Yadin, "Tefillin (Phylacteries) from Qumran (XQPhyl 1–4)," *Eretz Israel* 9 (1969): 60–83 (in Hebrew). The article was subsequently reprinted as a book, and included an English translation (which is not entirely reliable); see Yigael Yadin, *Tefillin from Qumran (XQPhyl 1–4)* (Jerusalem: Israel Exploration Society and Shrine of the Book, 1970).

43. Although these were not formally published until 2000, Milik had first discussed

texts as witnesses for biblical verses, and their orthography and morphology. In his introduction, however, Milik provided a synthetic treatment of the texts of the finds, which included the range of verses from which these were drawn.[44] He observed that there had been no apparent requirement to include this entire range, that complete passages might be omitted, and that the distribution of verses/passages could be capricious. In addition, he pointed to the considerable recensional variety exhibited. He did, however, see a move toward standardization, which had already begun prior to the first Jewish revolt against the Romans.

This section was followed by a short note on the origins and propagation of *tefillin* and *mezuzah*.[45] Observing that the earliest finds were not to be dated prior to the second century B.C.E., and the absence of *tefillin* among Samaritans (who had earlier split off from other Jews), Milik concluded that a custom of wearing *tefillin* during prayer originated during the Maccabean epoch, as one of many manifestations of national, religious, and literary renaissance. As such, this custom had eventually spread to the Diaspora. Even though the authorities in Jerusalem had probably fixed the rough limits of the contained text sections, the practice seems to have remained private and "semi-sacred," which would explain the considerable internal variety. Milik referred to some of the *tefillin* as Essene-type, but noted that he did so for convenience. He seems to have done this merely to distinguish them from other exemplars that resembled rabbinic (or in his view Pharisaic) *tefillin* more closely, and not to make a genetic claim.[46]

A detailed and valuable encyclopedia entry on *tefillin* was published in 1982, by Jeffrey Tigay.[47] While its author is perhaps best known as a scholar of the Hebrew Bible, he had previously written an article to justify the identity of the Matthean *phylakteria* with *tefillin*,[48] published two others related to the larger topic,[49] and demonstrated considerable familiarity with rabbinic sources. Rejecting the association of the word *tefillin* with prayer, and doubtful of a claim by E. A. Speiser that the word

---

them in 1956. See J. T. Milik, "Le travail d'édition des manuscrits du désert de Juda," *Supplements to Vetus Testamentum* 4 (1956): 20.

44. Milik, "Tefillin, Mezuzot et Targums," 38–46.

45. Ibid., 46–47.

46. Some subsequent scholarship has interpreted his nomenclature more literally. See the work of Jacqueline Genot-Bismuth and of David Nakman, to be discussed below.

47. Jeffrey H. Tigay, "Tefillin," in *Encyclopaedia Biblica* (Jerusalem: Mosad Bi'alik, 1982), 8: 883–95 (in Hebrew).

48. Jeffrey H. Tigay, "On the Term Phylacteries (Matt 23:5)," *Harvard Theological Review* 72, nos. 1–2 (1979): 45–53.

49. Marvin H. Pope and Jeffrey H. Tigay, "A Description of Baal, Part 4," *Ugarit-Forschungen* 3 (1971): 124–27; Jeffrey H. Tigay, "On the Meaning of T(W)TPT," *Journal of Biblical Literature* 101 (1982): 321–31.

derived from the Akkadian and had originally meant an apotropaic object,[50] Tigay conjectured that it referred to protective power vis-à-vis God's wrath.[51]

In his discussion of the meaning of *tefillin* practice, which he argued was broad based, Tigay sought to distinguish between the "official" standpoint and the popular one, and between these and the origin of the obligation. Whereas the rabbis and Hellenistic Jewish writers stressed the educational/spiritual value of keeping God's words close to one's body, the common folk (and even the rabbis) believed in the protective power of *tefillin*. That said, *tefillin* included no magical content; their use as amulets was secondary, and their origin was unconnected to amuletic ritual. Tigay did not reconcile his hypothesis on the origin of the word *tefillin* with this position on the meaning of the practice. In concluding he acknowledged the impossibility, within the format of an encyclopedia entry, of a comprehensive analysis of the development of the ritual.

Although much of her evidence flowed from harmonizing the Dead Sea finds with rabbinic data, Jacqueline Genot-Bismuth suggested new ways of looking at the Qumran *tefillin*.[52] Hers was the first attempt to link the Dead Sea findings with a protective function for *tefillin*, as implied by the Greek *phylakterion*. (While Milik and others used its modern cognate words to describe *tefillin* parchments, they did not analyze the significance, if any, of the etymology.) She stressed that these *tefillin* are to be considered as complete objects and not merely as inscribed parchments that happen to be kept in a case, and analyzed Yadin's findings as to the way parchments were folded. In her view, the hermetically sealed cases, with their micrographical parchment contents, symbolized a fortress, which safeguarded those it sheltered (she related this to the Greek *phylax*, which can mean garrison). Genot-Bismuth found it inconceivable that there might be Essene-type *tefillin*, as she felt Milik had suggested, as such a strict group could not have been so anarchic with respect to the practice.[53] Instead, she hypothesized that Qumran *tefillin* finds, including those that seemed to her typologically closer to Pharisaic *tefillin*, consisted of ones deemed invalid by the inhabitants of Qumran, and were being stored there (as in a *genizah* cache). This suggestion seems unfounded, and based on preconceived notions rather than the evidence to hand.

Genot-Bismuth also proposed the idea of a prenormative period, during which the practice had not yet been codified but was already built

---

50. E. A. Speiser, "Palil and Congeners: A Sampling of Apotropaic Symbols," in *Studies in Honor of Benno Landsberger* (Chicago: University of Chicago Press, 1965): 389–93.

51. Tigay, "Tefillin," 884–85.

52. Jacqueline Genot-Bismuth, "Les Tefilim de Qumran: pour une approche anthropologique" (paper presented at the 10th World Congress of Jewish Studies, 1989).

53. For a similar view, see Norman Golb, *Who Wrote the Dead Sea Scrolls?* (New York: Scribner, 1995), 103.

around the verses understood to be prescribing the rite. In this period the function of the text passages was to serve as an extended motive clause for the practice. She pointed to the verses around the Decalogue in Deuteronomy 5 and 6, which deal with human contact with the divine and the need for precaution vis-à-vis such contact, and suggested that this was a source of anxiety to *tefillin*-wearing Jews. The primary function of *tefillin* was to assure the harmlessness of contact with the sacred, and wearing *tefillin* was taken as a sign that attested to protection from this danger. The function of *tefillin* as "reminder" (implied by Exod 13:9) was designed to signify, however, that this sacred protection was not in essence magical. Rather, it was a reward for submission to the biblical command. *Tefillin* were the material expression of the fundamental Deuteronomic idea that a human life lived to its term is divine recompense for an existence in conformity with the Torah code. These sacred objects were rooted in the deepest kinds of human anguish—those due to death, and to the terror attached to the taboo of the divine.

David Rothstein's doctoral dissertation of 1992 was a lengthy critical treatment of *tefillin* and *mezuzah* in antiquity.[54] He began by evaluating the ancient translations of biblical verses traditionally taken to mandate *tefillin* and *mezuzah* practice. This was done as a prelude to determining the original intent of these verses (his discussion focused on whether the verses concerned had been meant literally or figuratively), and the literary-religious matrix in which they ought be situated. Both of these concerns lie beyond the limits of my own topic. Rothstein then proceeded to argue for the impossibility of determining the identity of those circles in which the Judean Desert *tefillin/mezuzot* had originated. This was important for the large section of his study devoted to analysis of the scribal practices exhibited by these exemplars, in the light of rules preserved in rabbinic (especially tanna'itic) texts.

In a review of DJD 6, Lawrence Schiffman argued that Milik paid insufficient attention to rabbinic data,[55] and this section of Rothstein's work seems to have been designed to fill in the gap that Schiffman addressed. The objective was "to use the rabbinic texts and the Dead Sea exemplars to explicate one another and, secondly, to compare the scribal practices reflected in the exemplars with those preserved in rabbinic texts."[56] Rothstein also attempted to explain the choice of contents exhibited by the

---

54. David Rothstein, "From Bible to Murabba'at: Studies in the Literary, Textual and Scribal Features of Phylacteries and Mezuzot in Ancient Israel and Early Judaism" (Ph.D. diss., UCLA, 1992). More recently, a doctoral dissertation restricted to the study of *mezuzah* has covered rabbinic literature on the subject up to the early-modern period. See Eva-Maria Jansson, *The Message of a Mitsvah: The Mezuzah in Rabbinic Literature* (Lund, 1999).

55. Lawrence H. Schiffman, *Journal of the American Oriental Society* 100, no. 2 (1980): 170–72.

56. Rothstein, "From Bible to Murabba'at," xx.

Judean Desert *tefillin* and *mezuzot* as a reflection of particular exegetical tendencies, which he related to rabbinic midrash.

In practice just about all Rothstein's tanna'itic evidence for scribal practices is from sources that will not, for the purposes of my own work, be considered as reliably tanna'itic.[57] Even if this methodological difference is set aside, I still have misgivings about important elements of his work. Underlying Rothstein's discussion is the idea that Judean Desert scribal practices can be seen as synonymous with a set of scribal norms, regarding *tefillin* and *mezuzot*, to which there was conscious adherence. I will argue against this notion below, and find little relevance to his claims that Judean Desert scribal practice can rarely be shown to be *inconsistent* with tanna'itic rules, as these are often ill defined or the subject of dispute. Additionally, the idea that the Dead Sea documents can be illuminated by consideration of later rabbinic texts is a controversial one. (It is also to be noted that Rothstein based the scribal "norms" he analyzed on photographs of the original fragments rather than the fragments themselves— this seems a problematic approach when analyzing *tefillin* texts, in view of their tiny script and numerous folds.[58])

Yadin had confusingly claimed that the passages in Qumran *tefillin* texts followed their biblical order, in line with rabbinic prescriptions, and that apparent deviations from this order had only been considered acceptable for those passages not known (from rabbinic literature) to be "classical" *tefillin* contents.[59] Although Yadin had criticized Kuhn for claiming otherwise,[60] the publications in DJD 6 demonstrate that the latter's understanding had been correct. In a recent article, David Nakman has now made a fresh attempt to reconcile the contents of Qumran *tefillin* with rabbinic rules.[61] Here he took issue with Milik, as well as with Emanuel Tov (whose ideas as to the sectarian nature of many of the Qumran *tefillin* will be addressed in chapter 3).

Nakman set out to show that there were halakic rules for writing correct *tefillin* passages, evidenced by the Qumran *tefillin*, and that these represent an early phase of the rules that developed into rabbinic halakah.[62] His work seems, to some extent, to assume what he claims to prove.[63] Much of it is dedicated, in effect, to demonstrating that his views cannot be *disproved*, but they are hardly a plausible explanation for the data,

---

57. See below for further discussion of this point.

58. See Milik, "Tefillin, Mezuzot et Targums," 33.

59. Yadin, *Tefillin from Qumran (XQPhyl 1–4)*, 15 n. 28, 32–34.

60. Kuhn, *Phylakterien aus Höhle 4 von Qumran*, 29.

61. David Nakman, "The Contents and Order of the Biblical Sections in the Tefillin from Qumran and Rabbinic Halakah," *Cathedra* 112 (2004): 19–44 (in Hebrew).

62. Ibid., 19–20.

63. See, in particular, section 4 of his article.

much less a compelling one. They will be discussed in further detail in chapter 3.

Unexplored Questions

Earlier scholars have tended to take much of the development of *tefillin* practice as a given, rather than investigating why it might have taken the specific form that it did. Although the Dead Sea scrolls provide an unparalleled opportunity to examine the early ritual in depth, it seems fair to say that this opportunity has largely been spent on implausible harmonizations of Qumran practice with later practice. Such efforts, inevitably, minimize the significance of evidence for the evolution of the ritual. In addition, no attempt has been made to evaluate *tefillin* practice against comparative evidence from other cultures in this period.

In particular, prior scholarship does not seem to have addressed the question of the magical function of *tefillin* satisfactorily,[64] including their depiction as *phylakteria* in Greek sources. Blau's assertion that the protection from wearing *tefillin* was no different than that afforded by Torah and other commandments warrants further investigation, and Schürer's suggestion relied on a connection between *tefillin* and prayer that seems dubious. So too for the ideas of Strack-Billerbeck and Genot-Bismuth, that any such function was, in essence, a reward. The above-mentioned denial by Gaster of any protective element, as late as the second century c.e., seems unconvincing. A protective function for *tefillin* cannot simply be dismissed by virtue of a parallel belief that the Torah had commanded it. Here an observation of Moshe Idel's looks particularly apt: "The more non-magical perceptions of Judaism, especially the ancient forms of this religion, evident even in the writings of scholars that were deeply interested in the phenomena connected to magic, require substantial qualifications."[65]

---

64. With regard to the Qumran *tefillin* and *mezuzot*, however, the question has been raised in Philip S. Alexander, "Magic and Magical Texts," in *Encyclopedia of the Dead Sea Scrolls*, ed. Lawrence H. Schiffman and James C. VanderKam (Oxford and New York: Oxford University Press, 2000).

65. Moshe Idel, "On Judaism, Jewish Mysticism and Magic," in *Envisioning Magic*, ed. Peter Schaefer and Hans G. Kippenberg (Leiden: Brill, 1997), 214. For examples of the kind of qualification that Idel calls for, see Peter Schaefer, "Magic and Religion in Ancient Judaism," in *Envisioning Magic*, ed. Schaefer and Kippenberg, 19–43; Avriel Bar-Levav, "Death and the (Blurred) Boundaries of Magic: Strategies of Coexistence," *Kabbalah: Journal for the Study of Jewish Mystical Texts* 7 (2002): 51–64.

Some Background on Comparative Evidence

Jews and the Greco-Roman World

A large and increasing body of scholarly literature deals with the impact on Jewish society of its encounter with the Greco-Roman world. While the exact nature and extent of Hellenism are the subject of debate,[66] or continued inquiry, there is a consensus regarding a considerable degree of adaptation by Jews, in Palestine, Egypt, and elsewhere, to the larger Greco-Roman world to which they belonged.[67] The scholarship cannot be reviewed here, but has asserted little influence for Greco-Roman culture on the ways in which Jews may have interpreted their traditional religious rituals.[68] Thus, John Collins has concluded, "The most striking thing about the Jewish encounter with Hellenism . . . was the persistence of Jewish separatism in matters of worship and cult."[69]

Underlying this book is the idea that comparing an apparently uniquely Jewish ritual to Greco-Roman practices is nevertheless worthwhile. Given the importance of amulets/phylacteries in the Greco-Roman world, as will be discussed, did *tefillin* practice fit into the larger picture, and if so how? Here Erich Gruen's formulation of the premise to a fairly recent book seems apposite: "The inquiry can be formulated thus: how did Jews accommodate themselves to the larger cultural world of the Mediterranean while at the same time reasserting the character of their own heritage within it?"[70]

---

66. See Lee I. Levine, *Judaism and Hellenism in Antiquity: Conflict or Confluence* (Seattle and London: University of Washington Press, 1998), 13–15.

67. See Martin Goodman, "Epilogue," in *Hellenism in the Land of Israel*, ed. John J. Collins and Gregory E. Sterling (Notre Dame, Ind.: University of Notre Dame, 2001), 302–5. However, see Louis H. Feldman, *Jew and Gentile in the Ancient World* (Princeton: Princeton University Press, 1993), 42–44.

68. Works of considerable influence have included E. J. Bickerman, *Der Gott der Makkabäer* (Berlin: Schocken, 1937); Saul Lieberman, *Greek in Jewish Palestine* (New York: Jewish Theological Seminary of America, 1942); E. R. Goodenough, *Jewish Symbols in the Graeco-Roman Period* (Princeton: Princeton University Press, 1953–1968); Victor Tcherikover, *Hellenistic Civilization and the Jews* (Philadelphia/Jerusalem: Jewish Publication Society of America/Magnes Press, 1959); Martin Hengel, *Judentum und Hellenismus* (Tübingen: Mohr, 1969). The latter appeared in English shortly after its original publication—Martin Hengel, *Judaism and Hellenism: Studies in Their Encounter in Palestine During the Early Hellenistic Period*, trans. John Bowden, 1st English ed. (London: SCM, 1974). It is still extremely influential for the Second Temple period.

69. John J. Collins, "Cult and Culture: The Limits of Hellenization in Judea," in *Hellenism in the Land of Israel*, ed. Collins and. Sterling, 61.

70. Erich S. Gruen, *Heritage and Hellenism: The Reinvention of Jewish Tradition* (Berkeley: University of California Press, 1998), xiv.

The conclusions of some scholars, although looking at very different evidence to mine, have been suggestive. Martha Himmelfarb has argued that it was the centrality of the Torah that enabled the Jews to adapt Greek culture in ways that other Near Eastern societies could not do.[71] If she is correct, then it seems possible that the ways in which the Torah came to be interpreted were themselves informed by such adaptation. Gruen, while not investigating religious rituals, observed that the Jews' "adjustment to the Hellenistic world expressed itself not as accommodation but as reaffirmation of their own lustrous legacy."[72] In the light of such conclusions, it seems worth investigating *tefillin* practice not only as an internal Jewish matter, but also against a Greco-Roman backdrop.

(This is not to say that there was no adaptation to Jewish practice on the part of non-Jews. The Greek magical papyri, as well as other archaeological findings, attest to a belief in the power of Jewish elements to amuletic rituals, which may have resembled *tefillin* in some manner, among gentiles no less than Jews.[73])

Inscribed Amulets in the Ancient Mediterranean World

To the inhabitants of the ancient Mediterranean, the cosmos teemed with supernatural forces, which they often sought to influence by the use of amulets—the most pervasive of magical tools in antiquity.[74] From the fourth century B.C.E., these objects are known in Greek as *periapta* or *periammata*, which means "things tied around." Amulets included cords, bands, or sashes, as well as pendants, rings, and other objects, which frequently contained text. They were generally tied around a part of the body, such

---

71. Martha Himmelfarb, "The Torah between Athens and Jerusalem: Jewish Difference in Antiquity," in *Ancient Judaism in Its Hellenistic Context*, ed. Carol Bakhos (Leiden/Boston: Brill, 2005).

72. Gruen, *Heritage and Hellenism*, 246.

73. See Campbell Bonner, *Studies in Magical Amulets, Chiefly Graeco-Egyptian* (Ann Arbor: University of Michigan Press, 1950), 18, 26–32; Hans Dieter Betz, *The Greek Magical Papyri in Translation, Including the Demotic Spells*, 2nd ed. (Chicago: University of Chicago Press, 1992), xliv–xlviii; Gideon Bohak, "Hebrew, Hebrew Everywhere?," in *Prayer, Magic and the Stars in the Ancient and Late Antique World*, ed. S. Noegel, J. Walker, and B. Wheeler (University Park: Pennsylvania State University Press, 2003), 69–82; Gideon Bohak, "A Jewish Myth in Pagan Magic in Late Antiquity," in *Myths in Judaism*, ed. Ithamar Grünwald and Moshe Idel (Jerusalem: Zalman Shazar Center for Jewish History, 2004), 97–122 (in Hebrew).

74. See Georg Luck, *Arcana Mundi* (Baltimore: Johns Hopkins University Press, 1985), 19; John G. Gager, *Curse Tablets and Binding Spells from the Ancient World* (New York/Oxford: Oxford University Press, 1992), 12; Naomi Janowitz, *Magic in the Roman World* (London and New York: Routledge, 2001), 56–57; D. Ogden, *Magic, Witchcraft, and Ghosts in the Greek and Roman Worlds* (Oxford: Oxford University Press, 2002), 261.

as the neck, head, arm or leg, or attached to clothing.[75] Bonner's broad definition of an amulet, from 1950, still seems reasonable: "any object which by its contact or its close proximity to the person who owns it, or to any possession of his, exerts power for his good, either by keeping evil from him and his property or by endowing him with positive advantages."[76] The assertion that everyone wore amulets, "given the conventional cognitive map of that world, it would have been foolish and unreasonable to behave otherwise,"[77] may be no exaggeration. Galen, in the second century C.E., acknowledged their successful use for medical purposes, even where he could find no reason to account for their effectiveness.[78] He drew the line, however, at the use of images, characters and incantations.[79] (A flavor for the power of amulets in the ancient world can be obtained even today from practices in parts of the developing world—a recent newspaper article describes Thai Buddhist troops, who though they wore amulets anyway, were ordered to wear a particularly effective one by their commander or face imprisonment.[80])

The connection between *tefillin* and amulets calls for investigation, if only because early Christian sources characterize *tefillin* as phylacteries, that is, protective amulets. Both objects were worn on the body, and are frequently juxtaposed in rabbinic sources. In addition, as Roy Kotansky has shown, there is a well-established link between recited verses and ancient amulets,[81] so the presence in *tefillin* of verses recited by Jews as part of the *Shema* prayer is also suggestive.[82] It thus seems relevant to look to comparative data concerning inscribed amulets in the ancient Mediterranean world for any light that might be shed on *tefillin* practice. Later chapters will appeal to such data as appropriate, and here I will simply provide some general remarks.

---

75. For general discussions, see Bonner, *Studies in Magical Amulets*, 1–21; Andrea Becker, "Phylakterion," in *Brill's New Pauly (Encyclopedia of the Ancient World)* (Leiden: Brill, 2007).

76. Bonner, *Studies in Magical Amulets*, 2.

77. Gager, *Curse Tablets and Binding Spells from the Ancient World*, 220.

78. XII, 573.

79. See L. Thorndike, *History of Magic and Experimental Science*, vol. 1 (New York: Macmillan, 1923), 172–74.

80. Wassana Nanuam, "Soldiers Ordered to Wear Luang Poo Jiam Talismans at All Times in Pattani," *Bangkok Post*, January 1, 2008.

81. Roy Kotansky, "Incantations and Prayers for Salvation on Inscribed Greek Amulets," in *Magika Hiera: Ancient Greek Magic and Religion*, ed. Christopher A. Faraone and Dirk Obbink (New York: Oxford University Press, 1991), 108–10, 12–14. The entire article is particularly valuable.

82. For the use of biblical verses in the context of later Jewish magic, see Joseph Naveh and Shaul Shaked, *Magic Spells and Formulae : Aramaic Incantations of Late Antiquity* (Jerusalem: Magnes Press Hebrew University, 1993), 22–31.

The existence of written amulets has been traced back to Egypt, where the findings are dated no later than the eighth century B.C.E. While the contents of these oracular amulets and their case-inscriptions suggest that they were primarily intended for protecting the living, it seems possible that they were deposited in their owners' graves after death (although they were not discovered in tombs).[83] It has been suggested that the form of the earliest Greek amulets arose out of contacts with the Egyptians of Naucratis at the end of the seventh century B.C.E., and/or that in adopting the Phoenician system of writing, Greeks also borrowed their practice of writing amulets.[84] Punic-Phoenician inscribed amulets in tubular capsules have been found, primarily in tombs, in Carthage and Sardinia, and dated from the seventh to the fifth century B.C.E.[85] Two silver Hebrew amulets have also been found, in a Jerusalem burial site, and dated to the seventh or sixth century B.C.E.[86] There is, in addition, Mesopotamian evidence for cylinder seals as having amuletic functions—in that they carry the inscribed wish that the wearer attain a long and prosperous life, or include an incantation;[87] as well as Mesopotamian plague amulets/house blessings containing written text.[88] (The Aramaic magic bowls, are, however, from a later period than is covered here.[89])

For the late classical period (around 400–330 B.C.E.) there have been findings of so-called Orphic *lamellae*—inscribed slips of metal foil. These were usually placed unrolled on corpses to protect the dead from the dangers of the underworld, and their precise connection to later amulets is a matter of debate. It is quite possible that the dead were the initial wearers of inscribed text in many cultures, with the living protected by more

---

83. See I. E. S. Edwards, *Hieratic Papyri in the British Museum, Fourth Series: Oracular Amuletic Decrees of the Late New Kingdom*, vol. 1, *Text* (London: Trustees of the British Museum, 1960), xiii–xxiii; John Ray, "Two Inscribed Objects in the Fitzwilliam Museum, Cambridge," *Journal of Egyptian Archaeology* 58 (1972): 251–53; J. D. Bourriau and J. D. Ray, "Brief Communications," *Journal of Egyptian Archaeology* 61 (1975): 257–58.

84. Peter W. Schienerl, "A Historical Survey of Tubular Charm-Cases up to the 7th Century A.D.," *Ornament* 4, no. 4 (1980): 13; Kotansky, "Incantations and Prayers for Salvation," 124 n. 8.

85. See Kotansky, "Incantations and Prayers for Salvation," 115.

86. They will be discussed in further detail in chapter 2.

87. See Beatrice L. Goff, "The Role of Amulets in Mesopotamian Ritual Texts," *Journal of the Warburg and Courtauld Institutes* 19, nos. 1–2 (1956): 1–39; E. Reiner, "Magic Figurines, Amulets and Talismans," in *Monsters and Demons in the Ancient and Medieval Worlds*, ed. A. E. Farkas, P. O. Harper, and E. B. Harrison (Mainz on Rhine: Philipp von Zabern, 1987), 27–28.

88. See E. A. W. Budge, *Amulets and Talismans* (New Hyde Park: University Books, 1930; reprint, 1961), 86–97; E. Reiner, "Plague Amulets and House Blessings," *Journal of Near Eastern Studies* 19 (1960): 27–36.

89. See Shaul Shaked, "Form and Purpose in Aramaic Spells: Some Jewish Themes," in *Officina Magica*, ed. Shaul Shaked (Leiden: Brill, 2005), 1.

ephemeral oral utterances.[90] Unlike many later amulets, the Orphic *lamellae* contain no personal names.[91]

David Frankfurter has argued for the convergence, in the Hellenistic and Roman periods, of the oral element at the core of Greek amulet ritual with the written element at the core of its Egyptian counterpart.[92] During the Roman period, amulets seem primarily aimed at curing or preventing disease, often connected in their texts to "spirits," although this purpose is not always made clear—thus Homeric verses are frequently encountered as amulet contents, with no explicit indication of protection in the text itself. While many amulets list medical complaints, others were designed for general protection, and this latter function is likely to have preceded their use to cover other needs.[93]

Magical papyri sometimes give directions for a consecration ceremony, after an amulet had been inscribed, which might include a requirement for prior purification, and the recitation of special formulas (*logoi*).[94] Some amulets contain text in a foreign language or language of uncertain provenance (often in Greek characters)[95]—presumably because the precise use of the exotic formulas concerned was associated with their effectiveness. Lucian of Samosata challenged this apparently common notion regarding the use of "a holy name or a foreign phrase" in the second century c.e., in the context of incantations against fever or inflammation,[96] and it seems likely that their use on amulets was for similar reasons. Origen, in the third century, explicitly observed that spells needed to be in their native language in order to be effective.[97]

Archaeological discoveries cannot possibly reflect the extent of amuletic practice, as many amulets were written on perishable material, and metal ones would often have been recycled.[98] (The latter possibility seems less likely for ones that had been placed in tombs, where many surviving

---

90. See Kotansky, "Incantations and Prayers for Salvation," 115. On writing as a substitute for vocal utterance, see David Frankfurter, "The Magic of Writing and the Writing of Magic: The Power of the Word in Egyptian and Greek Traditions," *Helios* 21 (1994): 192.

91. Kotansky, "Incantations and Prayers for Salvation," 131 n.53.

92. Frankfurter, "The Magic of Writing and the Writing of Magic," 198–99.

93. See Gager, *Curse Tablets and Binding Spells from the Ancient World*, 220.

94. See Bonner, *Studies in Magical Amulets*, 14.

95. See Fritz Graf, *Magic in the Ancient World* (Cambridge, Mass.; London: Harvard University Press, 1997), 299 n. 34.

96. *Lucian: The Lover of Lies*, trans. A. M. Harmon (Loeb Classical Library 3; London: William Heinemann, 1913), 335. Cf. the third-century philosopher Porphry's questioning why foreign names for gods are "preferred to our own," in practices he derides as magic (*goeteia*); see A. R. Sodano, ed., *Porphry, Epistula Ad Anebonem* (Naples: Arte Tipografica, 1958), 22.

97. *Contra Celsum*, 1.25.

98. Kotansky, "Incantations and Prayers for Salvation," 110.

examples were found.[99]) By the height of the Roman Empire the manufacture of inscribed amulets was flourishing, and those wearing them seem to have been ubiquitous.[100]

Terminology and Methodology: Some General Observations

The Use of the Term "Magic"

Investigating the protective function of *tefillin*, as I intend to do, can locate the practice within a complex of ancient rituals known from the Greco-Roman world, often referred to as magical rituals. Indeed that world, to borrow a phrase from Michael Swartz, was "infused with magical conceptions at all levels of society."[101] That said, a characterization of *tefillin* as magical, while perhaps an intuitively appealing counterpoint to the more common view that they were simply worn in fulfillment of a biblical requirement, is no simple matter. Explaining the problems involved and trying to solve them call for some background on a scholarly debate, whose resolution continues to be elusive. However, after having gone through a phase where theorists seemed to insist that there was only one right way of looking at magic, more recent scholarship looks to be acknowledging the value of different standpoints.[102] In this spirit, I will not attempt to come down on one side of the debate itself, but rather will try to explain the approach that I intend to take in this study, against the debate's backdrop.

A clear distinction between three human activities—namely, magic, religion, and science—was famously made by J. G. Frazer.[103] Scholarship on magic in the ancient world essentially followed Frazerian lines, until well into the postwar period[104] (although some scholars, and here Blau in

---

99. Ibid., 130 n. 49

100. Ibid., 112, 14–16.

101. Michael D. Swartz, *Scholastic Magic* (Princeton: Princeton University Press, 1996), 14.

102. See Jens Braarvig, "Magic: Reconsidering the Grand Dichotomy," in *The World of Ancient Magic*, ed. David R. Jordan, Hugo Montgomery, and Einar Thomassen (Athens: Norwegian Institute at Athens, 1999), 21–54; C. A. Hoffman, "Fiat Magia," in *Magic and Ritual in the Ancient World*, ed. Paul Mirecki and Marvin Meyer (Leiden: Brill, 2002), 179–94. Hoffman starts out by citing the inspiration of Henk Versnel, and it seems to me that his article is in some sense a refinement/update of the latter's important piece (Henk S. Versnel, "Some Reflections on the Relationship Magic-Religion," *Numen* 38, no. 2 [1991]: 177–97).

103. J. G. Frazer, *The Golden Bough*, 1st ed. (London: Macmillan, 1890).

104. See Graf, *Magic in the Ancient World*, 14.

his work on ancient Jewish magic is to be included,[105] were more influenced by Frazer's predecessor Sir Edward Tylor[106]). Among anthropologists, however, Frazer's work was challenged much earlier.[107] That challenge came to relate in part to the phenomenon of accusations of magic (as deviant activity)[108]—an issue first taken up for the late-antique context by Peter Brown.[109] Simply put, that issue is of little relevance to this book, but it can serve to highlight a further issue of considerable relevance. Of necessity, ancient accusations deal with an indigenous category of magic, one generated within the society that is the subject of study. This raises the question of whether any other use of the term magic is meaningful and, if so, how that meaning is to be defined and what purpose it serves. Many studies, quite legitimately, do focus on the term magic as it was used in the ancient world—the so-called emic approach, taken quite often with respect to the Greco-Roman world[110] (where one of the words for magic, in both Greek and Latin, was similar to our own[111]). By previewing the evidence that will be adduced here, it is clear that such an approach has limited utility for the topic of my study. Although the categorization of *tefillin* as a protective amulet has been noted above, the connection made in the ancient world between a protective function and licit magical ritual is far from clear.[112]

Similarly, the specifically sociological take on the emic approach, which can often explain how one and the same practice could be seen as either admirable or deviant, depending on context,[113] would also have limited value. Instead, I will follow the alternative approach to magic, sometimes known as the etic approach, whereby the term magic will be

---

105. Blau, *Das altjüdische Zauberwesen*.

106. See Jonathan Lee Seidel, "Studies in Ancient Jewish Magic" (Ph.D. diss, University of California at Berkeley, 1996), 1–7.

107. In particular, by Marcel Mauss and Bronislaw Malinowski. Cf. Graf, *Magic in the Ancient World*, 15–17.

108. A much-cited challenge is based on anthropological fieldwork with the Nigerian Azande and appears in E. E. Evans-Pritchard, *Witchcraft, Oracles and Magic among the Azande* (Oxford: Clarendon, 1937).

109. P. Brown, "Sorcery, Demons and the Rise of Christianity: From Late Antiquity into the Middle Ages," in *Witchcraft Confessions and Accusations*, ed. Mary Douglas (London: Tavistock Publications, 1970), 17–45.

110. For a discussion of the dichotomy between approaches, see Graf, *Magic in the Ancient World*, 17–19. Graf's book is a prime example of a work that attempts to use the term "magic" as it was used in antiquity.

111. See the comments in Yuval Harari, "What Is a Magical Text? Methodological Reflections Aimed at Defining Early Jewish Magic," in *Officina Magica*, ed. Shaul Shaked (Leiden: Brill, 2005), 108–9.

112. See, in general, R. Styers, *Making Magic: Religion, Magic and Science in the Modern World* (Oxford: Oxford University Press, 2004).

113. See the comments in Versnel, "Some Reflections on the Relationship Magic-Religion," 182–83.

used without particular reference to its use in the culture being described. It seems to me that this standpoint provides value for the use of the term in analyzing *tefillin* practice.[114]

It is now commonly accepted by scholars that magic and religion are intertwined, either because one shades into the other on a continuum[115] or because magic is simply a part of religion,[116] or because there is a "family resemblance" between them.[117] Thus, for example, it has been argued that there is no essential distinction between spells and prayer, as they can use similar formulas in similar circumstances.[118] Such views are often used to emphasize that practices previously viewed as magical are less different than one might otherwise imagine from religious practices. The corollary, whereby stress is placed on practices previously viewed as religious as having a magical component, is perhaps encountered less frequently. In the case of Jewish practices, the issue may be particularly significant. Halakah, on the one hand, and antique rituals having magical effects, on the other, share a considerable interest in the quest for correct observance.

Without defining magic precisely, the utility of a position that regards *tefillin* as magical (in part, at least) can already be addressed. Consideration of the magical aspects of *tefillin* will, it is hoped, allow for a "thicker" description of the practice in the ancient world than has heretofore been provided. Clifford Geertz, an anthropologist whose work is frequently encountered in the study of ritual, observed, "What . . . most prevents . . . us . . . from grasping what people are up to is . . . a lack of familiarity with the imaginative universe within which their acts are signs."[119] Paraphrasing Geertz, an attempt will be made here to incorporate the concept of magic, in trying to become familiar with the imaginative universe of ancient *tefillin* practitioners, so as to help determine what people were up to when they observed the rite.

I will not try to provide a broad definition of magic, as a characteristic of ritual, that is broadly applicable to the ancient world in general, or even to Judaism as a whole.[120] Instead, I would claim that the word

---

114. For similar usage in a book that deals with a contemporary Jewish community, including inter alia its attitudes to *tefillin*, see Dein, *Religion and Healing among the Lubavitch Community.*

115. W. J. Goode, "Magic and Religion: A Continuum," *Ethnos* 14 (1949): 172–82.

116. "Magic should be included within religion as one type of the practices of which religious ritual is composed"; see Dorothy Hammond, "Magic: A Problem in Semantics," *American Anthropologist* 72, no. 6 (1970): 1349. See also Graf, *Magic in the Ancient World*, 211.

117. Harari, "What Is a Magical Text?" 115.

118. Versnel, "Some Reflections on the Relationship Magic-Religion," 180 and n. 7.

119. Clifford Geertz, *The Interpretation of Cultures* (New York: Basic Books, 1973), 13. The first chapter, in which the above quote appears, is entitled "Thick Description: Toward an Interpretive Theory of Culture."

120. Cf. "No definition of magic can be universally applicable. . . . Its meaning changes

is appropriately used in a study of *tefillin* because of the "family resemblance" that *tefillin* share with magical amulets; the latter were worn on the body, frequently had inscribed contents—that might additionally be connected to recited verses—and were often designated as *phylakteria*. The magical aspects of *tefillin* will be compared as such to that of other rituals that not only have other forms but also other functions and religious provenance. In doing this, I follow the theoretical position first staked out by Henk Versnel and subsequently elaborated by C. A. Hoffman, who have argued for the validity of the etic approach.[121] Versnel makes a case for an overarching concept of magic, to which individual magical practices belong, linked by "a complicated network of similarities overlapping and criss-crossing." Here I am quoting (following Versnel) from Ludwig Wittgenstein, who in discussing the type of classifications without sharp borders (specifically the so-called polythetic classes) used the example of "games" as a classification to which all sorts of disparate games belong, having "family resemblances."[122] Yuval Harari has championed Versnel's approach, for the study of early Jewish magic.[123]

To the extent that I will label aspects of *tefillin* practice as magical, I do not intend to relegate them "to the periphery of . . . culture, . . . the realm beneath religion . . . and other human activities of a more respectable sort."[124] Such an approach has long been discredited in academic discourse,[125] although it continues to surface as a straw man.[126]

---

as the context in which it is used changes. . . . All definitions of magic are relative to the culture and sub-culture under discussion" (Alan F. Segal, "Hellenistic Magic—Some Questions of Definition," in *Studies in Gnosticism and Hellenistic Religions*, ed. R. Van den Broek and M. J. Vermaseren [Leiden: Brill, 1981], 350–51).

121. Versnel, "Some Reflections on the Relationship Magic-Religion," 185–86. For a contrast between this position and the views of J. Z. Smith and John Gager, in particular, see Hoffman, "Fiat Magia," 192–94. For another scholar who explicitly eschews the approach that will be used here, see C. R. Phillips, "The Sociology of Religious Knowledge in the Roman Empire to A.D. 284," in *Aufstieg und Niedergang der römischen Welt*, 2.16.3 (Berlin: de Gruyter, 1986), 2718.

122. See Ludwig Wittgenstein, *Philosophical Investigations, Part 1*, trans. G. E. M. Anscombe (Oxford: Basil Blackwell, 1953), sections 66–67.

123. Yuval Harari, "Early Jewish Magic: Methodological and Phenomenological Studies" (Ph.D. diss., Hebrew University, 1998, in Hebrew), 111–18; Harari, "What Is a Magical Text?" 109–11.

124. The quote, regarding the attitude that he decries, is from John G. Gager, "A New Translation of Ancient Greek and Demotic Papyri, Sometimes Called Magical," *Journal of Religion* 67, no. 1 (1987): 81.

125. In the case of Judaism, it was first decisively overturned by Goodenough. See, in particular, Goodenough, *Jewish Symbols in the Graeco-Roman Period*, 2: 156.

126. Perhaps the last serious proponent of this view was A. A. Barb, "The Survival of Magic Arts," in *The Conflict between Paganism and Christianity in the Fourth Century*, ed. Arnaldo Momigliano (Oxford: Clarendon, 1963).

Popular Practice

The terms "popular religion" and "popular practice" call for some elaboration. In the absence of evidence to the contrary I will presume, as Peter Brown has expressed it, that when it comes to shared religious practices "differences of class and education play no significant role."[127] With respect to popular beliefs, a similar point was made by Arnaldo Momigliano.[128] Accordingly, the use of these terms or similar ones, while intended to imply that an aspect of practice or belief was not restricted to an elite, is not to be taken to imply that there were differences in regard to the practice, or to beliefs associated with it, between elites and others. The evidence for any such differences will be evaluated where found, but will not be otherwise assumed.

Approaches to the Scriptural Origins of Tefillin

Ancients, both Jewish and gentile, understood *tefillin* to be a practice commanded by scripture, and it is the *origin of this understanding* that will be my primary focus in evaluating the relevant biblical passages. These are considered relevant to this study, but chiefly insofar as the course of their reception, with respect to the *tefillin* ritual, can be examined. Accordingly, no attempt will be made to resolve the precise *intent* of these verses or their background. Rather, to use Robert Crosman's succinct formulation, it will be presumed for my purposes that "readers make meaning."[129] The approach taken to scripture will thus be akin to that of the literary criticism technique known as reception theory, which concentrates on the history of a literary work's reception rather than on its intention.[130]

---

127. P. Brown, *The Cult of the Saints: Its Rise and Function in Latin Christianity* (Chicago: University of Chicago Press, 1981), 19.

128. Arnaldo Momigliano, *Essays in Ancient and Modern Historiography* (Oxford: Blackwell, 1977), 156.

129. Robert Crosman, "Do Readers Make Meaning?," in *The Reader in the Text*, ed. Susan R. Suleiman and Inge Crosman (Princeton: Princeton University Press, 1980), 149–64.

130. For a theoretical framework, see Hans Robert Jauss, "Literary History as a Challenge to Literary Theory," *New Literary History* 2 (1970–71): 19–37. For its application to the Hebrew Bible, see, for example, William M. Schniedewind, *Society and the Promise to David* (New York: Oxford University Press, 1999). For a different approach, which in its orientation to Bible reception is more closely related to anthropology, see Philip F. Esler, "The Madness of Saul: A Cultural Reading of 1 Samuel 8–31," in *Biblical Studies/Cultural Studies*, ed. Cheryl J. Exum and Stephen D. Moore (Sheffield: Sheffield Academic, 1998), 220–62.

Approaches to Judean Desert Findings

I will endeavor to avoid harmonization of the Qumran data with rabbinic literature, which has shaped *tefillin* ritual into the modern era. Put simply, such harmonization is problematic because it calls on scholars to imaginatively reconstruct absent data, while at the same time it reads out of consideration data that are actually present. Attempts at harmonization run the risk of squandering the opportunity provided by the archaeological data to investigate the early practice of *tefillin* in depth, as they are doomed to minimize the significance of evidence for its development. In my opinion, which runs counter to the approach of Yadin and Nakman (discussed above), it is precisely by highlighting differences rather than similarities with the familiar that the value of the Qumran data may be realized. As Martin Goodman has observed, the significance of the Dead Sea scrolls "should not be weakened by forcing what they tell us into the straitjacket of what was already known from other sources."[131] I will try instead to follow the prescription of Robert Darnton: "we should make contact with the otherness in other cultures. My own suggestion about a way of making contact is to search for opacity in texts. . . . When we run into something that seems unthinkable to us, we may have hit upon a valid point of entry into an alien mentality."[132]

This approach necessitates investigating the Dead Sea data as though the later rabbinic data were irrelevant to understanding it. While this may seem strange to some readers, there is, in fact, no alternative if the goal, as here, is to investigate the origin of the practice and assess its development from Second Temple to rabbinic times. D. K. Falk has characterized the Qumran caves as the Galapagos Islands for prayer in Second Temple Judaism, and I would suggest that his observation also holds true for *tefillin* ritual.[133]

Observations on Tanna'itic Literature

Much of the evidence for *tefillin* practice is found in rabbinic literature, and any attempt to reconstruct the contours of the practice must engage its legacy. The relevant works most immediately reflect a culture that

131. Martin Goodman, "Josephus and Variety in First-Century Judaism," *Proceedings of the Israel Academy of Sciences and Humanities* 7, no. 6 (2000): 201–13.

132. Robert Darnton, *The Great Cat Massacre and Other Episodes in French Cultural History* (New York: Vintage Books, 1985), 261–62.

133. D. K. Falk, "Qumran Prayer Texts and the Temple," in *Sapiential, Liturgical and Poetical Texts from Qumran*, ed. D. K. Falk, Florentino García Martínez, and Eileen M. Schuller (Leiden: Brill, 2000), 106.

arose subsequent to the destruction of the Temple and flourished among a limited circle in the Galilee in the aftermath of the Bar-Kokhba revolt. I am persuaded by those who have argued that the early rabbis were in their own time rather marginal figures; in Shaye Cohen's formulation, they "were but a small part of Jewish society, an insular group which produced an insular literature."[134] Archaeological evidence, material as well as documentary, points to this conclusion, as does consideration of other literature; and it can even be justified by analysis of the tanna'itic corpus in isolation.[135] Thus, although the literature had an enormous impact on Judaism as it subsequently developed, it presumably carried relatively little weight in its own day. Nor, in view of its idealizing tendencies, can it be viewed as a simple indicator of what Jews were actually doing at the time, and the line between its descriptive and prescriptive aspects is blurry[136] (in some measure because of the nature of tanna'itic Hebrew, which, to give one example, often does not distinguish clearly between descriptions of mandatory behavior and of merely sanctioned behavior[137]). Reading between the lines will therefore be an essential component of my analysis.

During and indeed beyond the period that will be considered here, it seems likely that much rabbinic "literature" was not committed to writing.[138] Its components did not initially take shape as strictly discrete corpora, but rather as accretions of oral traditions. Partly as a result, perhaps, rabbinic lore's self-image is that of a continuum, which began (at the latest) with the revelation at Sinai.[139] In addition, the literature generally (if not always) looks as though it takes its own attribution of sayings to individual rabbis, as well as its other reportage, as weighty representations

---

134. Shaye J. D. Cohen, "The Place of the Rabbi in Jewish Society," in *The Galilee in Late Antiquity*, ed. Lee I. Levine (New York: Jewish Theological Seminary of America, 1992), 173.

135. The seminal work, which focused on material remains, was Goodenough, *Jewish Symbols in the Graeco-Roman Period*. For more current (and perhaps less contentious) studies that shed light on this issue, see Martin Goodman, *State and Society in Roman Galilee* (Totowa, N.J.: Rowman & Allanheld, 1983; reprint, 2000); E. P. Sanders, *Judaism: Practice and Belief 63 B.C.E.–66 C.E.* (London: SCM, 1992); Hayim Lapin, "Early Rabbinic Civil Law and the Literature of the Second Temple Period," *Jewish Studies Quarterly* 2 (1995): 149–83; H. M. Cotton, "The Rabbis and the Documents," in *Jews in a Graeco-Roman World*, ed. Martin Goodman (Oxford: Clarendon, 1998), 167–79; Shaye Cohen, "The Rabbi in Second-Century Jewish Society," in *Cambridge History of Judaism* (Cambridge: Cambridge University Press, 1999), 922–90; Seth Schwartz, *Imperialism and Jewish Society, 200 B.C.E.–640 C.E.* (Princeton: Princeton University Press, 2001).

136. See Goodman, *State and Society in Roman Galilee*, 6.

137. See, for example, M. *Pesahim* 1:4.

138. See, most recently, Yaakov Sussmann, "Torah Shebe'al Peh, Peshutah Kemashma'ah," in *Mehqerei Talmud*, vol. 3, part 1, ed. Yaakov Sussmann and David Rosenthal (Jerusalem: Hebrew University Magnes Press, 2005, in Hebrew).

139. See, in particular, M. *Avot* 1:1.

of reality.[140] Until the 1970s, critical scholarship viewed the literature, in these respects, in a somewhat similar light to the way it viewed itself. In the most extreme form of this approach medieval midrashim could be cited as evidence for a facet of early rabbinic thought, whose origins might be dated to the Pharisees of the late–Second Temple period. Moreover, Judaism was thought to be co-extensive with rabbinic Judaism, in part no doubt as a result of this approach, and even the earliest rabbis were considered without foundation to be the leaders of the Jews.[141] (Goodenough's work was a notable exception, but it did not engage rabbinic literature to a significant extent.)

Although there is still some attempt to adhere to this approach, it has largely been discredited, in particular by Jacob Neusner and his followers.[142] A more skeptical way of using tanna'itic literature to write Jewish history has since developed, and is the approach that I will try to follow here.[143] It presumes that early rabbinic dicta can be viewed in a critical fashion as a reflection of the society in which the tanna'im found themselves—even though they neither shaped it nor represented it (much as they might have liked to), nor sought to describe it.[144] In addition, of course, these dicta are an important window into the tanna'itic subculture itself.

The Individual Tanna'itic Texts and Their Treatment of *Tefillin*[145]

Early rabbinic literature consists, in the first place, of the Mishnah, the Tosefta, and the various Midreshei Halakah, and the bulk of its traditions are probably to be dated to the first half of the third century or earlier. In

---

140. For a nuanced discussion of the rabbinic attitude to attribution, albeit limited to the Bavli, see Sacha Stern, "Attribution and Authorship in the Babylonian Talmud," *Journal of Jewish Studies* 45 (1994): 28–51.

141. See the comments in Cohen, "The Rabbi in Second-Century Jewish Society," 924–25.

142. The start of this revolution is to be dated to Jacob Neusner, *Development of a Legend: Studies on the Traditions Concerning Yohanan Ben Zakkai* (Leiden: Brill, 1970). Cf. Seth Schwartz, "Historiography on the 'Talmudic Period'," in *The Oxford Handbook of Jewish Studies*, ed. Martin Goodman (Oxford: Oxford University Press, 2002), 100–102.

143. The approach was perhaps first put to use (on a far larger scale than I will be undertaking) in Goodman, *State and Society in Roman Galilee*.

144. See Cotton, "The Rabbis and the Documents," 179; Martin Goodman, "Jews, Greeks and Romans," in *Jews in a Graeco-Roman World*, ed. Martin Goodman (Oxford: Clarendon, 1998), 9.

145. There is certain potential for confusion in common nomenclature, which I will try to avoid by using the following conventions:

    1. The smallest Mishnaic unit will be spelled "mishnah" (plural "mishnayot"), whereas the entire work will be spelled "Mishnah."

part, these reflect conditions preexisting the destruction of the Temple; to give one example from the *tefillin* context, M. *Sanhedrin* 11:3 and M. *Kelim* 18:8 both refer to four-compartment *tefillin* cases, which are already in evidence in Qumran. It is, however, often difficult to determine when individual traditions came into being.[146]

Tefillin are treated in an offhand manner in both Mishnah and Tosefta, where they are not the subject of primary interest for a single chapter, much less any one tractate. They are, so to speak, a "black box," and when mentioned they are essentially presumed to be entirely familiar objects, whose contents and construction, together with the "when and how" of wearing them, merit almost no comment. Rulings governing *tefillin* are, however, by no means absent in these works, although in almost all cases the discussion seems to provide incidental information while dwelling on other matters.

The Midreshei Halakah, which cite the same first- to third-century rabbis as the Mishnah and Tosefta, arose from a similar cultural milieu but are quite different in genre. In commenting on four Pentateuchal books, from Exodus to Deuteronomy, they serve to correlate tanna'itic halakah/legend with scriptural antecedents by deriving the former from scriptural sources.[147] In discussing *tefillin*, these works devote much of their attention to exactly how and when to wear them, and what they contained. Their purpose in doing so is not so much to list *tefillin* rules as to derive them from biblical texts, but they provide a rich source for how the rabbis wanted the practice to be observed. It is also likely that the tanna'im were, in deriving such details from scripture using midrashic methods, largely referring to previously well-established practices. (It is worth noting that some of the prerabbinic practitioners had likely tried to derive correct *tefil-*

---

2. The smallest Toseftan unit will be spelled "tosefta," whereas the entire work will be spelled "Tosefta."

3. The word used to describe rabbinic law/s will be written "halakah" (plural "halakot").

4. The corpus of Tanna'itic Midrashim will be referred to as "Midreshei Halakah," whereas the method of deriving halakah from scripture will be referred to as "midrash" or "midrash halakah." Individual derivations will be referred to as *"derashot"* (singular *"derashah"*).

146. See H. L. Strack and Günter Stemberger, *Introduction to the Talmud and Midrash*, trans. Marcus Bockmühl (Minneapolis: Fortress, 1996), 150–58. By and large, the Tosefta looks as though it is commenting or otherwise relating to the Mishnah, suggesting that its traditions are relatively late, although it has also been argued that many Toseftan traditions are actually older than their Mishnaic counterparts. For recent treatments, see Shamma Friedman, *Tosefta Atiqta* (Ramat Gan: Bar-Ilan University Press, 2002, in Hebrew); Judith Hauptman, *Rereading the Mishnah* (Tübingen: Mohr Siebeck, 2005).

147. The works include *Mekhilta Derabbi Yishma'el, Mekhilta Derabbi Shimon bar Yohai, Sifra, Sifre Bamidbar, Sifre Zuta, Sifre Devarim* and *Midrash Tanna'im.* See Strack and Stemberger, *Introduction to the Talmud and Midrash*, 247–75.

lin performance from scripture, and some *derashot* in Midreshei Halakah may similarly reflect prerabbinic origins.)

As the immediate context for a *derashah* is the verses to which it relates, it is not surprising that the overwhelming majority of relevant material is to be found in the Mekhiltot and in *Sifre Devarim/Midrash Tanna'im*, whose foci are the book of Exodus, in the case of the former, and Deuteronomy, in the case of the latter.[148] In large measure the different Midrashim are, as far as *tefillin* is concerned, engaged in deriving the same halakot, and there is much repetition over the various works. It is, however, worth noting that they do not always cover the same ground. Thus, although the Mekhiltot and *Sifre Devarim* seem to be in accord with respect to the precise texts to be included in *tefillin* parchments, the former show no interest in justifying the choice to omit alternative texts. *Sifre Devarim*, on the other hand, unlike the Mekhiltot, contains no passages discussing who wore *tefillin* and when they were worn. Where there is repetition I have generally (and arbitrarily) cited *Mekhilta Derabbi Yishma'el* over *Sifre Devarim*, with references to the latter in the footnotes. I have also cited *Mekhilta Derabbi Yishma'el/Sifre Devarim* in preference to *Mekhilta Derabbi Shimon bar Yohai/Midrash Tanna'im*, respectively, where these repeat each other. Editions of the latter are, strictly speaking, reconstructions of texts that are no longer extant in other than fragmentary form.[149]

It is also to be noted that the Gemara, redacted much later in both of its varieties (Yerushalmi and Bavli), also contains much material that is purportedly tanna'itic (as well as other material that is purportedly from the third century[150]). This is in the form of *baraitot*—material ostensibly omitted from the Mishnah but in currency at the same time as its formation, as well as legends about tanna'im. To the extent that these are not paralleled in other sources, namely, the Tosefta and Midreshei Halakah, modern scholars consider their early provenance suspect. This is because some are demonstrably post-tanna'itic, and the idea that most are not seems of little consequence (these sections may often have been drafted in order to seem older than they really were, and there may simply be no good way of telling the difference).[151] Accordingly, it seems best to omit them, at any rate in the first instance, when considering the evidence of

---

148. *Sifre Zuta* is highly fragmentary and includes no reference to *tefillin*; the relevant Deuteronomy verses were not recovered. See Menahem Kahana, *Sifre Zuta on Deuteronomy* (Jerusalem: Magnes, 2002).

149. See Strack and Stemberger, *Introduction to the Talmud and Midrash*, 247–75.

150. For example, traditions attributed therein to R. Yohanan, a third-century Palestinian amora.

151. Louis Jacobs, "Are There Fictitious Baraitot in the Babylonian Talmud?," *Hebrew Union College Annual* 42 (1971): 185–96; Louis Jacobs, "How Much of the Babylonian Talmud Is Pseudepigraphic?," *Journal of Jewish Studies* 28, no. 1 (1977): 45–59; Strack and Stemberger, *Introduction to the Talmud and Midrash*, 177–78 and 98–99.

the first to third centuries. While treating them as reliable evidence from the tanna'itic era might present a different picture than will be painted here, as well perhaps as provide further evidence for some of my conclusions, it is beyond my scope to do so.

Another work, *Massekhet Tefillin*, which resembles the Mishnah and Tosefta in genre, will also be omitted from consideration. The first attestation to the seven minor tractates, in which *Massekhet Tefillin* is traditionally included, is by Nahmanides in the thirteenth century,[152] and it seems best to view the work as an assemblage of talmudic material on *tefillin* that is itself to be dated to the Geonic era (after the advent of Islam).[153] Much like other *baraitot*, *Massekhet Tefillin* is ostensibly tanna'itic,[154] but this provenance is highly questionable for similar reasons. Andreas Lehnardt's argument for early dating, on the grounds that *Massekhet Tefillin* seems more interested than the Bavli in promoting the wearing of *tefillin* throughout the day, does not seem at all compelling.[155] In fact, it seems more likely to me, if this is the case, that the work postdated the Bavli; I argue below that *tefillin* were routinely worn throughout the day in tanna'itic times, and there may well have been no particular engagement with the issue, even as late as the Bavli.

While chapter 4 will provide further discussion, a few other observations can already be made here:

a. Within this period I intend to take a broadly synchronic approach to the literature, while analyzing evidence for development to the extent that I find it.

b. Later rabbinic reflections on the history of the tanna'itic period will not be considered relevant, as the rabbis concerned were not engaged in historiography (and may indeed have known quite little about the period).

c. Later rabbinic interpretations, of the passages to be discussed, extend from the time of their composition to the twenty-first century, and will usually not be cited. Such interpretations are generally concerned, even if not by design, with other considerations than establishing the most plausible meaning of ancient texts. This is because they are often motivated by such factors as the resolution of incon-

---

152. See Andreas Lenhardt, "Massekhet Tefillin—Beobachtungen zur literarischen Genese eines kleinen Talmud-Traktates," in *Jewish Studies between the Disciplines*, ed. K. Herrmann, M. Schlüter, and G. Veltri (Leiden and Boston: Brill, 2003), 30 and n. 9.

153. See Louis Rabinowitz, "Tefillin," in *Encyclopaedia Judaica* (Jerusalem: Keter, 1972); Robert Brody, *The Geonim of Babylonia and the Shaping of Medieval Jewish Culture* (New Haven and London: Yale University Press, 1998), 109–10.

154. See M. B. Lerner, "The External Tractates," in *The Literature of the Sages*, ed. S. Safrai (Maastricht and Philadelphia: Assen, 1987), 367–403.

155. See Lenhardt, "Massekhet Tefillin." Lehnardt's article is an in-depth treatment of Massekhet Tefillin, and here I am only taking issue with this particular claim.

sistencies or the denial of redundancy, or are at any rate unwilling
to contest prior interpretations that were motivated by those factors.

The next three chapters follow a historical framework. Chapter 2 dis-
cusses the period prior to the Jewish encounter with Hellenistic culture;
chapter 3 deals with the late–Second Temple era, and chapter 4 focuses on
the nature of the practice from 70 c.e. until the third century. The meaning of the *tefillin* ritual, particularly during this latter period, will be discussed separately in chapter 5.

2

Deuteronomy to Alexander
(Seventh Century B.C.E. to 331 B.C.E.)

This chapter will investigate whether the practice of wearing *tefillin* was already in existence during the late-monarchic, exilic, and/or Persian periods. It should be stated at the outset that there is no archaeological evidence that would date the ritual to this era, or an earlier one. Nor does the literature covered in this chapter depict any individual as wearing *tefillin*[1] (excluded here is any midrashic understanding of biblical passages as containing a depiction of this kind).

The Hebrew Bible

The "Traditional" Tefillin References

The basis for *tefillin* practice has traditionally been associated with four Torah verses—Exod 13:9 and 16, and Deut 6:8 and 11:18—that were taken to refer to wearing objects containing inscribed text, on the arm and on the head. Specifically, as will be discussed in chapter 3, late–Second Temple era archaeological findings demonstrate a link between *tefillin* and these verses, and Hellenistic writings may do the same (for the Deuteronomy verses, at least). *Tefillin* practice continued to be connected to these verses

---

1. Jeffrey Tigay, however, interpreted the word *tply*, in a Ugaritic description of Baal, as referring to a head ornament with apotropaic functions worn by the god. See Marvin H. Pope and Jeffrey H. Tigay, "A Description of Baal, Part 4," *Ugarit-Forschungen* 3 (1971): 124–26. Alternative suggestions for interpreting the Ugaritic have been offered; see Pope and Tigay, "A Description of Baal, Part 4," 127; David Rothstein, "From Bible to Murabba'at: Studies in the Literary, Textual and Scribal Features of Phylacteries and Mezuzot in Ancient Israel and Early Judaism" (Ph.D. diss., UCLA, 1992), 79–80.

in rabbinic and patristic sources, as will be shown in chapter 4. The issue at stake here is whether an understanding of certain sections of the Torah as referring to the practice of *tefillin* is likely to have predated the late Second Temple period. For purposes of this discussion the verses themselves will be presumed to predate the Babylonian exile. This seems a suitably cautious position, and at least as likely as the alternative.[2]

(It is to be noted, however, that there is little consensus regarding the date to be assigned to Moses' speech in Exod 13:3–16, which includes two of the above-mentioned verses.[3] Brevard Childs and Martin Noth categorize these verses as Deuteronomic/Deuteronomistic,[4] while Walter Houston sees them as part of a much earlier J strand.[5] M. Caloz [following N. Lohfink[6]] argued that they were to be dated prior to the Josianic reform,[7] and Molly Zahn, that they belonged to the very latest layers of the Pentateuch.[8] The similarities between the four *tefillin* verses have played a role in the argument for the Deuteronomic redaction of the Exodus speech—as has the correspondence between the mention of spoken Torah in Exod 13:9 and a similar theme in Deut 6:7 and 11:19.[9]

The passages from Deuteronomy that include 6:8 and 11:18 are generally dated, with much of the book, to the seventh century B.C.E. at the earliest. Arguments have been made for considering various parts of Deuteronomy as later compositions, with the possibility that the relevant passages are postmonarchic.[10])

---

2. See Nahum M. Sarna, "Exodus, Book of," in *The Anchor Bible Dictionary* (New York: Doubleday, 1992), 694–95; Moshe Weinfeld, "Deuteronomy, Book of," in *The Anchor Bible Dictionary* (New York: Doubleday, 1992), 171–74; Bultmann, "Deuteronomy," 136–37; Houston, "Exodus," 75–76.

3. See Cornelis Houtman, *Exodus*, trans. S. Woudstra (Kampen: Kok, 1996), 2:147–48.

4. Martin Noth, *Exodus*, trans. J. S. Bowden (London: SCM, 1962), 101; Brevard S. Childs, *Exodus* (London: SCM, 1974), 184.

5. Walter Houston, "Exodus," in *The Oxford Bible Commentary*, ed. John Barton and John Muddiman (Oxford: Oxford University Press, 2001), 19–20 and 75.

6. N. Lohfink, *Das Hauptgebot: Eine Untersuchung literarischer Einleitungsfragen zu Dtn 5–11* (Rome: Pontifical Biblical Institute, 1963), 121.

7. M. Caloz, "Exode, xiii, 3–16 et son rapport au Deutéronome," *Revue Biblique* 75 (1968): 5–62.

8. Molly M. Zahn, "Remember This Day: Grounding Law in Narrative through Redactional Composition (Exod 13:1–16)" (M.Phil. diss., University of Oxford, 2003), 44.

9. See J. Philip Hyatt, *Exodus* (Grand Rapids: Eerdmans, 1980), 142. An alternative approach sees the Deuteronomy *tefillin* verses as dependent on the earlier Exodus ones; see Michael V. Fox, "The Sign of the Covenant," *Revue Biblique* 81 (1974): 568.

10. See A. D. H. Mayes, *Deuteronomy* (Grand Rapids: Eerdmans, 1981), 81–82; Moshe Weinfeld, *Deuteronomy 1–11*, Anchor Bible (New York: Doubleday, 1991), 17; Christoph Bultmann, "Deuteronomy," in *The Oxford Bible Commentary*, ed. John Barton and John Muddiman (Oxford: Oxford University Press, 2001), 135–37; J. G. McConville, *Deuteronomy* (Leicester: Apollos, 2002), 26–28; Richard D. Nelson, *Deuteronomy* (Louisville: Westminster John Knox, 2002), 6–7. Tigay gives eighth–seventh centuries B.C.E. as the likely date; see Jeffrey

As I stated in chapter 1, it is not the verses' original meaning, in the sense of "authorial intent," that is of importance for this study but rather their reception; specifically, my concern is simply to determine when they were first understood to refer to the practice of *tefillin*, as known from the Dead Sea scrolls and other sources. Accordingly, the culture that produced the verses is not of primary concern (although that would change if the practice were to be dated as far back as the origin of the verses).[11] In order to evaluate the likely course of reception, the first steps will be to lay out their apparent meaning and literary context.

The Meaning of the Four Verses[12]

Exodus 13:9: Translation

And it will[a] become[b], for you, like a sign[c] on your hand[d] and a reminder[e] between your eyes[f], in order that YHWH's instruction be in your mouth, that[g] YHWH took you out of Egypt with a strong hand.

Translation Notes

a.   The idea that the Exodus verses entail a prediction will be contextualized below. Others have translated this as "shall," connoting an exhortation rather than a prediction.[13]

H. Tigay, *The JPS Torah Commentary, Deuteronomy* (Philadelphia: Jewish Publication Society, 1996), xx–xxi.

11. For a fuller evaluation of literary-cultural issues, contemporary with the biblical texts, see Rothstein, "From Bible to Murabba'at," 38–123.

12. For variants of the Hebrew verses, see A. F. Von Gall, *Der hebräische Pentateuch der Samaritaner* (Giessen: Töpelmann, 1918); Avraham and Ratson Sadaqa, *Jewish and Samaritan Version of the Pentateuch* (Israel: Rubin Mass, 1961–64); Yigael Yadin, *Tefillin from Qumran (XQPhyl 1–4)* (Jerusalem: Israel Exploration Society and Shrine of the Book, 1970); J. T. Milik, "Tefillin, Mezuzot et Targums," in *Discoveries in the Judaean Desert*, vol. 6 (Oxford: Oxford University Press, 1977); *Biblia Hebraica Stuttgartensia* (Stuttgart: Deutsche Bibelgesellschaft, 1984); Weinfeld, *Deuteronomy 1–11*; Judith E. Sanderson, "4QExod^d," in *Discoveries in the Judaean Desert*, vol. 12 (Oxford: Clarendon, 1994); Abraham Tal, *The Samaritan Pentateuch* (Tel Aviv: Tel Aviv University, 1994); Sidnie White Crawford, "4QDeut^c," in *Discoveries in the Judaean Desert*, vol. 14 (Oxford: Clarendon, 1995); Sidnie White Crawford, "4QDeut^p," in *Discoveries in the Judaean Desert*, vol. 14 (Oxford: Clarendon, 1995); William H. C. Propp, *Exodus 1–18*, Anchor Bible (New York: Doubleday, 1999); M. Morgenstern and M. Segal, "XHev/SePhylactery," in *Discoveries in the Judaean Desert*, vol. 38 (Oxford: Oxford University Press, 2000).

13. See, for example, Robert Alter, *The Five Books of Moses* (New York: W. W. Norton, 2004).

b.   The Hebrew *hayah le-* frequently relates to "becoming,"[14] and can further connote resemblance.[15] Thus, in Num 33:55 this form clearly refers to "becoming like" something, and it can be interpreted in similar fashion in Gen 11:3. Other possibilities are closer to "be," or "be like."[16]

c.   The translation of the Hebrew *ot* will be considered in further detail at the end of this section.

d.   This seems a better solution than "arm,"[17] as hand is the normal meaning of the Hebrew word *yad*.[18]

e.   Alternatively, *zikkaron* might be "memorial,"[19] or "remembrance."[20]

f.   This seems better than "on your forehead" as a literal translation, although the Hebrew expression might connote this (or perhaps "on your head").[21] Biblical Hebrew does have its own way of expressing "forehead," namely, the word *metsah*.[22]

g.   The word *ki* has been rendered "that," being taken as introducing the content signified by the sign to which the verse refers.[23] It could have been rendered "for," and thus read as introducing the motive for having a sign.[24] Another possibility is "namely that," as in Rashi, introducing God's role in the exodus as the subject of the opening word *vehayah*.

Exodus 13:16: Translation

And it will become like a sign on your hand, and *totafot*[a] between your eyes, that YHWH took us out of Egypt with strength of hand.

---

14. See *The New Brown–Driver–Briggs–Gesenius Hebrew and English Lexicon* (Peabody, Mass.: Hendrickson, 1979), 512. Cf. "and they shall become," in Deut 11:18 (Alter, *The Five Books of Moses*).

15. Interestingly, in Num 13:33 "in our eyes" and "in their eyes" are themselves to be understood as expressing resemblance, much as they might in the English idiom. Although "between your eyes," in the verses under consideration here, is a different Hebrew construction than "in our/their eyes" in Numbers 13, the two might not be far apart in meaning.

16. See *The Cambridge Annotated Study Bible: N.R.S.V.* (Cambridge: Cambridge University Press, 1993); Propp, *Exodus 1–18*.

17. But see Propp, *Exodus 1–18*.

18. See P. R. Ackroyd, "Yad," in *Theological Dictionary of the Old Testament* (Grand Rapids: Eerdmans, 1986), 5:400.

19. See Propp, *Exodus 1–18*.

20. See Alter, *The Five Books of Moses*.

21. See the notes in Weinfeld, *Deuteronomy 1–11*, 335; Propp, *Exodus 1–18*, 423.

22. See, for example, Exod 28:38.

23. See Cornelis Houtman, *Exodus*, trans. J. Rebel and S. Woudstra (Kampen: Kok, 1993), 1:33–34.

24. For a list of verses where *ki* may similarly introduce the provision of a rationale, see Michael Fishbane, "The Biblical *Ot*," *Shnaton, an Annual for Biblical and Ancient Near Eastern Studies* 1 (1975): 219 and n. 22 (in Hebrew).

Translation Note[25]

    a.   In view of the singular verb *vehayah*, it seems plausible that the noun is also singular (cf. two Samaritan variants, where both verb and noun are plural), but the Masoretic vocalization reads *totafot* rather than the singular—which would presumably be vocalized as *totefet*. Its meaning will be considered below.

Deuteronomy 6:8: Translation

And you shall tie them as[a] a sign on your hand; let them be[b] as *totafot* between your eyes.

Translation Notes[26]

    a.   There is no biblical parallel that might shed light on the precise meaning of the preposition *le-* in the words *uqeshartam le'ot*.[27]

    b.   This rendering attempts to incorporate the ambiguity of the Hebrew, and thus allows for the possibility that *vehayu* here anticipates the outcome of binding and might not constitute a separate injunction.[28] "And they shall become" would have a similar effect.[29]

Deuteronomy 11:18—Translation

You are to place these my words upon your heart and upon your soul[a], and you shall tie them as a sign on your hand; let them be as *totafot* between your eyes.

Translation Note[30]

    a.   The word *nefesh* here has also been rendered "self,"[31] and "being."[32] Another possibility is "neck" (as in Jon 2:6, Prov 3:22 and Ps 69:2).[33]

---

25. See also the notes to the previous translation.
26. See also the notes to the previous translations.
27. See J. Gamberoni, "Totapot," in *Theological Dictionary of the Old Testament*, ed. H Ringgren (Grand Rapids: Eerdmans, 1986), 5:321.
28. See Rothstein, "From Bible to Murabba'at," 9–10.
29. See Deut 11:18 in Alter, *The Five Books of Moses*.
30. See also the notes to the previous translations.
31. *Tanakh: A New Translation* (Philadelphia and Jerusalem: Jewish Publication Society, 1985); Alter, *The Five Books of Moses*.
32. Everett Fox, *The Five Books of Moses* (New York: Schocken, 1995).
33. I owe this suggestion to John Day and Hugh Williamson, who read an early draft of this chapter.

The most problematic issue in an initial rendering of these verses is the meaning of *totafot*, which although quite likely a singular form in origin, has traditionally been vocalized as a plural.[34] The word is otherwise unattested in the Bible and has inspired a variety of reasoned etymologies and translations.[35] The most widely accepted views are that the word refers specifically to a headband, or, more generally, to something that encircles (a body part such as the head) or, alternatively, to a pendant. In Jeffrey Tigay's view, *totafot* might have its origins in the characteristic head-straps of Syria/Israel, as depicted in Egyptian and Assyrian drawings of people from that region. The scriptural *totafot* would then be understood as reflecting a known custom of wearing an adornment or charm on the forehead, held in place by such straps.[36] With meager evidence for any of the alternatives, a clear-cut understanding remains elusive.[37] It is, however, worth noting the consensus that the word, while having no connotation of including written text, denotes a concrete entity (to be contrasted with the "reminder" in Exod 13:9).[38] On the other hand, the earliest translation, which is in the Septuagint, does not refer to a concrete entity;[39] thus, if modern scholars are correct as to this aspect of the word's original meaning, then the latter was apparently obscure to at least some readers of these verses by the third century B.C.E., if not earlier.

Somewhat less attention has been paid to the precise meaning of the word *ot* in these four verses, routinely rendered by "sign." The English word will continue to be used here for brevity and convenience, but the sign, if such it is, would have no signified object in the Deuteronomy verses (the lack of a signified object was already noted, in so many words, by Philo[40]). This alone makes the conventional translation problematic. *Ot* is most often to be understood in the Bible as denoting wondrous acts or predictions, whether by God or by prophets, demonstrating divine power

---

34. See Jeffrey H. Tigay, "On the Meaning of T(W)TPT," *Journal of Biblical Literature* 101 (1982): 321–22; Weinfeld, *Deuteronomy 1–11*, 334; Rothstein, "From Bible to Murabba'at," 45–46; Propp, *Exodus 1–18*, 373.

35. See E. A. Speiser, "TWTPT," *Jewish Quarterly Review* 48 (1957–58): 208–17; Tigay, "On the Meaning of T(W)TPT," 321–22; Weinfeld, *Deuteronomy 1–11*, 333–34; Rothstein, "From Bible to Murabba'at," 38–56.

36. Tigay, "On the Meaning of T(W)TPT," 328–30.

37. See Gamberoni, "Totapot," 5:321. Most recently Weinfeld has observed that "it must be admitted that the large amount of ink spilled in the effort to decipher the derivation and original meaning of this word has not led to conclusive results" (Moshe Weinfeld, *The Decalogue and the Recitation of "Shema": The Development of the Confessions* [Tel Aviv: Hakibbutz Hameuchad, 2001], 139 [in Hebrew]).

38. This is in accord with the next recorded use of the word, which is in the Mishnah; see *M. Shabbat* 6:1 and 6:5, paralleled in *T. Shabbat* 4:6.

39. The Septuagint's translation will be discussed in chapter 3.

40. See *De specialibus legibus* 4.26.138: "Of what it is a sign he has not definitely stated." Philo's comments will be discussed in chapter 3.

or divine agency at work. One example, in the books under consideration here, is from Exod 4:8–9, where the word refers to specific supernatural powers given to Moses, in order that the people believe that God appeared to him. In Deut 13:2–3 *ot* refers to an oracular utterance performed by a prophet or dreamer that calls for worshiping other gods. Scholars have analyzed the word in a variety of biblical contexts, and it seems fair to say that "sign," on its own, inadequately conveys the word's meaning.[41]

One English word, whose semantic field seems close to a common biblical usage of *ot*, is "oracle."[42] In other instances, the English "portent," or "omen," seems to capture the meaning most closely.[43] The word has also been rendered "mark"[44] or "guarantee."[45] Michael Fox classified the *ot* in all four of the verses under consideration here as mnemonic signs, which seems to work well in Exodus, but at first sight is less compelling for Deuteronomy.[46]

The Verses in Their Scriptural Context

Exodus 13:9 and 13:16

These two verses are part of Moses' address to the people in Exod 13:3–16, which begins with the instructions to remember the event of the exodus and God's strength of hand in bringing it about, and to refrain from eating anything leavened. In vv. 4 and 5, Moses tells the people that God is to be served, after bringing them to the promised land, during the month in which the exodus took place. Mention is made of "this service," which might refer to the previous chapter's *Pesah* meal, but more likely relates to the ensuing verses.[47] Here, in vv. 6–7, Moses specifies a seven-day period during which unleavened bread is to be eaten and leavened products are to be eschewed, with a festival on the seventh day. In verse 8 Moses further instructs the people to tell their children on that day about

---

41. See N. H. Tur-Sinai, *"Otot* in the Bible and in the Lachish Letters," in *J. N. Epstein Jubilee Volume* (Jerusalem: Magnes Press, Hebrew University, 1950), 49–57 (in Hebrew); Fox, "The Sign of the Covenant," 559–62; Fishbane, "The Biblical *Ot*," 214–29. In his important article Fox criticized the approach of Tur-Sinai, and argued for an alternative perspective.

42. See Fishbane, "The Biblical *Ot*," 214–29.

43. Thus, for example, 1 Sam 14:10.

44. Famously in Gen 4:15, the mark of Cain.

45. See James Kugel, *How to Read the Bible* (New York: Free Press, 2007), 717 n. 23.

46. Fox, "The Sign of the Covenant," 563–64, 67–69. See F. J. Helfmeyer, "Oth," in *Theological Dictionary of the Old Testament* (Grand Rapids: Eerdmans, 1977), 1:179–81; M. Z. Kaddari, "Ot," in *A Dictionary of Biblical Hebrew* (Ramat Gan: Bar-Ilan University Press, 2006).

47. See Houtman, *Exodus*, 2:212.

the connection of these practices to God's having effected the exodus.[48] Verse 9, one of the four verses translated above, is likely addressed directly to the people (although it has also been taken as continuing a quotation from the speech they are to make to their children[49]). Moses talks of a sign on the hand, and a reminder between the eyes. The referent of the verse is not entirely clear, but it seems to refer to eating *matsot*/no leaven, and to the festival mentioned in verse 6.[50] The tone is probably best taken as predicting that these will function as a sign and a reminder, rather than constituting supplementary instruction.[51] It seems that some sort of trope is involved, one that *reflected* a known practice of placing material objects or markings on the body as a commemorative sign. Alternatively, one might consider the possibility that the body parts in verse 9 are metonyms, so that *al yadekha* is not so much "on your hand" but rather "through you."[52] In this reading, the actions of the people (in eating *matsot*, and so on) come to signify to others that God effected the exodus with a strong hand. In addition to being a sign to others, these actions are at the same time a reminder in their own eyes of the same thing.[53]

(It is also noteworthy that in Josh 4:5–7 the motive for having a commemorative sign—an *ot* that is a *zikkaron*, as here—is to prompt its own explanation, in a speech to be given to future generations. A similar motive in Exod 13:8–9 could explain the otherwise difficult clause "in order that YHWH's instruction be in your mouth."[54] A connection between a child's question and a sign is to be found in Josh 4:6, as well as Deut 6:20-25.[55])

Scribal tradition has verse 10 as a part of the above section, although it might originally have opened the following one.[56] The verse mandates the continuing requirement to observe "this law." In the ensuing section (vv. 11–16), Moses addresses the people on the subject of firstborn consecration, of which God had spoken to him at the beginning of the chapter. Verses 11–13 describe the practice, to be undertaken after God has brought the people to the promised land. The following two verses then make a connection between firstborn consecration and God's having killed the Egyptian firstborn at the exodus, which is introduced by making that connection the answer that a parent is to give to a child who questions the

---

48. The precise intent of the prescribed utterance is unclear. See Propp, *Exodus 1–18*, 423.

49. For a discussion of this point, see ibid., 425. See also the reference in the following footnote.

50. See Houtman, *Exodus*, 2:213–14.

51. See ibid., 214; Tigay, *The JPS Torah Commentary, Deuteronomy*, 443.

52. For examples of metonymic usage of *yad*, see Gen 42:37 and Jer 18:21.

53. See Num 13:33.

54. See Houtman, *Exodus*, 2:214.

55. See Mayes, *Deuteronomy*, 175.

56. See Propp, *Exodus 1–18*, 425.

practice (in a parallel, of sorts, to verse 8). As part of the answer, mention is also made of the strength of God's hand in taking the people out of Egypt, which echoes vv. 3 and 9. Verse 16 (one of the four translated above) might be a continuation of this answer, although it seems more likely that it is not,[57] and in either event parallels 13:9 very closely; indeed, the ambiguity itself is a characteristic shared with 13:9. Here, though, it is firstborn consecration (not eating *matsot*, or a festival) that is to become a sign on the hand and *totafot* (rather than the "reminder" in verse 9) between the eyes. Just as in 13:9, Moses seems in verse 16 to be anticipating the outcome of a ritual (here the firstborn consecration ritual), and not elaborating on its performance.[58] Thus, in context, there seems no good reason for understanding Exod 13:9 and 16 as calling for any physical act whatsoever; one can hardly put *matsot*, or a firstborn consecration ceremony, on one's body. It is noteworthy that the twelfth-century rabbinic exegete R. Samuel ben Me'ir (a grandson of Rashi) famously asserted in his commentary to Exod 13:9 that the sign on the hand most simply referred to a reminder—one permanently present, as if literally inscribed on the hand of the person to be reminded—despite centuries of rabbinic tradition that read verse 13:9 as referring to *tefillin*. He related his understanding to the decidedly non-literal usage in Song 8:6: "Set me as a signet on your heart, As a signet on your arm."

The idiom of Exodus in these verses has, of course, been the subject of inquiry by modern biblicists as well; Tigay, in particular, pointed to other biblical and ancient Near Eastern sources that mention items of clothing or adornment in metonymic usage, representing things constantly remembered, or held close, or viewed as dear by those who wear them.[59]

Deuteronomy 6:8

The larger context of Deut 6:8 begins with the Decalogue in Deut 5:6–21 and its aftermath.[60] Verse 5:22 refers to the Decalogue as "these words," spoken by God to the entire assembly and transcribed on two stone tablets that were given to Moses. Deuteronomy 5:23–31 describe the people's reluctance to continue hearing God's voice directly, and their assent to Moses acting as an intermediary. In 5:32–6:3 Moses tells the peo-

---

57. See ibid., 373.

58. See Houtman, *Exodus*, vol. 2, 218; Tigay, *The JPS Torah Commentary, Deuteronomy*, 443.

59. Several examples are collected in Tigay, "On the Meaning of T(W)TPT," 327.

60. The numbering of the verses in Deuteronomy 5 is not standardized over different editions, neither in Hebrew nor in English. For the sake of consistency with archaeologists' reconstructions of Judean Desert *tefillin* (which will be discussed in chapters 3 and 4) I herein follow a common "Christian" numbering; see *The Cambridge Annotated Study Bible: N.R.S.V.*

ple that they are to observe God's commands unwaveringly, speaking of the ones that were given him to teach to them. The people, fearing God, are to follow these in the land that they are about to possess. A motif of length of days appears in 5:16 in connection with honoring parents, and in a more general way in 5:33 and 6:2–3.

Deuteronomy 6:4–9 is the first part of the traditional Jewish *Shema* prayer. In vv. 4–5 Moses tells the people to listen to his declaration that YHWH their God is the one and only YHWH,[61] whom they are to love with all their heart, soul, and might. Verse 6 contains an interpretative crux for our purposes, because in its instruction that "these words" commanded by Moses on that day be on the people's heart it includes the referent for 6:8 (as well as its adjacent verses). One explanation is that "these words" refer to the prior two verses (that is, to their content after the introductory "Hear, Israel").[62] Deuteronomy 5:22 had, however, used the identical expression in referring to the Decalogue, also known as "words" in Deut 4:10, 12, 13, 36; 9:10; 10:2, 4, which accordingly suggests another possible referent. At first sight, the concomitant claim in verse 6:6 that it was Moses rather than God who had commanded the Decalogue might seem an inappropriate one for Moses to be making. There is, however, reason to embrace the possibility that 6:6 indeed refers to the Decalogue. For one thing, verse 5:5 (just before the Decalogue) states that Moses had intervened between God and the people at that time to tell them the word of God.[63] More importantly, perhaps, Moses is presented in Deuteronomy as reminding the people of events from many years earlier. Thus, on the day mentioned in verse 6:6, it is he and not God who repeats to them the commands of the Decalogue (similarly, in Deut 5:1, Moses is apparently including the Decalogue when referring to those things that "I speak in your hearing this day"). A third alternative for the referent of "these words" in Deut 6:6, focuses on the adjacent words, "that I command you." In 6:1–2 the commandment (*mitsvah*) seems to cover a broad range, not to be limited to the Decalogue, and the commanded words of 6:6 may accordingly be similar in scope, perhaps intended to include the entire book.[64]

---

61. Following the interpretation of S. R. Driver, *A Critical and Exegetical Commentary on Deuteronomy*, 3rd ed., International Critical Commentary (Edinburgh: T. & T. Clark, 1895 [1965 impression]), 89–90. Driver's view is also favored in Weinfeld, *The Decalogue and the Recitation of "Shema,"* 127. For an elaboration of possible meanings, see McConville, *Deuteronomy*, 140–41.

62. See Othmar Keel, "Zeichen der Verbundenheit," in *Mélanges Dominique Barthélemy*, ed. Pierre Casetti, Othmar Keel, and Adrian Schenker (Fribourg: Editions Universitaires, 1981), 165.

63. Deuteronomy 5:5 is apparently contradicted in this respect by Deut 5:4; 5:22; and others. See Weinfeld, *Deuteronomy 1–11*, 240.

64. See Eduard Nielsen, *Deuteronomium* (Tübingen: Mohr-Siebeck, 1995), 87; Tigay, *The*

In any event, Deut 6:7–9 proceeds to refer to these words. They are to be impressed upon children and recited both at home and away from home, on lying down and on arising. Verse 8 (one of the four translated above) is a parallel to Exod 13:16, which had mentioned neither words nor tying. Verse 9 ends the section with the instruction that the words be written on (or possibly over) the doorposts of houses and (city[65]) gates.

Deuteronomy 11:18

Deuteronomy 11:18–20 is a close parallel to 6:6–9, but with changes in sequence. 11:18 (the fourth of the verses translated above) echoes 6:6 and 6:8, with 11:19 echoing 6:7, and 11:20 identical to 6:9.[66] In 11:18, "these my words" are the referent for pronouns throughout vv. 18–20. They might refer to the adjacent verses,[67] although scholars have tended to view them as applying in a more general way to the discourse of the entire book.[68]

The larger context for Deut 11:18–20 is to be found in the verses that bracket them. Deuteronomy 11:8–9 urge the people to observe the commandments, so as to gain the strength to take possession of the promised land flowing with milk and honey and enjoy length of days there. In vv. 10–12, Moses explains that the land will not be like Egypt; rather, it is dependent on rainfall, and hence on God's providence. Verses 13–17 include the assurance that provided the commandments to love and fully serve God are obeyed, the people's agricultural endeavors will flourish. Moses warns them, however, that if they serve other gods, then YHWH will be angry and withhold rain, the earth will not yield its produce, and they will quickly perish from the land. The section continues with verse 21 (which echoes 6:2–3[69]): "In order that your days may be many, along with the days of your children, on the soil that YHWH swore to your fathers, to give them (as long) as the days of the heavens over the earth." Verses 22–25 may be viewed as concluding this section, with further discussion of entry into the promised land.

JPS Torah Commentary, Deuteronomy, 78; Jean-Pierre Sonnet, *The Book within the Book: Writing in Deuteronomy* (Leiden: Brill, 1997), 52–55; Nelson, *Deuteronomy,* 91.

65. See Mayes, *Deuteronomy,* 178; Tigay, *The JPS Torah Commentary, Deuteronomy,* 79.

66. See Nielsen, *Deuteronomium,* 126. There are changes from singular to plural forms, both within 11:18–20 and when compared to 6:6–9, that are characteristic of Deuteronomy. See Duane L. Christensen, *Deuteronomy 1:1–21:9* (Nashville: Thomas Nelson, 2001), xcix–ci; Nelson, *Deuteronomy,* 5–6.

67. Keel, "Zeichen der Verbundenheit," 165–66.

68. See Weinfeld, *Deuteronomy 1–11,* 340.

69. See McConville, *Deuteronomy,* 142.

Deuteronomy and Exodus: Distinctions between the Four Verses

Instead of referring to Exodus's *matsot* and festival, or firstborn consecration, Deut 6:8 and 11:18 refer to certain "words" whose identity is not spelled out, and include the additional detail (also absent in Exodus) that these are to be *tied* on the hand. Missing in the overall context of the Deuteronomy verses is any indication of what is signified by the tied *ot*. Additionally, the idea that a ritual (such as firstborn consecration) might become a sign—as was suggested earlier for the Exodus verses—does not fit the context in Deuteronomy. Rather, these verses entail an *injunction*, that words are to be tied. The words be(com)ing *totafot*, however, might well represent the outcome of tying them, rather than a separate injunction. The meaning, then, would be that they are to be tied on the hands of the people, and will thus become like a cherished adornment, between their eyes.[70]

As mentioned earlier, Fox had classified the *ot* in the two Deuteronomy verses (as well as the two Exodus ones) as mnemonic signs.[71] He claimed that the words of the Torah have a mnemonic function in Deut 6:8 and 11:18 that echoes the usage of *ot* in Exod 13:9 and 16, but with memory itself as the goal in Deuteronomy rather than a particular signified object, as in Exodus. The understanding works well with the above idea, whereby the *ot* functions in such a way as to turn the words into a cherished object. It bears pointing out that the importance of memorizing words would, of course, be at odds with writing them down. Thus, any mnemonic signs would presumably not be written ones.

A speculative possibility, which might explain the lack of a signified object in Deut 6:8 and 11:18, is suggested by some Egyptian hieratic papyri. These early inscribed amulets contain text that is oracular, in which "the deity is represented as declaring that whatever promises have been included in the oracle will be fulfilled, as well as those of benefit to the owner which have been inadvertently omitted."[72] If *ot* is rendered as oracle instead of sign—a possibility raised above—then the Deuteronomy verses are perhaps to be understood as calling for the words to be tied, much as an oracular amulet would have been tied. There is no biblical evidence for the existence of such amulets, but the idea that written text has ritual power is not foreign to the Torah, being known from the *Sotah* rite

---

70. See Rothstein, "From Bible to Murabba'at," 9–10.

71. Fox, "The Sign of the Covenant," 567–68.

72. See I. E. S. Edwards, *Hieratic Papyri in the British Museum, Fourth Series: Oracular Amuletic Decrees of the Late New Kingdom*, vol. 1, *Text* (London: Trustees of the British Museum, 1960), xiii–xvii. The only papyrus to bear clear internal evidence of its date was placed between the tenth and eighth centuries B.C.E. Edwards points out that "these texts do not help in understanding the mechanical processes employed in obtaining oracular utterances."

in Num 5:11–31 (where the text concerned is written by a priest, as would presumably have been the case for the hieratic papyri as well).

Early Reception of the Four Verses

That Exod 13:9 and 16 were ultimately associated with the practice of *tefillin* undoubtedly calls for explanation, which I will endeavor to provide in chapter 3, but this is not to be confused with *evidence* for their initial reception, which simply does not exist. There seems to be no good reason for understanding these two verses as calling for any physical act whatsoever, and, consequently, no basis for imagining that their earliest readers might have seen things differently.[73] While the two Deuteronomy verses might have been viewed early on as calling for a physical practice, it is worth noting that the first part of Deut 11:18, which talks of placing "the words" on the *heart*, is most simply understood as a figure of speech,[74] and the rest of that verse may well have been taken figuratively—so too for the parallel passage in Deut 6:6–8.

It is, of course, entirely possible that no particular attention was paid to these two verses until well after the period of their production, when their idiom may have been quite unfamiliar. Nevertheless, a short discussion of authorial intent seems warranted here, if only because the currently most influential approach to the subject does imagine the Deuteronomy verses as calling for a physical practice that demonstrates that the wearer is bound to YHWH. The argument is made in an important article by Othmar Keel,[75] who adduced a variety of ancient Near Eastern evidence that he interpreted as demonstrating the special relationship between a wearer of marks, particularly ones on the forehead, and the relevant deity. Keel saw this as confirmation that the *totafot* of Deuteronomy were similarly supposed to be observed in a literal fashion.[76] He made a somewhat analogous suggestion for the background of the sign tied to the hand, which he related to evidence for bracelets belonging to kings, or given by them as a gift that signified the loyalty of the wearer (to a god or the king

---

73. For scholarship on the intent of these verses, which specifically engages the question of its possible association with a practice, see Driver, *A Critical and Exegetical Commentary on Deuteronomy*, 92–93; Jeffrey H. Tigay, "Tefillin," in *Encyclopaedia Biblica* (Jerusalem: Mosad Bi'alik, 1982), 8:891–93 (in Hebrew); Rothstein, "From Bible to Murabba'at," 38–123.

74. See Sonnet, *The Book within the Book*, 55. The suggestion has however been made that placing "on the heart" is to be viewed as analogous to a tangible practice, namely, Aaron's breastplate in Exod 28:29–30. See B. Couroyer, "La Tablette du Coeur," *Revue Biblique* 90 (1983): 419–20.

75. Keel, "Zeichen der Verbundenheit."

76. Ibid., 193–212.

himself).[77] Keel argued that the Deuteronomic "words" becoming *totafot* meant that they were to assume concrete form, but *not* that they were to be inscribed within such objects.[78] Viewing *tefillin* as an overly precise, formulaic, and casuistic interpretation of a spiritual requirement, he disavowed any connection between the findings in Qumran and the type of literal fulfillment that he understood the verses to be calling for.[79]

It is, however, not at all clear that Keel's Near Eastern evidence can shed much light on whether the verses are to be understood as mandating a tangible practice, or rather as simply suggesting an analogy to such practice. His own contention was that the signs in Deuteronomy could not be virtual, but must instead refer to something tangible. Correctly observing that words merely held in someone's consciousness cannot be called a sign, he claimed that the Deuteronomic "words" must be apprehended as taking physical form.[80] This seems to sidestep the issue of whether the intent of the verses is that the words literally become a sign, or whether instead they are simply to resemble a sign in some way, such as having a mnemonic function. As pointed out above, the signs in Deuteronomy have no apparent signified object, and thus do not seem to function as conventional signs. Indeed, one might argue, in a reverse of Keel's view, that nothing tangible is being called for by these verses, since words as such can hardly be tied.

Put more generally, the very notion of binding or tying would have included a metaphorical valence, a phenomenon known from a variety of cultures.[81] The ambiguity of the biblical Hebrew therefore calls into question the actual possibility for correctly discriminating between a bound material sign—that was *also* to be understood as a sympathetic metaphor for some form of close attachment, and (conversely) a sign that was *not* to be in material form—but was nevertheless to be symbolically bound. It seems that the issue of distinguishing between literal and figurative authorial intent cannot be resolved.

Innerbiblical Evidence for Reception of the "Tefillin Verses"

The only positive evidence for reception that may date to the period covered by this chapter is innerbiblical, and points strongly toward a

---

77. Ibid., 212–15.

78. Ibid., 195.

79. Ibid., 216–17.

80. Ibid., 181. See "The senses must be able to perceive a sign, or else it is not a sign" (Helfmeyer, "Oth," *Theological Dictionary of the Old Testament*, 1:180).

81. See chap. 3 in Mircea Eliade, *Images and Symbols: Studies in Religious Symbolism*, trans. Philip Mairet (London: Harvill, 1961).

figurative approach to Deut 6:8 and 11:18.[82] The context is Prov 1–9, now commonly held to be a product of the Second Temple period.[83] What is striking about Proverbs is that verses there similarly include injunctions that words/precepts/teachings are to be tied, without any hint of a literal understanding. The issue, for our purposes, is the light shed by these verses not so much on how Deut 6:8 and 11:18 are to be understood but rather on how these Deuteronomy verses *were* understood during the biblical era.

Proverbs 6:20–22 read as follows:

20. Keep, my son, your father's precepts,
forsake not your mother's teaching.
21. Bind them always upon your heart,
tie them about your throat.
22. When you walk about it will guide you,
when you lie down it will watch over you,
when you wake up it will converse with you.[84]

Here, a writer in the wisdom genre views parental instruction, clearly oral in nature,[85] as something to be cherished and held close, that will guide and protect its adherent. A connection with Deut 6:6–8 and 11:18–19 is easily drawn from the common element of binding/tying in Prov 6:21, as well as the other remarkable parallels in vv. 20 and 22. The juxtaposition of parental instruction with lying down/arising from sleep/walking around is surely no coincidence.[86] The "heart" and "throat" in Prov 6:21 are likely a further allusion to Deut 11:18, with *nefesh* having been taken by Proverbs to mean "neck" (as in Prov 3:22) rather than "soul."[87]

---

82. See Hermann L. Strack and Paul Billerbeck, "Die Tephillin (Gebetsriemen)," in *Kommentar zum neuen Testament aus Talmud und Midrasch*, vol. 4, part 1 (Munich: C. H. Beck'sche, 1928), 251.

83. See Michael V. Fox, *Proverbs 1–9*, Anchor Bible (New York: Doubleday, 2000), 6; Lester L. Grabbe, *Judaic Religion in the Second Temple Period* (London and New York: Routledge, 2000), 21. Whether these chapters are to be dated to the Persian or early Hellenistic periods is an open question, and they are addressed here because they may date to the former period.

84. All Proverbs translations are taken from Fox, *Proverbs 1–9*.

85. See William M. Schniedewind, *How the Bible Became a Book* (Cambridge: Cambridge University Press, 2004), 11.

86. For the idea that the bound precept or teaching serves not merely to remind and admonish the wearer, but also as a protective companion, see Patrick D. Miller, "Apotropaic Imagery in Proverbs 6:20–22," *Journal of Near Eastern Studies* 29 (1970): 131–32. It has, however, been observed that the teachings here are a substitute for an amulet, rather than a virtual amulet themselves; see Fox, *Proverbs 1–9*, 229.

87. John Day, "Foreign Semitic Influence on the Wisdom of Israel and Its Appropriation in the Book of Proverbs," in *Wisdom in Ancient Israel: Essays in Honour of J. A. Emerton,*

The idea that Proverbs is to be taken metaphorically, and may have repercussions for the meaning of our verses, is not a new one. The twelfth-century exegete Ibn Ezra raised the implications of Proverbs for the literal understanding of *tefillin*, only to reject them and thereby counter earlier Karaite claims.[88] Of greater significance here, however, is the implication of Proverbs 6 for the reception of Deuteronomy in the Second Temple period.[89] The writer, clearly alluding to the *tefillin* verses in Deuteronomy, has taken a metaphoric tack. In addition, he or she has changed the locus of tying from the hand/head (or maybe just the hand, as there is no reference in scripture to *tying* on the head) to the heart/throat.[90] There is nothing that would suggest a connection between Proverbs' understanding of the Torah verses and a known ritual practice. In the idiom of Proverbs, both writing instruction as well as tying it are simply figures of speech (see 3:3 and 7:3), and its references to tying or binding parental instruction are most simply understood as reflecting a known practice of wearing valued jewelry, or garlands. Thus, compare Prov 1:8–9, which reads:

> 8. Listen, my son, to your father's instruction;
> neglect not your mother's teaching,
> 9. for they are a graceful garland for your head,
> and a necklace for your throat.[91]

In addition to their implications for the reception of Deuteronomy, the verses from Proverbs are striking evidence for Tigay's claim, mentioned above, that the Bible uses objects worn on the body as a metonymic device.

---

ed. John Day, R. P. Gordon, and H. G. M. Williamson (Cambridge: Cambridge University Press, 1995), 68.

88. See Ibn Ezra's commentary on Exod 13:9. See A. M. Habermann, "The Phylacteries in Antiquity," *Eretz Israel* 3 (1954): 174 n. 2 (in Hebrew); Tigay, "Tefillin," 891.

89. The idea that biblical passages comment on earlier ones has been developed extensively in Michael Fishbane, *Biblical Interpretation in Ancient Israel* (Oxford: Oxford University Press, 1985). The Proverbs 6 passage has also been viewed as a parallel to Deuteronomy verses, rather than commentary on them; see Moshe Weinfeld, *Deuteronomy and the Deuteronomic School* (Oxford: Oxford University Press, 1972), 298–303. Deuteronomy, however, is generally considered to be older than Proverbs; see Keel, "Zeichen der Verbundenheit," 230 n. 127.

90. The heart is also mentioned in Deut 6:6, and in 11:18, where it precedes any mention of tying.

91. Similarly, in Prov 4:9, wisdom will "place a graceful garland on your head; grant you a splendid diadem." For the point that the necklace connotes an object of value, as do the other references to placing objects on the body, see Keel, "Zeichen der Verbundenheit," 182.

Amulets (and Body Marking?)

Any literal understanding of the *tefillin* verses would seem to presume either worn objects or a practice of body marking, which would include tattooing, painting, cutting, and even shaving (for which see Deut 14:1, the only biblical parallel to the repeated use of "between your eyes" in our four verses). Ezekiel 9:4–6 shows an instance of approved biblical body marking, and so perhaps does Gen 4:15; but Lev 19:28 and Deut 14:1 show forbidden counterparts.[92] There is, however, no evidence for the reception of our verses ever being connected to body marking, and I will accordingly concentrate in this section on evidence for worn objects, specifically, since *tefillin* contain text, their possible connection to *inscribed* amulets. Is there any reason to imagine that the use of such artifacts during the period under consideration might have influenced or reflected the understanding of our four verses?

Inscribed Hebrew Amulets

An archaeological find in Jerusalem has demonstrated that there were inscribed Hebrew amulets around the beginning of the period covered by this chapter, although there are no other findings of Hebrew amulets to be dated to the period.[93] The two scrolled silver plaques concerned were found in a Jerusalem burial chamber.[94] They are generally dated to the late seventh or early sixth century B.C.E., prior to the canonization of the Pentateuch; their inscriptions, however, include text that bears a remark-

---

92. For a more expansive list of sanctioned/mandated biblical body markings, see M. Bar-Ilan, "So Are They to Put My Name Upon the Children of Israel," *Hebrew Union College Annual* 60 (1989): 19–31 (in Hebrew). For the argument against the אות in Genesis 4:15 (the so-called mark of Cain) referring to a mark, see Tur-Sinai, "*Otot* in the Bible and in the Lachish Letters."

93. It should also be noted as a general matter that there is no meaningful evidence for Achaemenid inscribed amulets in other languages either (personal communication with Shaul Shaked, September 2004).

94. G. Barkay, "The Priestly Benediction on the Ketef Hinnom Plaques," *Cathedra* 52 (1989): 37–76 (in Hebrew); Ada Yardeni, "Remarks on the Priestly Blessing on Two Ancient Amulets from Jerusalem," *Vetus Testamentum* 41 (1991): 176–85; G. Barkay, "The Priestly Benediction on Silver Plaques from Ketef Hinnom in Jerusalem," *Tel Aviv* 19 (1992): 139–94. The second of the Barkay articles, in English, is described as a revised translation of the earlier Hebrew article. Yardeni was apparently the one to decipher the most significant part of the plaques, but Barkay's 1992 work was the official publication. A recent republication utilized technological innovations to buttress the dating originally claimed by Barkay, which had been questioned by a minority of scholars; G. Barkay et al., "The Amulets from Ketef Hinnom: A New Edition and Evaluation," *Bulletin of the American Schools of Oriental Research* 334 (2004): 41–71.

able resemblance to the Priestly Blessing in Num 6:24–26.[95] The publisher of the find pointed to the hollow in the scrolls as a place through which some attachment to the body would have been threaded. He viewed their prototype as the amuletic hieratic papyri from Egypt, discussed above, but the reasoning behind his comparison is unclear, and the analogy seems problematic. For one thing, the Egyptian papyri were not found in tombs, and, for another, their content strongly suggested that they were used for living individuals.[96] The same cannot be said for the Hebrew amulets, which were found in a burial chamber and whose content seems entirely appropriate for protecting the dead in the afterlife.[97] Although one cannot rule out their having been used by the living and then placed in graves, there seems no good reason to prefer that possibility.

It was also suggested that the plaques were an early intimation of *tefillin*, in that they reflect an early tradition about fulfilling the injunctions in Deut 6:8 and 11:18.[98] It is difficult to see how this could have been the case, because the Priestly Blessing seems entirely unrelated to the "words" whose binding is called for in Deuteronomy.[99]

The Priestly Blessing is clearly apotropaic in nature (and might indeed have originated in an apotropaic formulation), but it is to be noted that the plaques contain no references to malevolent forces, angels, magic formulas or oaths. In this respect, the Hebrew amulets are to be contrasted with inscribed clay plaques, dating to a similar time, from Arslan Tash in northern Syria.[100]

Is *Tefillin* Practice Reasonably to Be Dated to This Period?

In the absence of any evidence for the practice of *tefillin*, one is left with trying to reconstruct the early reception of those verses known to have been viewed, at a later date, as referring to the practice. I argued above

---

95. In addition, Deut 7:9 was assigned as a possible source for part of one plaque, although this identification seems less certain. See Barkay, "The Priestly Benediction on Silver Plaques from Ketef Hinnom in Jerusalem," 155. See also Menahem Haran, "The Priestly Blessing on Silver Plaques: The Significance of the Discovery at Ketef Hinnom," *Cathedra* 52 (1989): 77–89 (in Hebrew).

96. Pace Barkay, "The Priestly Benediction on Silver Plaques," 181. See Edwards, *Hieratic Papyri in the British Museum*, xiii and xix.

97. See Baruch A. Levine, *Numbers 1–20*, Anchor Bible (New York: Doubleday, 1993), 242–44.

98. Barkay, "The Priestly Benediction on Silver Plaques," 183–86.

99. The idea has nevertheless gained some traction. See Schniedewind, *How the Bible Became a Book*, 105–6.

100. See Barkay, "The Priestly Benediction on Silver Plaques," 185–86.

that there seems no reason to imagine that the Exodus verses, on their own, would have been taken to mandate such a practice. The two Deuteronomy verses, on the other hand, warrant additional focus, not only because of their content and context but also because Deuteronomy may be the one candidate for a biblical work that was already recognized as authoritative scripture in the preexilic period.[101] The limited evidence in Proverbs for the likely reception of our verses was addressed above, but at some point they *did* become associated with *tefillin* practice. How likely is it that this turn of events took place during our period?

Here it is to be noted that only by interpretation could an understanding of the verses have been augmented so as to imply their referring to the written word, since Deut 6:8 and 11:18 contain no explicit mention of writing the words to which the verses refer. In the first place, then, the likelihood that such an interpretation preceded the exile seems remote. For one thing, the evidence for Deuteronomy's early authority is limited to some of the cultic issues with which it is concerned. Even if, however, the entire book of Deuteronomy had become authoritative at the time of the Josianic reforms (around 620 B.C.E.), there is no evidence to suggest interpretation of obscure passages at this early stage. Additionally, although some measure of scribal skill may have been common before the exile, it is difficult to imagine that the understanding of Deuteronomy would have been expanded, so as to see writing where it was not explicitly called for. The other uses of *ot* in Deuteronomy refer, after all, to divine acts, or prophetic oracles (6:22; 13:2–3; 26:8; 28:47; 34:11). All in all, it seems quite unlikely that the verses would have been understood to refer to a *tefillin* practice in the late-monarchic era (nor any particular reason to imagine a change, in this respect, during the period of the Babylonian exile).

The Persian period needs to be treated separately, as it was then that the books of the Torah became viewed as canonical. By canonical I mean merely to imply the fixture of certain texts as authoritative, with the concomitant stress on their precise and hence more or less unwavering transmission, which was now in writing.[102] This, in turn, would have been followed by the need for their interpretation, as they could no longer be changed so as to clarify any troubling and obscure passages that they contained. Resolution of inconsistencies and explanation of gaps would have presumably begun to assume importance at this time. One particular aspect of canonization, which should be highlighted, is the development of a process whereby parts of the canon are used to shed light on other parts.[103]

---

101. See Weinfeld, *Deuteronomy 1–11*, 16–18.
102. This differs from the Christian concept of canon; see James Barr, *Holy Scripture: Canon, Authority, Criticism* (Philadelphia: Westminster Press, 1983), 48–53.
103. See, in general, chap. 1 in Moshe Halbertal, *People of the Book: Canon, Meaning and Authority* (Cambridge: Harvard University Press, 1997).

Exactly how and when this change occurred is debatable. The biblical book of Nehemiah refers to a written Torah that became authoritative in the mid-fifth century B.C.E., and such authoritative texts—by their nature—do not change a great deal. The largely invariant nature of Ezra's Torah (that is, the one mentioned in Nehemiah) thus seems likely. Although it is impossible to determine whether it was as comprehensive as the Pentateuch, there is no evidence for a later moment in time at which other parts of the Torah became authoritative. The translation of the Torah into Greek, probably around the mid-third century B.C.E., demonstrates that it was already canonical then in its (more or less) current form, and it seems quite reasonable to imagine that this same Torah had already been in existence for the previous two hundred years. For the purposes of the argument, therefore, it may be assumed that the Pentateuch was canonical by the middle of the Persian period. The implication of significance for this study is that all the *tefillin* verses, in the context that we find them, might have called for interpretation after this time.

The likelihood of a specific interpretation that called for *tefillin* practice must be considered, however, against the array of alternative explanations, an array that would only have increased in size as works other than Deuteronomy became accepted as authoritative. A list of such alternatives includes the following:

a.   Understanding the Deuteronomy verses in the light of the Exodus ones. A simple interpretation of the signs in Deut 6:8 and 11:18 might have been that the verses' referents be remembered, just as the signs in the Exodus verses seem to be mnemonic ones. The *zikkaron* ("reminder"), mentioned in Exod 13:9, might well have been used to shed light on the nature of the *totafot* in the other three verses.[104]

b.   Body marking, with Ezek 9:4–6 demonstrating God's endorsement of body marking for apotropaic purposes—a function that would presumably not have gone amiss, even if not apparent in Deuteronomy.

c.   Non-inscribed worn objects, which might have been seen as embodying "the words" in some kind of sign (for which see Keel's suggestion, discussed above).

d.   Wearing words written on metal, similar to the golden *tsits* of the biblical Aaron—which would constitute the sole biblical guideline to the appearance of a worn object that included inscribed text.[105]

e.   Interpretations that focus on an object worn on the heart or neck rather than, or in addition to, the hand and head—placing words on

---

104. See Keel, "Zeichen der Verbundenheit," 163.

105. See Exod 28:36–38 and 39:30–31. See also Z. W. Falk, "Forms of Testimony," *Vetus Testamentum* 11 (1961): 90.

the heart being mentioned in both Deut 6:6 and 11:18 (with 11:18 possibly having a reference to the neck, as mentioned earlier). Aaron's breastplate, known as a *zikkaron* in Exod 28:29, might have been seen as a model for a practice of this kind.

f. The metaphorical understandings reflected in Proverbs.

There is no apparent reason why interpreting the verses to refer to *tefillin* would have been preferred to any of these alternatives during this period. Indeed, that interpretation seems less likely than some alternatives. As discussed above, the only positive evidence for the reception of the verses that may date to our period (which is in Proverbs) demonstrates a figurative understanding, not a literal one. The idea that a literal writing practice originated at this time, without the Torah seeming to call for it, might well be considered implausible. In light of all the above, it seems that it might be more effective to look to subsequent periods for the origins of the practice.

3

Tefillin in the Later
Second Temple Period

In light of the argument presented in the previous chapter, it does not seem particularly likely that *tefillin* practice originated during or before the Persian period (although the possibility can certainly not be ruled out). The earliest archaeological evidence for *tefillin*, as will be discussed below, has provided a *terminus ante quem* for the practice in the second or first century B.C.E. Accordingly, it is within the Hellenistic period, which commenced in the late fourth century B.C.E., that the origins of the ritual will be sought. I will argue that *tefillin* were an invented tradition of the late–Second Temple era, functioning as a long-life amulet that arose from a literalist interpretation of scripture, and informed by knowledge of parallel Greek practices. Establishing this position will first require a rather detailed analysis of the material data from the Dead Sea scrolls, which will be followed by a shorter consideration of the more ambiguous literary record.

The earliest archaeological evidence has been dated to a period that coincides, more or less, with the Maccabean era. The Jews in Judea had earlier lived under either Ptolemaic or Seleucid rule, and thus in a Greek colony, from the time of Alexander the Great. The period subsequent to the Maccabean revolt saw them experiencing a national renaissance, which accompanied their recently found independence. The concluding section of this chapter will discuss the implications of these factors and integrate the archaeological and literary evidence for tefillin with more general features of the history of the period.

The Archaeological Evidence

The archaeological finds of *tefillin* (and *mezuzot*) at Qumran are to be counted among the earliest surviving material evidence of Jewish religious practice and are dated in some cases to the second century B.C.E.

Remnants from around forty-five separate parchment slips traced to Qumran were identified as belonging to *tefillin/mezuzot*, as well as around twenty-five *tefillin* housings.[1]

The Tefillin Housings[2]

Fourteen housings were published in some detail—one in considerable detail by Yigael Yadin, and subsequently thirteen others, by J. T. Milik. The remainder, reported several years before Yadin's work, and at a time when relatively few parchment slips had been published, received less attention. The housings, when closed, took the exterior form of a flattish leather pouch with one or more small protrusions; these were due to cells, inside which the slips had been placed. Although the housings were no longer stitched shut, as the sewing medium had disintegrated over their two millennia existence, the original thread holes were still visible. Several of the housings were essentially complete when found, albeit without straps or other means of attachment to the body.

Fourteen of the housings contained four cells each for holding texts, two had three cells, and the remainder had one cell each. The identification as *tefillin* housings is assured, because five were discovered with their parchment contents still inside, three *in situ* in Qumran Cave 4, one *in situ*

---

1. The final volume of the Discoveries in the Judaean Desert series lists only thirty-three such *tefillin* and *mezuzah* texts from Qumran. See Emanuel Tov, "Categorized List of the 'Biblical Texts': Appendix—Phylacteries (Tefillin) and Mezuzot," in *Discoveries in the Judaean Desert*, vol. 39 (Oxford: Oxford University Press, 2002), 182–83. The DJD 39 total is, however, a little misleading. It is due to some sets of multiple slips being treated as single items by their publishers, while others were not, as well as to some—but not all—indecipherable slips being ignored.

2. The word "housings" corresponds to the Hebrew *battim*, and I will use it here in preference to "*tefillin* cases," which might imply a more structured object than the ones found. References for the official publications are as follows:

Lankester G. Harding, "The Archaeological Finds: Introductory. The Discovery, the Excavation, Minor Finds," in *Discoveries in the Judaean Desert*, vol. 1 (Oxford: Oxford University Press, 1955), 1:7. See also plate 1.5–7.

R. de Vaux, "Archéologie: les grottes 7Q à 10Q," in *Discoveries in the Judaean Desert of Jordan*, vol. 3* *(Textes)* (Oxford: Oxford University Press, 1962), 31. See also vol. 3** *(Planches)*, VIII.5–6.

J. T. Milik, "Textes de la grotte 5Q: Phylactère," in *Discoveries in the Judaean Desert of Jordan*, vol. 3* *(Textes)* (Oxford: Oxford University Press, 1962), 178. See also vol. 3** *(Planches)*, XXXVIII.8.

Yigael Yadin, *Tefillin from Qumran (XQPhyl 1–4)* (Jerusalem: Israel Exploration Society and Shrine of the Book, 1970).

J. T. Milik, "Tefillin, Mezuzot et Targums," in *Discoveries in the Judaean Desert*, vol. 6 (Oxford: Oxford University Press, 1977), 34–35. See also plate VI.1–13.

in Cave 5, and one that was purchased. While none of the one-cell types happened to contain parchment, both three-cell exemplars and three of the four-cell ones were found with parchment slips inside. Out of these, one three-cell and one four-cell type contained decipherable slips; the contents of the other three housings that still held parchment were too distressed to be unrolled.

Most of the housings were formed of a single piece of leather, and their manufacturing process can be discerned from the publications. A single or multiple cell/s, designed to accommodate parchment slips, would have been formed on one side of the piece, alternatively on the opposite side as well. Yadin hypothesized that this was accomplished by stretching wettened leather over a wooden form,[3] which had been constructed for manufacturing *tefillin* housings, and Lankester Harding hypothesized a stamping process;[4] it seems quite likely that both these production methods would have been used. Occasionally, multiple cells within a housing were not uniform nor neatly next to each other in a straight line, but this was the exception.

After insertion of the slip/s into the hollow/s that had thus been created, the leather piece would have been doubled over. The two sides then formed a kind of shell around the slip/s. Before being sewn shut, a thong or thread, to be used for attachment to the body, would have been passed through the fold that was created when the piece was doubled over. Some housings still bore remnants of such an attachment, and many had traces of a bulge where the thong had passed through. At the final stage of manufacture, the piece would have been sewn shut. In other instances the whole process was varied slightly, with two separate pieces of leather being sewn together. In this latter case there was no remaining indication of how the housing would have been attached to the body, although thin flaxen thread of some kind was presumed. A third type of housing showed traces of yet another method of attachment, whose exact nature, however, remained a mystery to the archaeologists.[5]

The cells were simply slight protrusions for holding the parchment slips, and the housings were generally rectangular, but not square. In a few exemplars, the four cells fanned out, due to incisions between cells. In all these respects they are dissimilar to *tefillin* known from the modern era, in comparison to which they were also miniscule. The four-cell type was formed from a piece of leather that had typically been around 25mm x 25mm in size before the cells were formed and the piece doubled over to enclose their parchments, and the one-cell type was formed from a piece

---

3. Yadin, *Tefillin from Qumran (XQPhyl 1–4)*, 10.
4. Harding, "The Archaeological Finds," 7.
5. See Milik, "Tefillin, Mezuzot et Targums," 34–35.

that had typically been around 35mm x 10mm, on the same basis.[6] Another four-cell exemplar measured about 20mm x 28mm when stretched open, and 20mm x 13mm when closed.[7] A closed three-cell exemplar measured 23mm x 13mm.[8] The cells of single-cell housings were typically larger than the individual cells of the other types, presumably because the former contained more text.

One set of slips, forming a wad, demonstrates the existence of a much larger type of housing, although none of these were found.[9] Additionally, this set demonstrates that several slips might have been inserted into a single compartment, as a single wad of slips could hardly have been split up over several cells. In fact, many more such wads were traced to Cave 11; they share many characteristics with *tefillin*—thin and brittle, folded parchment, traces of thread marks where skin had been wrapped, tiny script, and hardly any space between the lines—but are quite unlike any other Qumran manuscripts. All Cave 11 wads were indecipherable, and DJD 23 argues that they were not *tefillin* or *mezuzot* on the grounds that no housings were found in Cave 11, that the wads were larger than the typical *tefillin*, and that there were too many wads to have constituted a single *tefillin* (or *mezuzah*).[10] None of these arguments is compelling, however, in light of the decipherable wad mentioned in the previous paragraph, which was the first Qumran *tefillin* exemplar to be published in DJD.

In the light of later rabbinic texts,[11] the four-cell exemplars were identified as belonging to head *tefillin*, and the one-cell type as belonging to arm *tefillin*. (This basis for classifying the objects was not always articulated by the publishers, but no better rationale for the identification is evident.) Accordingly, the taxonomy rests entirely on the presumption of a conservative nature to *tefillin* practice. It is naturally impossible to know whether that presumption is valid, but the three-cell exemplars (as well as the contained texts, which will be discussed below) may suggest otherwise. There is no evidence for use of three-cell types in rabbinic texts, and David Nakman has recently suggested that one of those found was in reality a large fragment from four-cell head *tefillin*.[12]

---

6. Ibid., 34.

7. Yadin, *Tefillin from Qumran (XQPhyl 1–4)*, 9.

8. Milik, "Textes de la grotte 5Q: Phylactère," 178.

9. Harding, "The Archaeological Finds," 7. See also plate XIV.0, for a picture of the wad.

10. "11QUnidentified Wads," in *Discoveries in the Judaean Desert*, vol. 23, ed. Florentino García Martínez, Eibert J. C. Tigchelaar, and Adam S. van der Woude (Oxford: Clarendon, 1998), 445–46.

11. Some of the earliest are *M. Sanhedrin* 11:3, *T. Kelim (Bava Batra)* 4:1, and most explicitly *Mekhilta Derabbi Yishma'el, Bo Parashah* 17.

12. David Nakman, "The Contents and Order of the Biblical Sections in the Tefillin from Qumran and Rabbinic Halakah," *Cathedra* 112 (2004): 30 (in Hebrew).

Along related lines, it is also tempting to imagine that the one-cell and four-cell types represent *two* elements (namely, arm and head) of a *single* practice. There is, however, no basis at this early stage for presuming as much. Indeed, the different types may simply reflect alternative understandings of how the practice was to be observed, with individual practitioners conceivably wearing only one housing. The variety of practices implied by the findings is anyway quite striking, and one can readily view it as having been rather haphazard.

The Parchment Slips[13]

The majority of Qumran slips were published by Milik in DJD 6, as Cave 4 findings. It is to be noted, however, that only three slips were actually found in Cave 4; all others that received a 4Q designation were obtained via purchase. Others were found in Caves 1, 5, and 8 (although none found in Cave 5 were decipherable). The four slips purchased by Yadin, many years after all caves had been excavated, were designated as XQPhyl 1–4. This was to signify that their cave of origin was unknown, although believed to have been in Qumran.

It should be noted that comparatively few slips were found during organized campaigns; the remainder were purchased, directly or otherwise, from local Bedouin. Around half the housings were similarly purchased. In this regard, it is interesting to consider the implications of archaeologist Roland de Vaux's diary entries, which demonstrate that the "unofficial" excavators, as well as their intermediaries, were understandably reluctant to disclose the existence of caves of which archaeologists

---

13. References for the official publications are as follows:

D. Barthélemy, "Textes bibliques: Phylactère," in *Discoveries in the Judaean Desert*, vol. 1 (Oxford: Oxford University Press, 1955), 72–76. See also plate XIV.

K. G. Kuhn, *Phylakterien aus Höhle 4 von Qumran* (Heidelberg: Abhandlungen der heidelberger Akademie der Wissenschaften, Phil.-Hist. Klasse 1, 1957). These texts were republished in DJD 6 by Milik, who identified further fragments as being from the same slips and also corrected some of Kuhn's readings.

Milik, "Textes de la grotte 5Q: Phylactère," 178. The three slips were indecipherable.

M. Baillet, "Grotte 8: Phylactère, Mezouza," in *Discoveries in the Judaean Desert of Jordan*, vol. 3* *(Textes)* (Oxford: Oxford University Press, 1962), 149–61. See also vol. 3** *(Planches)*, XXXII–XXXIV.

Yadin, *Tefillin from Qumran (XQPhyl 1–4)*.

Milik, "Tefillin, Mezuzot et Targums," 33–85. See also plates VII-XXVII.

Since the publications use "Phyl" in parchment designation—e.g., 4QPhyl H to refer to slip H from Qumran Cave 4—I follow their practice when referring to a particular *tefillin* slip. (I have otherwise avoided the somewhat loaded word "phylacteries" in this book, which is devoted in part to determining whether such usage is indeed appropriate.)

were not yet aware.[14] He documents that this led to an initial tendency on the part of resellers to falsely claim Qumran origin for fragments that apparently came from the subsequently identified site of Murabba'at. Similarly, documents later proven to have originated in Nahal Hever were said by their sellers to have originated in Wadi Seiyal—in this case because they were found in Israel but sold in Jordan.[15] In many other instances too it may just have seemed simpler, or more profitable, for the sellers to say that an object was found in a particular location than to give a more truthful report. Thus, for example, in the only instance where decipherable slips were inside a *tefillin* housing when purchased, Yadin determined that one of the slips concerned had been inserted at a late date to complete a set of four.

In light of the above, some of the definitive statements made about provenance are to be treated with greater caution than seems to have been exercised in their descriptions by the archaeologists concerned. Here it seems worth repeating William F. Albright's remarks on the provenance of the Nash Papyrus, which had similarly been purchased: "the Nash papyrus may actually have been found anywhere in Egypt; the authority of a dealer is generally quite valueless in itself. The fact that widely publicized finds had then recently been made at Oxyrhynchus and elsewhere in the Faiyum was quite enough to suggest to a dealer that the mention of this provenience might enhance the value of his wares. All archaeologists working in the Near East are familiar with the tendency in question."[16] For simplicity, however, I use "found" or "discovered" for items discussed, even though many were purchased. Those slips found *in situ* will be identified as such.

Discriminating between Tefillin and Mezuzot

There is occasional uncertainty expressed by the publishers of the finds as to whether an inscription is a *tefillin* slip or a *mezuzah* slip. Six decipherable *tefillin* slips were found in housings that would have been worn on the body, so that the identification of some slips as *tefillin* was based on more data than the identification of others as *mezuzot*; none of the putative *mezuzot* was found in a housing of any kind. While there were Exodus

---

14. R. de Vaux, "Archéologie: historique des découvertes," in *Discoveries in the Judaean Desert*, vol. 2* *(Texte)* (Oxford: Oxford University Press, 1961), 3–8.

15. Jonas C. Greenfield, "The Texts from Nahal Se'elim (Wadi Seiyal)," in *The Madrid Qumran Congress*, ed. Julio Trebolle Barrera and Luis Vegas Montaner (Leiden: Brill, 1992), 661–65.

16. W. F. Albright, "A Biblical Fragment from the Maccabaean Age: The Nash Papyrus," *Journal of Biblical Literature* 56 (1937): 145.

passages in the Qumran *mezuzot*, none were from Exodus 12:1–23, which mentions the protective function of blood on the *mezuzot* (literally, door-posts), at the event of the exodus. Rather, they were from the same Exodus passages as contained in the Qumran *tefillin*, and which are similarly not known from later rabbinic *mezuzah* practice.

The rationale for identifying some as *tefillin* slips and others as *mezuzot* is evident in the work of Milik, who published all but one of the *mezuzot*, and Maurice Baillet, who published the other one. In the latter case (8QMez) presentation seems to have played a role in the way it was written, and the concern for writing to be as small as possible seemed to be absent (in both cases when compared to 8QPhyl, the set of *tefillin* slips published by Baillet together with 8QMez).

This is evidenced by the following:

- the quality of the calligraphy
- the general presence of intervals between words
- margins on both left and right
- extensions of last letters on some lines as a way of filling out blank space
- somewhat greater letter size
- much greater intervals between lines (about 3mm, as opposed to 1mm in the case of the 8QPhyl *tefillin* slips).[17]

These features might have been inappropriate for *tefillin* slips, which could anyway not be read once placed in the tiny housings, which would have been sewn shut.

Milik distinguished between 4Q *tefillin* and *mezuzot* based on the thickness of the parchment used, although he also found the *mezuzot* to demonstrate a more classic literary hand, of the kind found in other scrolls. On this latter basis, he questioned whether two slips he classified as *tefillin* might in fact have been *mezuzot*, and similarly whether one of the so-called *mezuzot* might really have been a *tefillin* slip. The thickness of the *mezuzot* was similar to that of other scroll parchments and would seem to have been inappropriate for *tefillin*, in view of the need to fold them so as to fit into their tiny cells. Any difference in textual content, as a factor in discriminating between the two objects, was denied by Milik, and indeed is not apparent from the findings. Milik characterizes *tefillin* script as showing little variation at Qumran, down to the first century C.E. Those slips identified as *mezuzot*, however, show palaeographic development similar to other Qumran scrolls.[18]

---

17. Baillet, "Grotte 8: Phylactère, Mezouza," 158.
18. Milik, "Tefillin, Mezuzot et Targums," 35–39.

Reasons for placing *tefillin* but not *mezuzot* in sealed housings might have been related to purity concerns specific to objects worn on the body. Additionally, the size of *tefillin* slips might have been determined by the need to wear them conveniently, particularly if they were worn at all times. Whether these are sufficient reasons to imagine that larger parchments belonged to *mezuzot* is another matter. In the absence of rabbinic literature, one would likely have imagined any practice evolving from Deut 6:9 and 11:20 as associated with writing *on* doorposts and gates, rather than on parchment that was placed on doorposts and gates. Additionally, the rabbinic record does not allow for Exodus verses in *mezuzot*, so that viewing some of these Qumran parchments as *mezuzot* entails not merely harmonization with later practice but selective harmonization at that. It therefore seems possible, at least, that the so-called *mezuzot* are merely large *tefillin*, worn in larger housings than those that were found.[19] As pointed out above, there is evidence for the existence of such larger housings, even though none were found.

Introduction to the Inscriptions

The tables below show all *tefillin* and *mezuzot* inscriptions from the period under discussion in this chapter. For a variety of reasons, scholars have used different designations when referring to the same slip, and I will use the ones listed in the name-columns in DJD 39.[20] Where relevant, I have subdivided items on the DJD list and have omitted indecipherable slips that were listed there, as well as post–70 c.e. findings, which will be discussed in chapter 4. (Other inscriptions, apparently similar to *tefillin* and *mezuzot* but not included in the DJD list of these items, are presented separately, in a third table.)

By their nature *tefillin* slips were particularly difficult to decipher. Not only was the writing microscopic, but they were rolled up and folded in a variety of ways before being placed in their housings. In the case of XQPhyl 1, for example, Yadin identified nine separate folding stages for a parchment slip that had measured less than 3cm x 5cm before folding began! This all led to extremely crumpled texts, parts of which were sometimes stuck to each other when unrolled. (Milik observed a preference for deciphering *tefillin* slips based on originals rather than photographs,

---

19. For similar reservations about discriminating between *tefillin* and *mezuzot*, see Hartmut Stegemann and Jürgen Becker, "Zum Text von Fragment 5 aus Wadi Murabba'at," *Revue de Qumran* 3, no. 11 (1961): 444–45.

20. See Tov, "Categorized List of the 'Biblical Texts.'" The list also provides a corresponding text number for each of these names.

particularly because letters were frequently identified in folds, and these simply did not show up in two-dimensional representations.[21]) In addition, many slips were found in fragmentary form. Sometimes parts of a fragment were decipherable, while others were not. It is beyond the scope of this work to replicate the exact inscriptions preserved, which are best viewed in the original publications.

The data does however lend itself to reconstruction of the original inscriptions, although some element of subjectivity is clearly inherent to any process of reconstruction. I have presented below in tabular form the publishers' reconstructions of the original Qumran inscriptions. All table entries are based on the readings in DJD or, in the case of XQPhyl, on the readings of Yadin.[22] It is important to note that disagreements among scholars, as to the verse-by-verse reconstruction of the inscriptions, generally revolve around the extent of text that had originally been present, rather than variations in the reading of the preserved texts.

The publishers of the *tefillin* and *mezuzot* implicitly presumed the following:

- Unless there was reason for believing otherwise, the identification of part of a verse was evidence for the original presence of the entire verse. Thus a "preserved" verse need not have been preserved in its entirety to be considered as such.

- Unless there was reason for believing otherwise, the identification of any verses from a passage was evidence for the original presence of all intervening verses. For the purposes of this presumption, the "passages" were defined as three large groups of scriptural text, in which identified scriptural verses originated. These are Exod 12:43–13:16, Deut 5:1–6:9 and Deut 10:12–11:21. The special case of Deuteronomy 32 in 4QPhyl N will be discussed below. No other preserved scriptural text fell outside these limits, with occasional snippets from the Decalogue in Exodus 20 seen simply as a reflection of harmonization between Exodus and Deuteronomy (due perhaps to scribes writing from memory).[23]

---

21. Milik, "Tefillin, Mezuzot et Targums," 33. However, Milik himself did republish, on the basis of photographs, those parts of 4QPhyl A, B, H, and J that had previously been published by Kuhn.

22. Yadin's readings of the slips he published were subsequently corrected slightly; see M. Baillet, "Nouveaux phylactères de Qumran (XQPhyl 1–4). A propos d'une édition récente," *Revue de Qumran* 7, no. 27 (1970): 403–15.

23. For discussion of harmonization in Qumran *tefillin* and *mezuzot*, see Esther Eshel, "4QDeut^n—a Text That Has Undergone Harmonistic Editing," *Hebrew Union College Annual* 62 (1991): 117–54; Innocent Himbaza, "Le Décalogue du Papyrus Nash, Philon, 4Qphyl G, 8Qphyl 3 et 4Qmez A," *Revue de Qumran* 20, no. 79 (2002): 411-28; George J. Brooke, "Deuteronomy 5–6 in the Phylacteries from Qumran Cave 4," in *Emanuel: Studies*

The tables follow these two presumptions, which seem reasonable. My reconstructions of *tefillin* and *mezuzot* have also followed the publishers when they conjectured the original presence of a beginning or end (which in some instances was of considerable length) to a particular set of preserved verses, or the original presence of text from an entirely unpreserved passage. I am thus, in a sense, first giving the publishers the benefit of the doubt. It seems to me that this is a sensibly cautious approach to material with which they had greater familiarity than it is possible for subsequent scholars to have. In all such cases I have, however, highlighted by use of parentheses the absence of internal textual evidence for the expansive limits ascribed to the preserved text. The tables do not follow the publishers' reconstructions of entirely hypothetical slips.

In general I have not noted differences between the text preserved and other witnesses to it, for which the publications may be consulted (as well as subsequent literature on the relevant biblical passages[24]), but I have done so in the case of seemingly deliberate omissions and additions that are peculiar to the corpus of *tefillin* and *mezuzah* slips. The tables also show the presence of unidentified text, if decipherable; entirely indecipherable text has been ignored.

The entries in the tables show the verse order that was preserved within each slip; these were, in general, written in a single column from top to bottom. Verse designations are the ones commonly found in Christian editions of the Bible, simply because these were the designations used by all the publishers, including Yadin.[25] Where the archaeologists identified a set of slips, coming from a single housing, the table groups them together before providing details of the text found on the individual slips.

---

in Hebrew Bible, Septuagint, and Dead Sea Scrolls in Honor of Emanuel Tov, ed. Shalom M. Paul et al. (Leiden: Brill, 2003): 57-70.

24. See, in particular, Baillet, "Nouveaux phylactères de Qumran (XQPhyl 1–4)"; Alexander Rofé, "Deuteronomy 5:28–6:1, Composition and Text in the Light of Deuteronomic Style and Three Tefillin from Qumran," *Henoch* 7 (1985): 1–14; Carmel McCarthy, "Moving in from the Margins: Issues of Text and Context in Deuteronomy," in *Congress Volume Basel 2001*, ed. A. Lemaire, VTSup 92 (Leiden: Brill, 2002), 112–25.

25. See *The Cambridge Annotated Study Bible: N.R.S.V.* (Cambridge: Cambridge University Press, 1993). This is relevant for Deuteronomy 5, and for the occasional reference herein to Exodus 20, as Jewish and Christian editions typically differ in breaking down these "Decalogue chapters" into verses.

Table 1. The Reconstructed *Tefillin* Inscriptions

1QPhyl 1–4 (set of slips, found in a single wad):

1	Deut 5:1–5:27; (5:28–6:9)
2	Deut (10:12–16); 10:17–11:12
3	Exod 13:(1), 2–9, (10)
4	unidentified decipherable text including, possibly, Exod 13:15–16

4QPhyl A recto/verso	Deut 5:1–6:3 (with omission); 10:12–11:17/Deut 11:18–21; Exod 12:43–13:7, (8–16)
4QPhyl B recto/verso	Deut 5:1–6:5 (with omission); (6:6–9); (10:12–11:21); (Exod 12:43–13:8)/Exod 13:16a, 9b–15
4QPhyl C	Exod 13:1–16; Deut 6:4–9; 11:13–21

4QPhyl D, E, F (set of slips, found inside a housing):

Phyl D	Deut 11:13–21
Phyl E	Exod 13:1–9 (10)
Phyl F	Exod 13:11–16

4QPhyl G, H, I (identified as originating in one set of slips):

Phyl G recto/verso	Deut 5:1–21 (with omissions/additions/transpositions)/Exod 13:11–12
Phyl H recto/verso	Deut 5:22–6:5 (with omissions/additions)/Exod 13:14b–16
Phyl I recto/verso	Deut 11:13–21; Exod 12:(43) 44–13:10 (with omission)/possibly Deut 6:6–7

4QPhyl J, K (identified as originating in one set of slips):

Phyl J recto/verso	Deut 5:1–24a (with omission)/Deut 5:24b–6:3 (with omission)
Phyl K recto/verso	Deut 10:12–11:7a/Deut 11:7b–12

4QPhyl L, M, N (identified as originating in one set of slips):

Phyl L	Deut 5:(1–6), 7–24, (25–33)
Phyl M recto/verso	Exod 12:(43), 44–13:10/Deut 5:33–6:5
Phyl N	Deut 32:(1–13), 14–20, (21–31), 32–33
4QPhyl O recto/verso	Deut 5:1–16, (17–21)/Deut 6:(4–6), 7–9
4QPhyl P recto/verso	Deut 10:22–11:3, (4-?)/11:(?–17), 18–20, (21)
4QPhyl Q recto/verso	Deut 11:4–18/Exod 13:4–9
4QPhyl R recto/verso	Exod 13:1–7a/Exod 13:7b–10
4QPhyl S	Deut 11:(18), 19–21

Table 1. The Reconstructed *Tefillin* Inscriptions (*cont.*)

8QPhyl I-IV (identified as originating in one set of slips)[26]:

I	Exod 13:1–10; 13:11–16; Deut 11:13–21; Deut 6:4–9
II	Deut 6:1–3; 10:20–22 (with addition/omissions), as well as unidentified decipherable text
III	Deut 10:12–19; Exod 12:43–51; Deut 5:1–14 (with omissions); Exod 20:11
IV	uncertain text, Deut 10:21–22; 11:1; 11:6–12 (with omissions/addition), as well as unidentified decipherable text

XQPhyl 1–3 (set of slips, found inside a housing)[27]:

1	Exod 12:43–13:10; Deut 10:12–19
2	Deut 5:22–33; 6:1–9
3	Deut 5:1–21; Exod 13:11–16

Table 2. The Reconstructed *Mezuzah* Inscriptions

4QMez A	harmonized Decalogue, corresponding to Deut 5:11–16, with omissions
4QMez B	Deut 6:(4) 5–6; 10:14–11:2 (3–21)
4QMez C	Deut 5:(1–26) 27–6:9; 10:12–20 (10:21–11:12); unidentified decipherable fragment
4QMez D	Deut 6:5–7
4QMez E	Deut 11:17–18
4QMez F	Exod 13:1–4
4QMez G	Exod 13:11–16
8QMez	Deut 10:12–11:21

---

26. The claim that these were from a set had been made by Baillet, their publisher, and was disputed in Yadin, *Tefillin from Qumran (XQPhyl 1–4)*, 15 n. 28 and p. 34.

27. The entire XQPhyl 4 slip was essentially indecipherable, and its reconstruction so tentative that I have omitted it from the table. Although found in the same housing as the other three slips, it was determined to have originated elsewhere and was not part of the same set. See Yadin, *Tefillin from Qumran (XQPhyl 1–4)*,11–13.

Table 3. Other Excerpted Qumran Texts, Resembling *Tefillin* in Content[28]

4QDeut[j]	Deut 5:1–6:3; 8:5–10; (10:12–11:5); 11:6–13 (14–21); Exod 12:43–13:5, (6–16); Deut 32:(1–6), 7–8, (9); unidentified decipherable fragments
4QDeut[kl]	Deut 5:28–32; 11:6–13; 32:17–18, 22–23, 25–27
4QDeut[n]	Deut 8:5–10; 5:1–6:1
4QDeut[q]	Deut 32:(1–8), 9–43
4QExod[d]	Exod 13:15–16; 15:1
4QExod[e]	Exod 13:3–5

The Nash Papyrus

Some fifty years earlier than the findings at Qumran, a Hebrew papyrus was discovered in Egypt. Its contents were the Decalogue, followed by an "insertion" that appears in similar form in the Septuagint (but is absent in the Hebrew Bible), and Deut 6:4–5.[29] Although initially dated to the second century C.E.,[30] which would place it beyond the scope of this chapter, the Nash Papyrus is now generally dated to the second half of the second century B.C.E. (with extreme limits roughly the same as those of the Maccabean era, 165–37 B.C.E.).[31] The papyrus was purchased in Egypt, where writing on leather was very rare; and Egyptian provenance is further buttressed by the similarity of its textual insertion to the one in the Septuagint.

---

28. For the other Qumran texts identified here as resembling *tefillin* in content, see Judith E. Sanderson, "4QExod[d]," in *Discoveries in the Judaean Desert*, vol. 12 (Oxford: Clarendon, 1994), 127–28; Judith E. Sanderson, "4QExod[e]," in *Discoveries in the Judaean Desert*, vol. 12 (Oxford: Clarendon, 1994), 129–31; Sidnie White Crawford, "4QDeut[n]," in *Discoveries in the Judaean Desert*, vol. 14 (Oxford: Clarendon, 1995), 117–28; Julie Ann Duncan, "4QDeut[j], 4QDeut[kl]," in *Discoveries in the Judaean Desert*, vol. 14 (Oxford: Clarendon, 1995), 75–98; Patrick W. Skehan and Eugene Ulrich, "4QDeut[q]," in *Discoveries in the Judaean Desert*, vol. 14 (Oxford: Clarendon, 1995), 137–42. For the excerpted nature of all these texts, see also Julie Ann Duncan, "Excerpted Texts of Deuteronomy at Qumran," *Revue de Qumran* 18, no. 69 (1997): 43–62. The feature was first noted with respect to 4QDeut[n] in Hartmut Stegemann, "Hinweis auf eine uneditierte Handschrift aus Höhle 4Q mit Exzerpten aus dem Deuteronomium," *Revue de Qumran* 6, no. 22 (1967): 217-27.

29. For a detailed reconstruction, see Ernst Würthwein, *The Text of the Old Testament. An Introduction to the Biblia Hebraica*, 2nd ed. (Grand Rapids: Eerdmans, 1995), 144–45.

30. See the *editio princeps*, Stanley A. Cook, "A Pre-Masoretic Biblical Papyrus," *Proceedings of the Society of Biblical Archaeology* 25 (1903): 34–56.

31. See Albright, "A Biblical Fragment from the Maccabaean Age," 145-76; N. Avigad, "The Palaeography of the Dead Sea Scrolls and Related Documents," in *Scripta Hierosolymitana*, vol. 4, ed. Chaim Rabin and Yigael Yadin (Jerusalem: Magnes Press, Hebrew University, 1958), 58-67. For the view that this papyrus might simply reflect an archaic script, and equally be dated to the beginning of the Common Era, see Milik, "Tefillin, Mezuzot et Targums," 37.

It seems fair to say that until the discovery of the Dead Sea scrolls the Nash Papyrus was viewed as simply reflecting the liturgical significance of the Decalogue, together with the first two verses of the *Shema*. More recently, however, it has been viewed as a *mezuzah* or *tefillin* slip,[32] not only because of its content but also owing to physical similarities between it and the Qumran exemplars (the papyrus was smallish and had been folded, as was also typical of *tefillin/mezuzot*[33]). While it thus can be taken as evidence for *tefillin* or *mezuzah* practice in Egypt, it remains possible that the text merely signifies the liturgical significance of its contents. As will continue to be seen, it is difficult to tease such apparently distinct possibilities apart.

Evaluating the Qumran Inscriptions

Initial Observations

Scriptural passages identified in the Qumran *tefillin* and *mezuzot* fell within three pericopes, namely, Exod 12:43–13:16; Deut 5:1–6:9; and Deut 10:12–11:21.[34] One of the four *"tefillin* verses" concludes the first of these pericopes, and another is the penultimate verse of the second. The third pericope also contains one of these verses, shortly before its ending, and the remaining one is found in the middle of the first pericope (at Exod 13:9).

It is noteworthy that the first *tefillin* slips to be published were not found inside housings. Accordingly, their earliest identification as part of a worn object was largely based on the resemblance of their contents to rabbinic *tefillin* texts. Even without such data, however, the very fact of an excerpted set of texts that mentioned tying would have been suggestive. Subsequently, 4QPhyl D, E, F and XQPhyl 1–3, which had been found inside their original housings, were published, so that the identification of these texts came to rest on even more certain footing. Both of the above housings contained parchments that preserved the two salient Exodus verses. In addition, one of the two Deuteronomy verses was preserved in the 4QPhyl D, E, F housing, and the other in the XQPhyl housing. The

---

32. For the initial suggestion, see Kuhn, *Phylakterien aus Höhle 4 von Qumran*, 24. See also Milik, "Tefillin, Mezuzot et Targums," 39 and 47; Othmar Keel, "Zeichen der Verbundenheit," in *Mélanges Dominique Barthélemy*, ed. Pierre Casetti, Othmar Keel, and Adrian Schenker (Fribourg: Editions Universitaires, 1981), 166–67; Eshel, "4QDeutⁿ," 123 n. 36. However, see Duncan, who still refers to it as a lectionary text ("Excerpted Texts of Deuteronomy at Qumran," 55).

33. See Colette Sirat, *Les papyrus en caractères hébraïques trouvés en Égypte* (Paris: Centre National de la Récherche Scientifique, 1985), 26 and 29 n. 30.

34. 4QPhyl N, a clear exception, will be discussed in further detail below.

characteristic script observed by Milik, combined with the overall textual similarity of the many exemplars to one another, reinforce the view that other slips containing verses from the same passages originated in *tefillin*.[35] Significantly, the four verses are clearly the main common element to the Exodus and Deuteronomy pericopes, which are otherwise quite disparate. Their placement together, whether in housings or single slips, seems quite incongruous unless adherents of the practice saw a scriptural foundation to it, with the verses taken to refer to wearing inscribed text. As discussed in chapter 2, such an understanding, particularly of the two Deuteronomy verses, could certainly have evolved from a particular interpretation of their meaning.

The reception of these verses as involving a practice of *tefillin* is thus to be dated no later than the second or first centuries B.C.E., which is the period to which the earliest of these slips was dated.[36] The practice is likely to have been driven initially by the two Deuteronomy verses, with their reference to tying words on the hand or arm. Indeed, hand/arm *tefillin* may have developed earlier than head *tefillin*; it is conceivable that the *totafot* clauses in these verses were interpreted as predicting the outcome of tying words, rather than suggesting an ancillary practice, and the meaning of *totafot* may in any case have been obscure. [37]

In any event, an initial evaluation clearly points to a practice associated with the reception of scripture. It does, however, immediately raise the following questions:

- Is a proto-halakah of *tefillin* exhibited at Qumran?
- Are the Qumran *tefillin* to be viewed as sectarian exemplars?

A Proto-Halakah for Tefillin?

Despite the common features exhibited by the Qumran *tefillin*, the corpus as a whole is remarkable for its diversity,[38] and it evidences significant differences with later rabbinic dicta (which will be discussed in detail in chapter 4). Table 4 illustrates the latter point, simply by showing the

---

35. For an interesting approach, in an entirely different context, to the way in which Qumran findings reinforce the interpretation of one another, see Edna Ullmann-Margalit, *Out of the Cave: A Philosophical Inquiry into the Dead Sea Scrolls Research* (Cambridge: Harvard University Press, 2006).

36. See Milik, "Tefillin, Mezuzot et Targums," 37.

37. See chap. 2.

38. See ibid., 46–47; Norman Golb, *Who Wrote the Dead Sea Scrolls?* (New York: Scribner, 1995), 102–4.

observed range of texts among the Qumran finds, when compared to rabbinic *tefillin*.

Table 4. Range of Qumran *Tefillin* Contents[39]
(Compared to Rabbinic *Tefillin*)

Exod 12:43—13:16 (rabbinic *tefillin*: Exod 13:1–16)
Deut 5:1—6:9 (rabbinic *tefillin*: Deut 6:4–9)
Deut 10:12—11:21 (rabbinic *tefillin*: Deut 11:13–21)
Deut 32:1—33 (–43?[40]) (rabbinic *tefillin*: absent)

More importantly, the evidence of Qumran points away from *any* consistently applied understanding of how the practice was to be performed.[41] The varying scope of the contained verses and the ways these were split up are readily apparent from Table 1. Other variations are as follows:

1. In eight of the twelve *tefillin* slips containing text from both Deuteronomy and Exodus, verses from the former book preceded any from the latter; this order is reversed in the case of the other four (the slips were essentially written in a single column, and here I am referring to their top-to-bottom order).

2. There were several other variations in layout:

   • Vacats were used sometimes but not consistently.

   • There is evidence for some degree of word separation in 4QPhyl C; this is not found elsewhere in the corpus of *tefillin* slips.[42]

   • In 8QPhyl I the third and fourth pericopes were written in a kind of multicolumn format. Specifically, Deut 11:13–21 was written in the shape of a backwards "L" (one that has been rotated through 180 degrees around the vertical axis). Each side of the "L" contained multi-

---

39. See Milik, "*Tefillin, Mezuzot* et Targums," 38.

40. 4QPhyl N ended at v. 33. On the basis of that exemplar, however, it seemed likely that the entire Song of Moses, which ends at 32:43, was considered suitable as a *tefillin* text; see ibid.

41. The comprehensive work by David Rothstein has been discussed in chap. 1. It seems fair to say that for purposes of comparison with rabbinic halakah he presumed the existence of scribal-practice halakah at Qumran for both *tefillin* and *mezuzot*, without however attempting to explain other variations. I am not persuaded as to the presence of such halakah by his finding that Judean Desert practice can rarely be shown to be inconsistent with tanna'itic scribal rules, as these are often ill defined or the subject of dispute, as his study shows. See Rothstein, "From Bible to Murabba'at: Studies in the Literary, Textual and Scribal Features of Phylacteries and Mezuzot in Ancient Israel and Early Judaism" (Ph.D. diss., UCLA, 1992), 181–427.

42. See ibid., 269–70.

ple lines of text, and Deut 6:4–9 was inscribed inside the space bounded by these two sides.

- In three slips from a single housing, XQPhyl 1, 2 and 3, words at the end of a line were frequently split up, but generally not by writing the second half of a word at the beginning of the line following the first half (although this too was occasionally observed). Rather, the scribe inserted the last letter/s of the split word toward the *end* of the line below it or above it, or inserted the first letter/s of the split word toward the end of the line above it, or both. A single word might thus be written over three lines, and ends of lines could consist of an accumulation of letters from adjacent lines. All of this would probably have rendered parts of the text quite unintelligible to anyone not already familiar with it. Yadin believed that the scribal practice exhibited was designed to utilize all available space, but his hypothesis does not explain the data.[43] Thus, a word might be split, even though there would have been room on the line for the entire word,[44] and sometimes an entire word was inserted out of place toward the end of a prior or subsequent line.[45] Additionally, it bears pointing out that the full utilization of space could, seemingly more intelligibly, have been accomplished by writing the end of a word at the beginning of a subsequent line. As an alternative to Yadin's hypothesis, therefore, one might suggest a deliberate effort to render the text confusing, or perhaps just a very idiosyncratic scribe.

- The unusual layout of 4QPhyl J will be discussed separately below as a significant anomaly for understanding the development of the practice.

3. Some slips were inscribed on both recto and verso, while others were not.

4. Some slips were written on the hair side of the skin, others on the inside.

5. Harmonization was practiced, but not in any consistent fashion over the corpus of slips[46]:

- Harmonization of Deuteronomy with the Decalogue in Exodus 20 was observed in 4QPhyl G, 4QPhyl J, 8QPhyl III, and XQPhyl 3, as well as 4QMez A. This was also noted for the Nash Papyrus and 4QDeut[n] but was not found in other slips that included the Decalogue.[47]

- To the extent that the verses preserved on the verso of 4QPhyl B are out of sequence, as shown in Table 1, it seems due to harmonization of

---

43. Yadin, *Tefillin from Qumran (XQPhyl 1–4)*, 21–22.
44. See slip 2 lines 9 and 10, where the Tetragrammaton seems to have been deliberately split over two lines.
45. See slip 3 lines 25, 26, 27, and 28.
46. See Brooke, "Deuteronomy 5–6 in the Phylacteries from Qumran Cave 4," 62.
47. See Eshel, "4QDeut[n]," 142–47; Himbaza, "Le Décalogue du Papyrus Nash," 427–28.

Exod 13:9 (which does not include the word *totafot*) with its close parallel, Exod 13:16 (which does).

If these instances of harmonization were not done deliberately then they can be put down to a habit of writing texts from memory,[48] which would seem equally unconcerned with precise textual fidelity.

6. There were additions/omissions throughout the corpus of slips, and some will be discussed separately below as anomalies whose significance is particularly important for understanding the development of the practice. Others too may be linked to contextual factors, rather than textual variations. Thus,

   • In 4QPhyl G, an omission in Deut 5:5 eliminates mention of Moses' role in transmitting God's word. This is possibly due to harmonization with the previous verse, which had stressed God's face-to-face communication with the people.

   • In 4QPhyl H, an addition/omission in Deut 5:25 implies that the people had not feared death from hearing God's voice per se, but rather from hearing it "speaking from the fire"—possibly a harmonization with the following verse.[49]

7. The existence of text from outside the three "core" passages was not limited to 4QPhyl N (which is the most obvious example), or to harmonization with the Exodus Decalogue. Thus, there were other identifiable additions to the scriptural text found in 4QPhyl G, 4QPhyl H, 8QPhyl II and IV, while 1QPhyl, 8QPhyl II and 8QPhyl IV contained clusters of letters that could not be linked to any of the observed pericopes.

8. 1QPhyl was found in a single wad, too large for any of the housings observed (several similar—albeit indecipherable—wads were also found).

Most important, however, is the enormous variation between the preserved texts within the three major passages. Although reconstruction reduces the implications of such variation for the contents of the original slips, it does not eliminate the likelihood of significant differences. On its face, the precise nature of the "correct" practice was vague, and under those circumstances one ought not be surprised by such variety. Indeed, one must question whether the practice always included some element from each scriptural passage, and here the evidence is inconclusive.[50]

The recently published idea that there was a well-defined halakah as to the extent of the inscribed verses, but none as to their order within a passage, is fanciful;[51] in fact, the preserved inscriptions are positive evi-

---

48. See Himbaza, "Le Décalogue du Papyrus Nash," 427–28.

49. See Brooke, "Deuteronomy 5–6 in the Phylacteries from Qumran Cave 4," 62.

50. For opposing views on the subject, see Milik, "Tefillin, Mezuzot et Targums," 38–39, 48, 55–56; Nakman, "The Contents and Order of the Biblical Sections."

51. See Nakman, "The Contents and Order of the Biblical Sections," 37–40. His

dence that verse order within a passage did matter to scribes, as Table 1 demonstrates, even though there were different practices with respect to the correct order of the passages themselves. So too for the oft-repeated assertion that variations in the Second Temple era *tefillin* findings reflect a halakic dispute, otherwise unknown before the Middle Ages, concerning the ordering of slips in head-*tefillin* housings and four-column arm-*tefillin* parchments.[52] The claim can be briefly addressed by noting that (a) in only two instances were Qumran slips found inside a housing, and in neither case did their contents conform to either of the two opinions in the medieval dispute, and (b) none of the Judean Desert *tefillin* were written in four columns.[53]

Are the Qumran Tefillin Sectarian?

The existence of distinct practices among Second Temple era sects is known from the writings of Josephus and others, and sectarian texts, most commonly identified with the Essenes, were found at Qumran. Indeed, long before the discoveries in the Judean Desert, Y. H. Schorr, basing his judgment on Josephus's description of their extraordinary piety, speculated that *tefillin* had been instituted by the Essenes.[54] With all *tefillin* finds from our period traced to Qumran, one thus needs to consider the possibility that these represent sectarian practice.

It is first to be noted that nothing in the Qumran community's literature suggests a *tefillin* ritual, much less one that was specific to its members. Interestingly, Norman Golb has observed that Qumran sectarians, authors of the Manual of Discipline, are not good candidates for having understood the *tefillin* verses literally, because they "evince the very opposite tendency to interpret the literal injunctions of the Pentateuch as

---

hypothesis requires passages to have been chopped up so as to allow for the possibility that their text might have been present, and the expansive reconstructions ignore the physical characteristics of the slips, as well as the apparently purposeful omissions that will be highlighted below. The article in general does not engage the positive data, and provides no rationale for the odd hypothetical verse order that it demands.

52. See Yadin, *Tefillin from Qumran (XQPhyl 1–4)*, 14–15; Ruth Fagen, "Phylacteries," in *Anchor Bible Dictionary*, ed. David Noel Freedman (New York: Doubleday, 1992); D. K. Falk, *Daily, Sabbath and Festival Prayers* (Leiden: Brill, 1998), 115; Lawrence H. Schiffman, "Phylacteries and Mezuzot," in *Encyclopedia of the Dead Sea Scrolls*, ed. Lawrence H. Schiffman and James C. VanderKam (Oxford and New York: Oxford University Press, 2000).

53. For a fuller analysis, see Yehudah Cohn, "Rabbenu Tam's Tefillin: An Ancient Tradition or the Product of Medieval Exegesis?," *Jewish Studies Quarterly* 14, no. 4 (2007): 319–27.

54. Y. H. Schorr, "Tefillin," *Hehaluts* 5 (1860): 15 (in Hebrew).

metaphors."[55] George Brooke investigated textual variants in the *tefillin* in order to compare these to views represented in Qumran sectarian compositions and could not establish a meaningful correlation.[56] In addition, it was argued above that these objects do not exhibit a proto-halakah of any kind, so that the onus of proof seems to rest with those who have claimed—to the contrary—that they actually demonstrate sectarian difference with respect to correct practice. As the debate is a significant one for the argument in this book, I will now discuss these claims.

The first to attempt a classification along sectarian lines was Milik, who identified two types of Qumran *tefillin*.[57] Those close to rabbinic practice in textual content, or at any rate not clearly deviating from it, he categorized as Pharisaic type. Others were branded as Essene type. Milik's labels rested on the idea that rabbinic practice was presumably Pharisaic in origin and that nonrabbinic Qumran *tefillin* were presumably Essene in origin. This position has been progressively undermined, with Nakman arguing that none of these *tefillin* were sectarian, and Yonatan Adler claiming that Milik's classification does not serve to discriminate between those that were sectarian and those that were not.[58]

The Talmud Yerushalmi (a text generally regarded as redacted in the fourth or fifth century c.e.[59]) highlights the removal of the Decalogue from the liturgy, associating the phenomenon with a claim by *minim* that its commandments alone were given to Moses at Sinai (*Y. Berakhot* 1:5 [3c]). This led Emanuel Tov to suggest that inclusion of the Decalogue in Qumran *tefillin* ought, by extension, to be ascribed to sectarian *minim*.[60] This idea seems dubious. The Decalogue was, according to an earlier rabbinic tradition in *M. Tamid* 5:1, recited daily in the Temple, and there is little reason to imagine that its removal from the liturgy preceded the destruction of the Temple.[61] Even if it had, the Decalogue

---

55. Golb, *Who Wrote the Dead Sea Scrolls?*, 103–4.

56. Brooke, "Deuteronomy 5–6 in the Phylacteries from Qumran Cave 4," 57–59 and 69–70.

57. Milik, "Tefillin, Mezuzot et Targums," 47. The classification continues to be used throughout the DJD 6 *tefillin* publications.

58. See Nakman, "The Contents and Order of the Biblical Sections"; Yonatan Adler, "Identifying Sectarian Characteristics in the Phylacteries from Qumran," *Revue de Qumran* 23, no. 1 (2007): 79–92.

59. See H. L. Strack and Günter Stemberger, *Introduction to the Talmud and Midrash*, trans. Marcus Bockmuehl (Minneapolis: Fortress, 1996), 170–71.

60. Emanuel Tov, "Tefillin of Different Origin from Qumran?," in *A Light for Jacob: Studies in the Bible and the Dead Sea Scrolls in Memory of Jacob Shalom Licht*, ed. Y. Hoffman and F. H. Polak (Jerusalem: Bialik Institute and Tel Aviv University, 1997), 44-54. His claims have recently been reiterated in Emanuel Tov, *Scribal Practices and Approaches Reflected in the Texts Found in the Judaean Desert* (Leiden: Brill, 2004), 270–71.

61. See E. E. Urbach, "The Role of the Ten Commandments in Jewish Worship," in *The Ten Commandments in History and Tradition*, ed. Ben-Zion Segal and Gershon Levi (Jerusa-

might well have persisted in *tefillin*. There is accordingly no reason to associate sectarian *minim* in particular with the Second Temple era *tefillin* that contained the Decalogue.

Adler (taking issue with other elements of Tov's argument) has recently whittled down the so-called Pharisaic slips, those that do not show Qumran scribal characteristics,[62] to 4QPhyl D, E, F and 8QPhyl I—the only ones, in this conception, that are *not* to be considered unique to the sectarian Qumran community.[63] Even that position looks dubious, if only because the identification rests on readings that are at variance with those of their publishers[64] (and there anyway seems to have been insufficient scribal practice data to make any determination regarding 4QPhyl D and E[65]).

Thus, there is no evidence for sectarian difference with respect to early *tefillin* practice, as no genuine basis for discriminating between sectarian and nonsectarian exemplars has been shown to hold water.

Significant Anomalies

I will now highlight some anomalies in the Qumran *tefillin* corpus and will appeal to their significance in the concluding section of this chapter, where a hypothesis for the development of the ritual will be proposed.

Deuteronomy 32 as a Tefillin Text

The most intriguing parchment slip to be identified as *tefillin* was 4QPhyl N, all of whose text was from the Song of Moses in Deuteronomy 32. Thus, uniquely, it bore no apparent connection to the four constitutive verses. In an attempt to reconcile the Qumran *tefillin* with a hypothetical reconstruction of early halakah, an attempt has recently been made to read 4QPhyl N out of the Qumran *tefillin* corpus,[66] but the idea is reductionist and highly problematic. For one thing, Milik claimed that the slip was part of a set that preserved otherwise unremarkable text from *tefillin* passages found elsewhere at Qumran (see Table 1). Just as important, perhaps, the asso-

---

lem: Magnes Press, Hebrew University, 1985), 168–81. *Bavli Berakhot* 12a is here viewed as unlikely to have historical value vis-à-vis the abandonment of Decalogue recital.

62. The most important discussion of Qumran scribal practice is now to be found in a monumental book, Tov, *Scribal Practices and Approaches*.

63. Adler, "Identifying Sectarian Characteristics in the Phylacteries from Qumran." For his disagreement with Tov, see nn. 33 and 44.

64. See the relevant publications and ibid., n. 40.

65. See Tov, *Scribal Practices and Approaches*, 271.

66. Nakman, "The Contents and Order of the Biblical Sections," 35–37.

ciation of Deuteronomy 32 with *tefillin* passages is not contingent on the validity of Milik's assertion, as can be seen by examining Table 3, where three of the texts seem particularly noteworthy.

Preserved text in 4QDeut[kl] consisted of part of Deuteronomy 32, together with some text from both of the extended Deuteronomy passages typically found in Qumran *tefillin*. 4QDeut[j], in addition to these three elements, contained a large piece of the extended Exodus *tefillin* passage, plus Deut 8:5–10. These latter six verses were also found in 4QDeut[n], together with the Decalogue and adjacent verses in Deut 5:1–6:1.

In addition, 4QDeut[j], 4QDeut[kl], and 4QDeut[n] each bore a certain physical resemblance to other *tefillin* and *mezuzah* texts; the former two exhibited signs of folding,[67] and the latter (which was exceptionally well preserved) had an unusually tiny script[68] and was written on a particularly small parchment for a Qumran scroll.[69] Deuteronomy 8:5–10, found in two of these scrolls, is to be compared to Deut 11:11–15, a section of a Qumran *tefillin* passage to which it show some resemblance; indeed, the promise in the first two words of Deut 8:10, "and you shall eat and be satisfied," is repeated verbatim in Deut 11:15. It is also noteworthy that Deuteronomy 32 verses in 4QDeut[j] and 4QDeut[kl] show no sign of stichometric presentation,[70] so that their inclusion seems only indirectly related to that chapter's salient poetic feature (the same characteristic was observed for 4QExod[d] but not for 4QDeut[q]). Thus, rather than reading out 4QPhyl N from the *tefillin* corpus in view of its inclusion of text from Deuteronomy 32, it is instead worth considering whether 4QDeut[j], 4QDeut[kl], and 4QDeut[n] ought to be read *in* to the Qumran *tefillin* corpus.[71]

I will not, however, press the point that these scrolls functioned as *tefillin*, as for now I am merely interested to demonstrate that they place the onus of proof on the claim that Milik incorrectly identified 4QPhyl N, which contains text from Deuteronomy 32 only, as part of a set of *tefillin* texts. No such proof has been offered, and the latter's identification is accordingly to be presumed correct.

---

67. Duncan, "4QDeut[j], 4QDeut[kl]," 75 and 93.

68. Duncan, "Excerpted Texts of Deuteronomy at Qumran," 49.

69. Eshel, "4QDeut[n]," 150.

70. Duncan, "4QDeut[j], 4QDeut[kl]," 90 and 93.

71. For alternative proposals, see Eshel, "4QDeut[n]," 151–52; Moshe Weinfeld, "Grace after Meals in Qumran," *Journal of Biblical Literature* 111, no. 3 (1992): 427-40. For reservations regarding these proposals, see Reuven Kimelman, "A Note on Weinfeld's 'Grace after Meals in Qumran,'" *Journal of Biblical Literature* 112, no. 4 (1993): 695-96; D. K. Falk, "Prayer in the Qumran Texts," in *The Cambridge History of Judaism*, ed. William Horbury, W. D. Davies, and John Sturdy (Cambridge: Cambridge University Press, 1999), 3:865. In any event, the best evidence from Qumran itself, for the content of any of these three scrolls to be viewed as liturgical, is owed to the presence of *tefillin* texts.

Aspects of Deuteronomy 32 are especially noteworthy, and I adduce them here for reference later in this chapter. While the Song of Moses itself, introduced as a *shirah* in 31:19–22 and 31:30, only extends from v. 1 to v. 43, v. 44 proceeds to refer to "the words of the song" and v. 45 talks of "these words," echoing Deut 6:6/11:18. (Verse 46 qualifies these words as testimony, and is to be compared to Deut 31:19, where the forthcoming song is described in similar terms.) Finally, v. 47, in its promise of length of days on the land, is a parallel of sorts to Deut 11:21.

Omissions and Layout

Leaving Deuteronomy 32 for now, other anomalies in the Qumran *tefillin* corpus are the presence of certain omissions, and the unusual layout of one of the parchments concerned. (In talking of omissions I am referring to those peculiar to the corpus of *tefillin* slips, when considered in relation to other important textual witnesses.[72])

Table 5. Omissions[73]

4QPhyl A	within Deut 5:32 (starting after *ushemartem*) to the end of 6:1[74]
4QPhyl B	within Deut 5:31 (starting after *telammedem*) to the end of 6:1[75]
4QPhyl H	*ulema'an ya'arikhun yamekha* in Deut 6:2[76]
4QPhyl J	within Deut 5:32 (starting after *lo*) to 6:2 (ending before *asher*)[77]
8QPhyl II	*kol yeme hayyekha ulema'an ya'arikhun yamekha* in Deut 6:2, and *asher yitav lekha va'asher tirhun me'od* in Deut 6:3[78]
8QPhyl IV	Deut 11:8 (replaced by *lema'an tihyu veyitbu yamim*)[79]
4QMez C	within Deut 5:32 (starting after *tsivvah*) to Deut 5:33 (ending before *veha'arakhtem*)[80]

---

72. It should go without saying that I am not addressing unpreserved text, which is of course entirely uninterpretable.

73. For further discussion, and a few other omissions in the *tefillin* corpus which are not relevant to my argument, see Brooke, "Deuteronomy 5–6 in the Phylacteries from Qumran Cave 4," 63–65.

74. Milik, "*Tefillin, Mezuzot* et Targums," 48–49.

75. Ibid., 52.

76. Ibid., 61.

77. Ibid., 64–67.

78. Baillet, "Grotte 8: Phylactère, Mezouza," 150 and 52.

79. Ibid., 156.

80. Milik, "*Tefillin, Mezuzot* et Targums," 82.

While one can never be certain that an omission was intentional, a clustering of omissions around particular verses or notions is suggestive and warrants investigation. Indeed, all omissions in Table 5 cluster around verses related to length of days. In Deut 6:2, in 4QPhyl H and 8QPhyl II, the omitted words are shown in the table. In 8QPhyl IV, Deut 11:8 is omitted; it specifies fulfillment of all the commandments as a condition for entering and possessing the land as well as achieving length of days on it (according to the next verse, which is a parallel to Deut 11:21). The range of words for the other omissions, in 4QPhyl A, B, and J, and 4QMez C, all include a connection between precise or complete observance of the commandments, at Deut 5:32, 5:33, and 6:2; and length of days, at 5:33 and 6:2.

While Milik had suggested homeoteleuton as a possible cause for the omitted text, in the case of 4QPhyl B (as well as 4QMez C), Alexander Rofé subsequently took issue with the possibility.[81] The latter proceeded to provide an explanation for the lacunae in 4QPhyl A, B, and J, to the effect that they resulted from an otherwise unattested *Urtext* (while acknowledging that this did not fully explain the missing text in 4QPhyl J). His basis for preferring this seemingly drastic suggestion to an intentional omission rested on a presumption as to the unlikelihood of the latter in a *tefillin* parchment.[82] This was based on the idea of a halakah of correct *tefillin* practice, whose unlikelihood has already been discussed; indeed, as mentioned with specific respect to harmonization, there is positive evidence that scribes were *not* concerned with textual fidelity.

A diametrically opposite suggestion has also been made, to the effect that text was abbreviated in Deut 5:32–6:2 because scribes found their content to be repetitive.[83] This seems implausible to me; *tefillin* scribes seem to have sought out innerbiblical repetition, as evidenced by the inclusion of Exodus verses, rather than avoided it.

A final piece of evidence that calls for interpretation is the uniquely strange layout on the verso of 4QPhyl J. The first verse in biblical sequence, Deut 5:24, starts in the middle of the parchment slip and is followed by vv. 5:25–28. Text from Deut 5:29–32 is upside down at the top of the slip and is accordingly out of sequence, and sandwiched in between it and Deut 5:24 is part of Deut 6:2 together with 6:3, which are written the right way up.[84]

---

81. Ibid., 52; Rofé, "Deuteronomy 5:28–6:1," 9–13. (I have brought the verse designations in the body of the latter article into line with those used here.) Pace Rofé, Milik did not focus on homeoteleuton as the cause of the omission in either 4QPhyl A or 4QPhyl J. It should also be noted that homeoteleuton might be a means for deliberate exclusion, rather than an accident. See George J. Brooke, *Exegesis at Qumran: 4QFlorilegium in Its Jewish Context* (Sheffield: JSOT Press, 1985), 111–12.

82. Rofé, "Deuteronomy 5:28–6:1," n. 26.

83. Brooke, "Deuteronomy 5–6 in the Phylacteries from Qumran Cave 4," 64–65.

84. Milik, "*Tefillin, Mezuzot* et Targums," 64 –67; and see Planche XIX.

In K. G. Kuhn's initial publication of 4QPhyl J, which preceded Milik's by twenty years, the former attempted to explain its layout with the suggestion that the scribe twice inverted the parchment when running out of space.[85] This implies that on two occasions the space required for the desired text was severely misgauged, but no other solution has heretofore been offered. I will return below to the phenomena highlighted in this section.

Are There References to *Tefillin* Practice in the Jewish Literature of the Period?

All literary evidence for our period is from the Egyptian Diaspora. It is broken down by document below.

The Septuagint

In Exod 13:16 the words *letotafot ben enekha* are rendered into Greek as *asaleuton*, or in another variant *saleuton, pro ophthalmon sou*.[86] The two variants mean "immovable before your eyes" and "moving before your eyes," respectively. The *lectio difficilior* is clearly the latter. Something bound or remembered (as suggested by the parallels in Exod 13:9, Deut 6:8, and 11:18) might readily be considered fixed or immovable, but "moving" seems more problematic. In Deut 6:8 and 11:18 the plural *asaleuta* and the singular variants *asaleuton* or *saleuton* are found.[87] Scholars have made suggestions for how the Septuagint arrived at its translation,[88] but for our purposes the more particular issue of interest is whether the Septuagint shows evidence of understanding the verses to imply a practice. According to J. W. Wevers, "LXX did not understand the word [i.e., *totafot*] at

---

85. Kuhn, *Phylakterien aus Höhle 4 von Qumran*, 6. (Kuhn referred to this slip as 4 q phylᵃ, and it is not to be confused with the slip designated 4QPhyl A by Milik; see Tov, "Categorized List of the 'Biblical Texts,'" 182–83).

86. J. W. Wevers, *Septuaginta, Exodus* (Göttingen: Vandenhoeck & Ruprecht, 1991). For the considerable problems inherent in identifying the original version of any LXX text, see Melvin K. H. Peters, "Septuagint," in *Anchor Bible Dictionary*, ed. David Noel Freedman (New York: Doubleday, 1992).

87. J. W. Wevers, *Septuaginta, Deuteronomium* (Göttingen: Vandenhoeck & Ruprecht, 1977). Since the referent is the plural "words," Wevers deemed the singular form secondary. See J. W. Wevers, *Notes on the Greek Text of Deuteronomy* (Atlanta: Scholars Press, 1995), 197.

88. See J. W. Wevers, *Notes on the Greek Text of Exodus* (Atlanta: Scholars Press, 1990), 202; Rothstein, "From Bible to Murabba'at," 3–6; Wevers, *Notes on the Greek Text of Deuteronomy*, 117. All focus on the *asaleuton* variant. For consideration of the *saleuton* variant see below, under the discussion of Philo.

all,"[89] and in any event the Septuagint could hardly have understood the verses to refer to a head-*tefillin* practice, given its choice of an adjective rather than a noun for *totafot*.[90]

There is also no particular reason to imagine that the Septuagint understood these verses to reflect a hand/arm-*tefillin* practice (although the possibility that it knew of a hand practice cannot be entirely ruled out). This is because its translation of the relevant clauses is unremarkable, so that the underlying ambiguity of the Hebrew *Vorlage* is preserved. (David Rothstein has argued that the Septuagint in Deuteronomy may be referring to a literal binding, which would ensure that the words become "immovable before your eyes." This suggestion of semantic parallelism between the two halves of a verse cannot be claimed for Exod 13:16, where there is no mention of binding, and Rothstein sees the Septuagint's translators as understanding that text in the light of its Deuteronomic counterparts.[91])

The (So-called) Letter of Aristeas[92]

The work is widely viewed as a composition of the second century B.C.E.[93] While claiming to be a gentile courtier, the writer is a Jew, with the implied audience being educated Jews, and possibly gentiles as well.[94] The relevant section is as follows:[95]

> 157. So he exhorts us to remember how the aforesaid blessings are maintained and preserved by divine power under his providence, for he has

---

89. See also Hermann L. Strack and Paul Billerbeck, "Die Tephillin (Gebetsriemen)," in *Kommentar zum neuen Testament aus Talmud und Midrasch*, vol. 4, part 1 (Munich: C.H. Beck'sche, 1928), 250.

90. See Moshe Weinfeld, *Deuteronomy 1–11*, Anchor Bible (New York: Doubleday, 1991), 335.

91. Rothstein, "From Bible to Murabba'at," 5–10.

92. The work is often referred to as the *Letter of Aristeas*, but that title is problematic, as is the more recent scholarly choice of *Pseudo-Aristeas*. See the introduction to Sylvie Honigman, *The Septuagint and Homeric Scholarship in Alexandria: A Study in the Narrative of the Letter of Aristeas* (London: Routledge, 2003).

93. See the extensive discussion in Geza Vermes, Fergus Millar, and Martin Goodman, eds., *The History of the Jewish People in the Age of Jesus Christ (175 B.C.–A.D. 135) by Emil Schürer, (Revised Version)*, volume 3, part 1 (Edinburgh: T. & T. Clark, 1986), 677–87.

94. See G. W. E. Nickelsburg, "Epistle of Aristeas," in *Jewish Writings of the Second Temple Period*, ed. Michael E. Stone (Assen: Van Gorcum, 1984), 75-80; Vermes, Millar, and Goodman, eds., *The History of the Jewish People in the Age of Jesus Christ*, 677–87; Honigman, *The Septuagint and Homeric Scholarship*, 2, 27–29.

95. The English citation is taken from R. J. H. Shutt, "Letter of Aristeas," in *The Old Testament Pseudepigrapha*, vol. 2, ed. James H. Charlesworth (Garden City: Doubleday, 1985).

ordained every time and place for a continual reminder of the supreme God and upholder (of all).

158. Accordingly in the matter of meats and drinks he commands men to offer first fruits and to consume them there and then straightaway. Furthermore in our clothes he has given us a distinguishing mark as a reminder, and similarly on our gates and doors he has commanded us to set up the "Words," so as to be a reminder of God.

159. He also strictly commands that the sign shall be worn on our hands, clearly indicating that it is our duty to fulfill every activity with justice, having in mind our own condition, and above all the fear of God.

160. He also commands that "on going to bed and rising" men should meditate on the ordinances of God, observing not only in word but in understanding the movement and impression which they have when they go to sleep, and waking too, what a divine change there is between them—quite beyond understanding.

The larger context is a report of the Jerusalem high priest Eleazar's lengthy discourse to Aristeas about Jewish law (covering sections 130–69). In particular, Eleazar utilizes allegorical technique to explain *kashrut* laws as expressions of the importance of living righteously. The section adduced here continues in a similar vein by reflecting on the themes of remembering and justice, with apparent references to *tsitsit*, *mezuzah*, and hand-*tefillin* practice.

A mention of *tefillin* is, however, not clear-cut. In particular it is worth noting that the writer explicitly associates "the words" (*ta logia*) with gates and doors, but *not* with the sign on the hand. Thus, if the reference is to a literal observance, it might have been one that did not involve written words.[96] In addition, although the passage has almost always been taken as a reference to a literal sign, and been employed to date the *tefillin* ritual,[97] it can also be viewed as simply a paraphrase of Deut 6:8/11:18,[98] and no less ambiguous than the Torah (or Septuagint) itself. Adjacent verses, after all, are paraphrased throughout this section.

Accordingly, the apparent reference to *tefillin* might instead merely be a figurative expression, albeit one having allegorical significance—the hand being associated with activity in paragraph 159—just as more practical laws do. If it is, on the other hand, a reference to an actual practice,

---

96. However, see André Pelletier, *Lettre d'Aristée à Philocrate* (Paris: Les éditions du Cerf, 1962), 178 n. 2., "Aristée . . . parle clairement des textes à attacher aux bras, mais il omet de préciser sur quel objet les écrire."

97. See Strack and Billerbeck, "Die Tephillin (Gebetsriemen)," 251; Rothstein, "From Bible to Murabba'at," 147.

98. See Keel, "Zeichen der Verbundenheit," 166.

then the absence of any mention of head *tefillin* is striking, and has led to speculation that Alexandrian Jews maintained the arm practice only.[99] The absence of any mention of an object worn on the head is, of course, equally explained by presuming that the author knew nothing of any actual practice and was simply paraphrasing the Septuagint (which also knows nothing of a head object).

Taken as a group, these particular references are, however, quite remarkable. For one thing they appear to have been forced into the context of a discussion of the apparently strange-seeming *kashrut* laws. More to the point, Eleazar mentions no other Jewish rituals whatsoever. John Barclay comments on this passage, "The Jewish concern with remembering the blessings of God—illustrated by their *mezuzoth* and phylacteries— is taken as a sign of their special piety."[100] Notable for their omission, however, are Shabbat and circumcision—either of which seems like a good candidate for illustrating the significance of remembering God. It is interesting to note that several elements in the passage can also be associated with *Shema* recital, including the allusion to Deut 6:7/11:19 in paragraph 160. Thus, the three paragraphs of the *Shema* liturgy may well have been a feature of Egyptian Jewish ritual, while *tefillin* perhaps were not (this point will be discussed in more detail below).

The writer has Eleazar stating that wearing the sign on the hands (whether literally or figuratively) signifies that "it is our duty to fulfill every activity with justice, having in mind our own condition, and above all the fear of God." If *tefillin* (or *mezuzah*) originated as a magical amulet, then there is certainly no trace of that fact in this record. Having said that, the writer is an Egyptian Jew addressing an Egyptian Jewish (and possibly gentile) audience while representing himself as a gentile addressing a gentile audience (Aristeas's "brother" Philocrates), and reporting a discourse by a Judean Jew (Eleazar) to a gentile (Aristeas) on ostensibly strange foreign laws. These convoluted circumstances make it particularly difficult to evaluate the details of any actual rituals known to its author. Indeed, it is altogether possible that, if these were common rituals that were viewed as magical, whether by gentiles or Jews, they were included in the work precisely because of the opportunity it granted the author to implicitly deny any such element to their practice.[101] As Sylvie Honigman has observed, the discussion seems to be part of "an endeavor to present Judaism as a religion of philosophers."[102]

---

99. Cf. Strack and Billerbeck, "Die Tephillin (Gebetsriemen)," 251.

100. John M. G. Barclay, *Jews in the Mediterranean Diaspora from Alexander to Trajan* (Edinburgh: T. & T. Clark, 1996), 146.

101. Note the observation that the work "is an apology whose object is not very clear, and a polemic whose referents remain unnamed" (Gabriele Boccaccini, *Middle Judaism* [Minneapolis: Fortress, 1991], 164).

102. Honigman, *The Septuagint and Homeric Scholarship*, 23.

Philo

Further evidence for *tefillin* among Egyptian Jews has been traced to Philo's *De specialibus legibus*, book 4.[103] Although Philo's exact dates are uncertain, he is known to have been an adult in 39–40 C.E., having been part of an embassy to Rome at that time. He also visited the Temple in Jerusalem. It has been observed that "the extent of his familiarity with Jewish thought and practice in contemporary Palestine (if indeed they differed markedly from those of Alexandria) remains open to dispute."[104] As he apparently knew little Hebrew, if any, his knowledge of scripture—as distinct from his knowledge of practice—centered on the Septuagint.

De specialibus legibus is a discussion of Mosaic laws, placed by Philo under the rubric of individual commandments in the Decalogue. The fourth book includes (relatively briefly) those laws that he considered under the last three of the ten commandments, followed by laws that are to be considered under the virtue of justice, which fit in with the entire Decalogue rather than any one of its commandments in particular. (This section of the book is thematically similar to another of his works, *De virtutibus*, which seems to be a continuation of it, and considers laws under the heading of other specific virtues.)[105] The relevant passage from section 26 is as follows:

137. The law tells us that we must set the rules of justice in the heart and fasten them for a sign upon the hand and have them shaking before the eyes. The first of these is a parable indicating that the rules of justice must not be committed to untrustworthy ears since no trust can be placed in the sense of hearing but that these best of all lessons must be impressed upon our lordliest part, stamped too with genuine seals.

138. The second shows that we must not only receive conceptions of the good but express our approval of them in unhesitating action, for the hand is the symbol of action, and on this the law bids us fasten and hang the rules of justice for a sign. Of what it is a sign he has not definitely stated because, I believe, they are a sign not of one thing but of many, practically of all the factors in human life.

139. The third means that always and everywhere we must have the vision of them as it were close to our eyes. And they must have vibration

---

103. Translations below are taken from *Philo*, vol. 8, trans. F. H. Colson, Loeb Classical Library (London: William Heinemann, 1939).

104. Jenny Morris, "The Jewish Philosopher Philo," in *The History of the Jewish People in the Age of Jesus Christ (175 B.C.–A.D. 135) by Emil Schürer, (Revised Version)*, volume 3, part 2, ed. Geza Vermes, Fergus Millar, and Martin Goodman (Edinburgh: T. & T. Clark, 1987), 818.

105. See ibid., 850–51; Suzanne Daniel-Nataf, "De Specialibus Legibus, Book 4," in *Philo of Alexandria, Writings, Exposition of the Law (Part 2)*, ed. Suzanne Daniel-Nataf (Jerusalem: Bialik Institute, 2000), 134 (in Hebrew).

and movement, it continues, not to make them unstable and unsettled, but that by their motion they may provoke the sight to gain a clear discernment of them. For motion induces the use of the faculty of sight by stimulating and arousing the eyes, or rather by making them unsleepful and wakeful.

140. He to whom it is given to set their image in the eye of the soul, not at rest but in motion and engaged in their natural activities, must be placed on record as a perfect man. . . .

141. Indeed he must be forward to teach the principles of justice to kinsfolk and friends and all the young people at home and in the street, both when they go to their beds and when they arise, so that in every posture and every motion, in every place both private and public, not only when they are awake but when they are asleep, they may be gladdened by visions of the just. . . .

142. He bids them also write and set them forth in front of the door posts of each house and the gates in their walls, so that those who leave or remain at home, citizens and strangers alike, may read the inscriptions engraved on the face of the gates and keep in perpetual memory what they should say and do, careful alike to do and to allow no injustice, and when they enter their houses and again when they go forth men and women and children and servants alike may act as is due and fitting both for others and for themselves.

Having covered the law courts and judges earlier in the work under the ninth of the ten commandments, Philo announced at the beginning of section 26 that his intention was to cover other aspects of the subject of justice.[106] The rest of the section is both a paraphrase and an explanation of Deut 6:6–9 and/or its parallel Deut 11:18–20.

Philo seems, in the first line of paragraph 137, to be referring to Deut 11:18, which he paraphrases (or alternatively, he is referring to a combination of Deut 6:6 and 6:8). He views the scriptural referent, namely, the words that are to be placed on the heart, and so on, as "the rules of justice." (The seal allegory, mentioned at the end of the paragraph, is an incorporeal idea in Philonic thought.[107]) His reference to "shaking before the eyes" makes it highly likely that his text of the Septuagint had the *saleuton* variant, mentioned above, and the theme of movement is repeated in paragraphs 139–41. Philo apparently understood this as connected to

106. Cohen argues that justice (*dikaiosyne*) here refers to "the righteousness expressed by religious observance." See Naomi G. Cohen, "The Jewish Dimension of Philo's Judaism—an Elucidation of De Spec. Leg. 4 132–150," *Journal of Jewish Studies* 38, no. 2 (1987), 165-86.

107. See Maren R. Niehoff, *Philo on Jewish Identity and Culture* (Tübingen: Mohr Siebeck, 2001), 203. However, see also Naomi G. Cohen, "The Elucidation of Philo's Spec. Leg. 4 137-8: "Stamped Too with Genuine Seals,"" in *Classical Studies in Honor of David Sohlberg*, ed. R. Katzoff (Ramat Gan: Bar-Ilan University Press, 1996), 153-66.

a requirement to talk of these rules when moving around (Deut 6:7 and 11:19), and the first sentences of paragraphs 140 and 141 seem to be alluding to that.[108] In this regard it is interesting to note that the *Letter of Aristeas* also refers to movement (paragraph 160); perhaps it too read the puzzling *saleuton* and looked to elaborate on it. (In another interesting parallel, both Philo and the *Letter of Aristeas* relate their discussion to justice.[109])

Some scholars have presumed that Philo understood Deuteronomy as referring to a *tefillin* practice,[110] and there has been some discussion as to whether he was actually familiar with this practice. Naomi Cohen, presuming that Philo had the *asaleuton* variant, has hypothesized that he was not primarily addressing the Septuagint but was rather focusing on a practice he knew of that entailed wearing dangling head *tefillin*.[111] (She also takes issue with suggestions that Philo could not have been familiar with actual *tefillin* practice,[112] noting that he had been to Jerusalem.) The idea that he was not referring to the Septuagint seems far-fetched, as his comments can readily be seen as reflecting the *saleuton* variant.

In reality, it is not at all clear that Philo is referring to a practice of any kind. Indeed, there is no clear distinction in this regard between the first of the elements of Deut 11:18 in paragraph 137 (placing the rules of justice "in the heart"), and the other two on which he proceeds to elaborate in paragraphs 138–39 (fastening them for a sign "upon the hand"; having them shaking "before the eyes"). In paragraph 139, in addition, the rules of justice are "as it were" (*kathaper*) close to the eyes, which militates against a literal interpretation. This seems further borne out by paragraph 140, where the rules are "in the eye of the soul." Although "the law bids us fasten and hang the rules of justice for a sign," in paragraph 138, might be more readily taken to refer to a practice, it is quite probably simply a restatement of one element of the (ambiguous) verses in Deuteronomy. It is worth noting that Philo does not make mention of *writing* the laws of justice, but does make an allegorical connection between the hand and human activities, observing explicitly that "the hand is the symbol of action" (much as Aristeas had [paragraph 159]). On balance, then, it seems

---

108. It has also been hypothesized that Philo's reading of the Septuagint envisioned an ornament suspended before the eyes and shaking. See Jeffrey H. Tigay, "On the Meaning of T(W)TPT," *Journal of Biblical Literature* 101 (1982): 330.

109. Also, as mentioned above, the *Letter of Aristeas* had considered these verses in the context of a discussion of *kashrut*. In Philo the immediately preceding section, covering the tenth commandment, included the consideration of *kashrut* laws.

110. See recently, for example, Daniel-Nataf, "De Specialibus Legibus, Book 4," 134.

111. See Naomi G. Cohen, *Philo Judaeus: His Universe of Discourse* (Frankfurt am Main: Peter Lang, 1995), 144–55.

112. As in Isaak Heinemann, *Philon's griechische und jüdische Bildung* (Breslau, 1932), 167.

entirely plausible that Philo is not referring to a practice,[113] which is not to say that he was unfamiliar with one. (Accordingly, one can derive nothing about possible Alexandrian *tefillin* practice from the fact that he talks of the hand rather than the arm.)

Philo may be referring to a known *mezuzah* practice in paragraph 142. As Othmar Keel astutely observed, however, this practice would seem to be very different from the one known from rabbinic literature. The latter does not entail the possibility that "those who leave or remain at home . . . may read the inscriptions engraved on the face of the gates." Here Keel and Cohen imagine Philo as referring to a practice that is similar to Samaritan *mezuzot*.[114] In any event, it seems that Deut 6:6–9 or 11:18–20 were of some significance to him. In similar vein to my comments on the *Letter of Aristeas*, it seems possible that *Shema* recital was a feature of the Jewish life that he knew.

The (Negative) Samaritan Evidence

Modern Samaritans do not practice *tefillin*,[115] and Milik found this significant when dating a *terminus post quem* for the origins of *tefillin* ritual to the second century B.C.E., with its major break between Samaritans and Judeans.[116] Presuming Samaritans had never practiced *tefillin*, it seemed quite likely to him that the ritual was equally unknown to Judeans prior to the split between the two groups. It is to be noted, however, that the absence of such practice—even if it dates back to late antiquity—is not an infallible guide for our period, because Samaritan rituals may simply have changed.[117] Accordingly, I consider this lack of evidence inconclusive for dating purposes. (A late antique Samaritan practice that entailed inscrib-

---

113. See Heinemann, *Philon's griechische und jüdische Bildung,* 167; Pelletier, *Lettre d'Aristée à Philocrate,* 178 n. 2.

114. See Keel, "Zeichen der Verbundenheit," 168 and n. 74; Cohen, *Philo Judaeus,* 164–67.

115. J. A. Montgomery, *The Samaritans* (Philadelphia: John C. Winston, 1907), 32. I am continuing to define the latter as a ritual connected to the verses discussed in the previous chapter. Samaritan amuletic practice, which is another matter, is discussed extensively in Moses Gaster, "Samaritan Phylacteries and Amulets," in *Studies and Texts,* vol. 1, ed. Moses Gaster (New York: Ktav, 1971 [this section first published 1915–1917]). The absence of Samaritan *tefillin* practice may also be implicit in rabbinic literature, where *kutim* (a word sometimes used there to describe Samaritans) are mentioned in a list of those deemed ineligible to write *tefillin,* because they do not wear them; the three parallel texts are *Midrash Tanna'im* to Deut 6:9, B. *Gittin* 45b and B. *Menahot* 42b.

116. Milik, "Tefillin, Mezuzot et Targums," 46–47.

117. See the closing comments regarding likely changes over time in Samaritan religion in John Bowman, "The History of the Samaritans," *Abr-Nahrain* 18 (1978/79): 101–15.

ing the Decalogue on stone lintels is viewed by some scholars as reflecting an understanding of the two *mezuzah* verses, Deut 6:9 and 11:20.[118])

Building a Hypothesis for Early Development of the Ritual

The foregoing has detailed the evidence for *tefillin* practice in the later Second Temple period. While extensive archaeological data from this period was found in the Judean Desert, indications from the Diaspora are ambiguous with respect to the existence of a *tefillin* ritual there. I will now try to build on the evidence and determine a likely course for the early development of the ritual, in an attempt to answer the following inter-related questions:

- How did *tefillin* practice come into being?
- Why did it develop as it did?
- How is it best to be situated within the context of late–Second Temple Judaism?
- How, if at all, is it to be connected to the Jewish interaction with the larger Greco-Roman world?

Literacy, Literalism, and the Interpretation of Scripture

The extent of literacy in ancient Jewish society is a matter of some debate.[119] Whatever its exact scope may have been, there seems good reason to imagine that reading and writing Hebrew became more widespread over the course of the late–Second Temple period than it had been during the Persian era.[120] This increase in literacy, under the Maccabees, has been connected to the administrative functions that newfound Jewish independence demanded.[121] There seems, in addition, to

---

118. See James D. Purvis, *The Samaritan Pentateuch and the Origin of the Samaritan Sect* (Cambridge, Mass.: Harvard University Press, 1968), 23–24; Keel, "Zeichen der Verbundenheit," 174–83; Joseph Naveh, "Script and Inscriptions in Ancient Samaria," in *The Samaritans*, ed. Ephraim Stern and Hanan Eshel (Jerusalem: Yad Ben-Zvi, 2002), 372–81 (in Hebrew).

119. See the survey of scholarship in Catherine Hezser, *Jewish Literacy in Roman Palestine* (Tübingen: Mohr Siebeck, 2001), 27–36.

120. See William M. Schniedewind, *How the Bible Became a Book* (Cambridge: Cambridge University Press, 2004), 174–77 and 98–99.

121. See Albert Baumgarten, "Literacy and the Polemic Concerning Biblical Hermeneutics in the Second Temple Era," in *Education and History: Cultural and Political Contexts*, ed. Rivka Feldhay and Immanuel Etkes (Jerusalem: Zalman Shazar Center for Jewish History, 1999, in Hebrew), 40.

have been a simultaneous increase in focus on the *relevance* of scripture around this time on the part of non-Priestly circles.[122] A characteristic associated with greater literacy is a concern for precision,[123] and, in the case of Jewish society, this expressed itself in greater literalism in the interpretation of the Torah (with an attendant scope for disputes as to correct interpretation).[124]

Along similar lines, Adiel Schremer has highlighted the evidence of Qumran as pointing to a return to the written text, in a move beyond tradition-based religious observance.[125] As he notes, a tendency toward returning to the text likely extended beyond the denizens of Qumran, although that group is clearly the best-documented example of such a stance. Schremer's position focuses on the innovative aspects of this development for the approach to halakic matters in the first century B.C.E. and thereafter. My own attention will center on a different implication of the return to the written text during this period, namely, its potential for engendering entirely new "traditional practices."

The Invention of Tradition

This subsection has been named after a much-cited work that elaborated on a phenomenon of the modern era.[126] The Scots tartan kilt, to give one notable example, was invented by an English industrialist in the eighteenth century, although by 1805 no less a figure than Sir Walter Scott was asserting that it would doubtless have been worn in the third century C.E.[127] The approach to analyzing such examples was initially focused on the fertile ground of the era following the industrial revolution, but it has since been applied to Jewish practices of the late–Second Temple period by Albert Baumgarten. Writing about the middle years of the second century B.C.E., the latter commented that "the stage is set for the invention of tradition, to be recorded as history, reinforced as liturgy and ceremony, cel-

---

122. Ibid., 37–38.

123. Walter Ong, *Orality and Literacy* (London: Methuen, 1982), 103-05.

124. Baumgarten, "Literacy and the Polemic Concerning Biblical Hermeneutics," 41–45.

125. Adiel Schremer, ""[T]He[Y] Did Not Read in the Sealed Book": Qumran Halakhic Revolution and the Emergence of Torah Study in Second Temple Judaism," in *Historical Perspectives: From the Hasmoneans to Bar Kokhba in Light of the Dead Sea Scrolls*, ed. D. Goodblatt, A. Pinnick, and D. R. Schwartz (Leiden: Brill, 2001), 105–26.

126. Eric Hobsbawm and Terence Ranger, eds., *The Invention of Tradition* (Cambridge: Cambridge University Press, 1983).

127. See Hugh Trevor-Roper, "The Invention of Tradition: The Highland Tradition of Scotland," in *The Invention of Tradition*, ed. Eric Hobsbawm and Terence Ranger (Cambridge: Cambridge University Press, 1983), 15–41.

ebrated as ritual." Relating to the momentous and rapid changes that had taken place during these years, he argued that the Maccabean elite had instituted new practices as a response, which invoked continuity with the past. (Specifically, Baumgarten addressed the creation of the half-sheqel Temple tax, and the recitation of the *Shema* in the Temple.)[128]

Following this argument for dating certain rituals to the Maccabean era, I would like to suggest a change in reception for the *"tefillin* verses" at around this time, which introduced a novel understanding that they referred to a practice. This would have gone hand in hand, in line with Eric Hobsbawm's formulation, with "the use of ancient materials to construct invented traditions of a novel type for quite novel purposes."[129] A change in reception of scripture would be consonant with the return to the written text of scripture, as well as the adoption of literalist conceptions of that text, which were outlined above. I will not, however, relate the genesis of *tefillin* practice to the political motivations asserted by Baumgarten for the Maccabean institution of *Shema* recital and the half-sheqel tax.[130] Instead I will now investigate a rather different inflexion point for Jewish society that, it will be suggested, led to the invention of the *tefillin* ritual.

Jews, Amulets, and the Encounter with Hellenism

If the assessment in chapter 2 is correct, then a Jewish practice of wearing inscribed text, connected to a novel reception of scripture, likely originated after the Jewish encounter with Greek culture. Although there is evidence for inscribed Hebrew amulets from a much earlier period, there is none for the intervening centuries. It seems, moreover, that the earlier evidence is unconnected to the reception of canonical scripture, to which *tefillin* must inevitably be linked.

Changes in the reception of literary works, as theorized by Hans Robert Jauss, are a function of the readers' "horizon of expectations," which are themselves affected by the evolution of cultural, political, and social conditions, and norms in the society at large.[131] It thus seems plausible

128. Albert Baumgarten, "Invented Traditions of the Maccabean Era," in *Geschichte— Tradition—Reflexion*, vol. 1: *Judentum*, ed. Peter Schaefer (Tübingen: Mohr Siebeck, 1996), 197–210. An "invention of tradition" approach, which does not however address religious practice as Baumgarten did, is also taken by Erich S. Gruen, *Heritage and Hellenism: The Reinvention of Jewish Tradition* (Berkeley: University of California Press, 1998).

129. Hobsbawm and Ranger, eds., *The Invention of Tradition*, 6.

130. Although Milik associated the origins of *tefillin* practice with the national renaissance of the Maccabean era, the suggestion on its own seems vague.

131. See Hans Robert Jauss, "Literary History as a Challenge to Literary Theory," *New Literary History* 2 (1970–71): 19–37; Susan R. Suleiman, "Introduction: Varieties of Audience-

that the interaction with Hellenistic culture, with its widespread use of protective amulets, would have led Jews toward an integration of Greek practice with their own paramount source of authority, namely, the Torah. Roy Kotansky has observed that "amulets were usually used to cure medical complaints (both injuries or illnesses) and to thwart the daemonic influences often held responsible for disease."[132] One can readily imagine that Jews would have been just as eager as gentiles to avail themselves of such useful objects.

The appeal of apotropaic amuletic practice to Jews might be viewed as self-evident in light of our knowledge of the Hellenistic world in general. Additionally, however, it may be documented in literary form by 2 Macc 12:34–40.[133] Here the work describes a battle against Gorgias, governor of Idumea, in which "a few of the Jews fell." After an intervening Shabbat, "Judas and his men went to recover the bodies of the fallen. They found under the tunics of every one of those who had fallen objects which had been consecrated (*ieromata*) to the idols of Jamnia, forbidden to Jews by the Torah. It was clear to all that for this very reason the men had fallen."[134]

It seems most likely that the text is referring to protective pagan amulets worn by the soldiers.[135] Robert Doran refers to the fallen as "image-wearers,"[136] and worn images would indeed have functioned as protective amulets. The interpretation can be reinforced by the observation that in Deut 4:23–26 the Torah associates the use of graven images with forgetting the covenant, provoking God's jealousy, and an early demise. This could

---

Oriented Criticism," in *The Reader in the Text*, ed. Susan R. Suleiman and Inge Crosman (Princeton: Princeton University Press, 1980), 36.

132. Roy Kotansky, "Incantations and Prayers for Salvation on Inscribed Greek Amulets," in *Magika Hiera: Ancient Greek Magic and Religion*, ed. Christopher A. Faraone and Dirk Obbink (New York: Oxford University Press, 1991), 107.

133. All translations below are taken from Jonathan A. Goldstein, *II Maccabees* (New York: Doubleday, 1983).

134. For a comparison of the narratives in 2 Maccabees 12 with 1 Maccabees 5, see Robert Doran, *Temple Propaganda: The Purpose and Character of 2 Maccabees* (Washington D.C.: Catholic Biblical Association of America, 1981), 14–15. Whereas the Gorgias of 2 Maccabees is governor of Idumea, in 1 Maccabees he commands the forces of Jamnia.

135. See "These *ieromata* were small portable idols, worn as amulets" (J. Moffatt, "II Maccabees," in *The Apocrypha and Pseudepigrapha of the Old Testament*, ed. R. H. Charles [Oxford: Clarendon, 1913], 149). See also Campbell Bonner, *Studies in Magical Amulets, Chiefly Graeco-Egyptian* (Ann Arbor: University of Michigan Press, 1950), 28; Judah Goldin, "The Magic of Magic and Superstition," in *Aspects of Religious Propaganda in Judaism and Early Christianity*, ed. Elisabeth Schüssler Fiorenza (Notre Dame, Ind.: University of Notre Dame, 1976), 116; John G. Gager, *Curse Tablets and Binding Spells from the Ancient World* (New York/Oxford: Oxford University Press, 1992), 218. It has, however, also been argued that the objects referred to are gold and silver spoils of war, removed from idols, and prohibited to the Jews by Deut 7:25; see Goldstein, *II Maccabees*, 448–49; D. R. Schwartz, *The Second Book of Maccabees* (Jerusalem: Yad Ben-Zvi, 2004), 244.

136. Doran, *Temple Propaganda*, 110.

in turn explain the clear connection, to which 2 Macc 12:40 refers, between the soldiers' actions and their fate (it is to be noted that Doran has, in general, connected divine intervention in 2 Maccabees to the worldview of Deuteronomy[137]).

If the above interpretation is correct, then 2 Maccabees shows a contested Jewish interest in pagan amulets. The assertion of an amuletic custom with unquestionably Jewish pedigree could well have served to neutralize such an interest and channel it into an unproblematic form. The above-mentioned verses from Deuteronomy 4, for example, may have been taken to imply that *uninscribed* amulets could backfire as a method of assuring protection for oneself or one's loved ones. Some such amulets, after all, could presumably risk classification as the *pesel temunat kol* to which Deut 4:23 and 4:25 refer (other uninscribed amulets, commonly made of vegetable matter, might have been less problematic). It should therefore come as no surprise to find Jews, in a Hellenistic context and at a time when Hebrew scribal culture was flourishing,[138] gravitating toward a scriptural text that might be interpreted as assuring protection for wearers of *inscribed* amulets. In a world where such amulets were ubiquitous, one might well expect Jews, given their relationship to scripture at this time, to mine the Torah for instruction as to what text such amulets ought to contain, how they ought to be worn, and what they might accomplish. It is this last feature, namely, the rationale for presuming *tefillin* to be efficacious amulets, that will round out my hypothesis of a novel reception for some biblical texts.

A Deuteronomic Promise of Length of Days

Common Greek terms for amulet are derived from the verb *periaptein* (to tie on), thus highlighting that these objects were tied and not merely worn. A remarkable parallel to a known practice of tying inscribed text onto one's body so as to assure a favorable outcome might readily have been found in Deut 11:18–21. A possible interpretation of these verses, after all, would have Moses instructing the people in 11:21 to tie words to their hands (or arms) "in order that your days may be many, along with the days of your children, on the soil that YHWH swore to your fathers, to give them (as long) as the days of the heavens over the earth." Other specified actions lead to the identical outcome in these verses, to be sure, but this observation need not have detracted from the powerful correspondence that stood ready to be drawn between the Torah's instructions

---

137. See ibid.
138. See Schniedewind, *How the Bible Became a Book*, 199.

and a widely known contemporary practice.[139] Taking into account literalist tendencies in scriptural interpretation (discussed above), it thus seems quite plausible that *tefillin* originated in an understanding of the Torah as showing Jews how to accomplish a long life, both for themselves and their children, via amuletic ritual.

I am suggesting, in other words, that Deut 11:21 came to be seen as elaborating the anticipated outcome for an inscribed amulet, which had been alluded to a few verses earlier. While Deut 11:18 makes no reference to writing, it does refer to tying the words mentioned in the earlier part of the verse, and these could hardly be tied without taking physical form. With the power of the written word being a well-attested feature of the ancient world,[140] reinforcement for the idea that wearing suitable written words might lead to length of days in the land, for adults and their children alike, would have been available from Deut 11:20, with its explicit mention of writing words on doorposts and gates. Here the protective role of the *mezuzah*, within the narrative of the exodus from Egypt (in Exodus 12), could only have added to the picture.[141] So too, perhaps, would the partial parallel to Deut 11:18 in Exod 13:9, where the word *zikkaron* takes the place of the word *totafot*, thus lending itself to the idea that an object described by this rare word might cause its wearer to be remembered by God.[142] Yet another affirming text might have been Deut 17:18–20, where (to a suitably disposed interpreter) the future king writes a copy of an entire Torah scroll "in order that he may prolong his days over his kingdom, he and his sons, in the midst of Israel" (with the word *lema'an* here echoing Deut 11:21).

Such an understanding of Deut 11:18 would have been accompanied, naturally enough, by two developments: (1) an insight that Deut 6:8, a close parallel to 11:18, makes the identical call for tying words, and (2) the need, in the case of both these verses, to define the extent of those words.

---

139. For a comprehensive survey, see Kotansky, "Incantations and Prayers for Salvation."

140. For a variety of cultural contexts, see Chester McCown, "The Ephesia Grammata in Popular Belief," *Transactions and Proceedings of the American Philological Association* 54 (1923), 128–40; Pedro Lain-Entralgo, *The Therapy of the Word in Classical Antiquity*, trans. L. J. Rather and John M. Sharp (New Haven and London: Yale University Press, 1970); Isaac Rabinowitz, *A Witness Forever* (Bethesda: CDL, 1993), 40–44; David Frankfurter, "The Magic of Writing and the Writing of Magic: The Power of the Word in Egyptian and Greek Traditions," *Helios* 21 (1994): 189–221.

141. For contextualizing *mezuzah* against the background of Greek lore, which is beyond my scope here, see Christopher A. Faraone, *Talismans and Trojan Horses: Guardian Statues in Ancient Greek Myth and Ritual* (New York/Oxford: Oxford University Press, 1992).

142. See Jacqueline Genot-Bismuth, "Les Tefilim de Qumran: pour une approche anthropologique" (paper presented at the 10th World Congress of Jewish Studies, 1989); Cohen, *Philo Judaeus*, 153.

The *Tefillin* Ritual as Known from Qumran

The above discussion provides the following hypothesis. *Tefillin*, an invented tradition of the late–Second Temple era, functioned as a long-life amulet, informed by knowledge of parallel Greek practices. It arose from a literalist interpretation of scripture, with Deut 11:21 seen to imply length of days, as an outcome of tying the words referred to by Deut 11:18. The evidence shows that the "words" were largely understood to consist of verses preceding, rather than subsequent to, the constitutive verses. This understanding may well have been driven by its application to Deut 6:8, whose preceding verses included the Decalogue, referred to as *devarim* on numerous occasions in Deuteronomy. Perhaps Deut 6:4–5, which begin the *Shema*, were also considered to be particularly significant prior verses.[143] It is far from obvious, however, why Deut 6:6–9 and 11:18–20 would have been viewed as included in the words to which they themselves refer. The incorporation of these verses into the *tefillin* ritual, together with ones from Exodus, will be addressed below.

Most significantly, the above hypothesis explains the anomalies that were highlighted earlier. The inclusion in *tefillin* of verses from the Song of Moses in 4QPhyl N can be explained by the association of Deut 32:44–47 with Deut 11:21. Once the latter verse was seen to imply length of days as an outcome for tying the words mentioned in Deut 11:18 ("these my words"), it could easily follow that words associated with Deut 32:44–45 ("the words of the song"/"these words") would, if tied, achieve a similar result. After all, 32:47 states (perhaps in even more dramatic fashion than 11:21), "indeed, no empty word is it for you, indeed, it is your (very) life; through this word you shall prolong (your) days upon the soil that you are crossing over the Jordan to possess."

There is another remarkable point of contact between Deuteronomy 11 and Deuteronomy 31–32. Deuteronomy 11:16–17 includes dire predictions for God's anger and Israel's future, followed by 11:18–21, with their possible suggestion of a written antidote. Deuteronomy 31:16–18 contains dire predictions that include similar language (cf. *veharah af* in 11:17 with *veharah appi* in 31:17), and are immediately followed in v. 19 by the first mention of the ensuing song, "But now; write yourselves down this song." This similarity would have reinforced the idea that the Song of Moses was appropriate for inclusion in *tefillin*—or perhaps engendered

---

143. While the age of the *Shema* is impossible to determine, it bears noting that according to M. *Tamid* 5:1 it was recited in the Temple. Some scholars see the Qumran Community Rule as alluding to its recital; see, for example, S. Talmon, "The "Manual of Benedictions" of the Sect of the Judaean Desert," *Revue de Qumran* 2, no. 8 (1960): 488–90.

this idea in the first place, in which case 32:44–47 would have provided the reinforcement.

In addition, it is to be noted that the 11QApocryphal Psalms scroll (11Q11) was identified in DJD as used for antidemonic purposes, and contained biblical text from Psalm 91, as well as two other songs against demons.[144] Psalm 91 concludes with a reference to length of life, so that such biblical references are known from sources other than *tefillin* to have been used for protective purposes.[145]

The hypothesis also explains the omissions in Table 5. Requirements for achieving length of days on the land, as detailed in Deut 5:32–6:2 and 11:8–9, included fulfillment of *all* that had been commanded (at 5:33; 6:2; and 11:8), and *precise* observance of the commandments (at 5:32). These prerequisites would, of course, have been far more onerous than the rather simple expedient of wearing an amulet. If *tefillin* practice were supposed to achieve the same outcome (that is, length of days on the land, as promised by Deut 11:21) then some scribes might have felt it best to omit other verses on this subject so as to avoid highlighting to God—or perhaps to *tefillin* practitioners—the stringent obligations they included. Indeed, it is worth noting that other scribes avoided these problematic verses altogether, beginning one of their Deuteronomy passages at 6:4, and the other at 11:13 (just as rabbinic *tefillin* do).[146]

In this context the upside-down writing of Deut 5:29–32 in 4QPhyl J is also particularly striking, for in 5:29 observance of *all* God's commandments (*kol mitsvotay*) is a precondition for eternal good befalling the people and their children, and 5:32 talks of unwavering adherence to God's command (*lo tasuru yamin usmol*). The right-side-up writing resumes in the second part of 6:2, with its mention of long life; the first part of that verse, which calls for observance of all the laws and commandments (*kol huqqotav umitsvotav*), is missing. The sympathetic or "persuasively analogical"[147] function of abnormal writing has been dated to a fourth century B.C.E. Attic curse, which was written backwards (from right to left) with the explicit wish that this form of writing have a concomitant effect.[148] The

---

144. "11QApocryphal Psalms," in *Discoveries in the Judaean Desert*, vol. 23, ed. Florentino García Martínez, Eibert J. C. Tigchelaar, and Adam S. van der Woude (Oxford: Clarendon, 1998), 181–205. See Esther Eshel, "Demonology in Palestine during the Second Temple Period" (Jerusalem: Hebrew University, 1999), 306–9 (in Hebrew).

145. See Bilhah Nitzan, "The Use of Scriptural Passages in 'Anti-Demonic Hymns' in Qumran and in Jewish Folklore," in *Qumran Prayer and Religious Poetry* (Leiden: Brill, 1994), 359–63.

146. 8QPhyl I and 4QPhyl C; see Baillet, "Grotte 8: Phylactère, Mezouza," 150–51; Milik, "Tefillin, Mezuzot et Targums," 53–55.

147. The expression is owed to S. J. Tambiah, "Form and Meaning of Magical Acts: A Point of View," in *Modes of Thought; Essays on Thinking in Western and Non-Western Societies*, ed. Robin Horton and Ruth Finnegan. (London: Faber, 1973), 211–13.

148. "Just as these words are cold and backwards (lit. *eparistera*—written right to left),

upside-down writing in 4QPhyl J, as well indeed as the omissions that were discussed earlier, can thus be seen as representing a wish for inversion/omission of the relevant conditions for achieving long life.[149]

In addition to its explanatory power vis-à-vis features that I have classified as anomalies, my hypothesis can also shed light on the choice of verses included in *tefillin*, as well as on particular features of their housings.

Exodus Verses in Tefillin, and Less-Than-Obvious Candidates from Deuteronomy

Once the two Deuteronomy verses—11:18, and by analogy its close parallel 6:8—were taken to call for an amuletic ritual, it seems that two Exodus verses (13:9 and 13:16) became associated with that ritual because of their remarkable correspondence to Deuteronomy. All four verses refer to an *ot* on the hand or arm, and three of them mention the *totafot* between the eyes. Exod 13:9, in other respects extremely similar to Exod 13:16, has a "reminder" in place of the word *totafot*, which suggests that the object concerned would function to remind God of its wearer. The two Exodus verses, moreover, might have suggested an origin for *tefillin* that could be connected to the great events of the exodus, surely a powerful source for any Jewish ritual.[150] In some sense then, all four verses seem to have been viewed as the mythical origins of the rite, even if the Deuteronomy verses were the ones to lead the way to its initial adoption.

Viewing the four verses in this light, one can also understand the phenomenon of their incorporation into the ritual itself, as the instructions on how to observe it—thus demonstrating its efficacy from within. Here one can point, as a parallel, to the common ancient phenomenon of incorporating the mythical origins of a practice of ritual power into the practice itself (such origin stories are often referred to by theoreticians of ancient

---

so too may the words of Krates be cold and backwards." See R. Wuensch, *Defixionum Tabellae Atticae* (Berlin, 1897), Text 67; Christopher A. Faraone, "The Agonistic Context of Early Greek Binding Spells," in *Magika Hiera: Ancient Greek Magic and Religion*, ed. Christopher A. Faraone and Dirk Obbink (New York: Oxford University Press, 1991), 6–10; D. Ogden, "Binding Spells," in *Witchcraft and Magic in Europe: Ancient Greece and Rome*, ed. B. Ankarloo and S. Clark (London: Athlone, 1999), 29–30.

149. For reflections on being upside down as being alien, see Jonathan Z. Smith, "Birth Upside Down or Right Side Up?," *History of Religions* 9 (1970): 281–302. For inversion in a Jewish context, see *venahafokh hu* in Esth 9:1.

150. See Yair Zakovitch's observation that "no other event in the history of Israel is given so much attention by biblical writers as is the exodus—as many as one hundred and twenty references in a variety of literary genres" (Yair Zakovitch, *And You Shall Tell Your Son . . .* [Jerusalem: Magnes Press, Hebrew University, 1991], 9).

ritual as "historiolae").[151] For *tefillin*, the mythical "events" consisted of the different places in the Torah in which Jews had been told to observe the ritual. The same idea would also explain the inclusion of Deut 6:6–7 and 11:19, which form the immediate context for 6:8 and 11:18 respectively. This is not to say that all of these verses were systematically written on *tefillin* slips; as can be seen from Table 1, there may have been considerable variation in this, as well as other, respects.[152]

While the importance of mythical origins would also justify the presence of an entire Exodus passage, the reason for inclusion of Deut 6:9 and 11:20 is less apparent but is perhaps to be accounted for by the explicit mention of writing in these two verses. The additional incorporation of Deut 11:21, in some instances, can be explained by its significance to the practice as a whole, as hypothesized earlier.

One further observation presents itself: the hypothesis may also shed light on the possible inclusion of Deut 8:5–10 in *tefillin*, as suggested above with respect to 4QDeut[j] and 4QDeut[n]. Deuteronomy 11:21 and the prior verses affirm not only God's promise of length of days on the land but also the assurance of God's bounty in the land, while referring to the possibility of losing the land when the people's actions arouse God's anger. In much the same way, Deut 8:5–10, while acknowledging that God punishes wrongdoers, is an affirmation that God promised sustenance on the land to those who are true to him (cf. "and you shall eat and be satisfied" in 8:10 and 11:15).

The Nature and Purpose of Tefillin Housings

The *tefillin* cases found in Qumran resemble aspects of other known practices; housings for text worn on the body are a well-known feature of ancient amuletic ritual. Although surviving exemplars from other cultural contexts are generally metal or wood, the practice of enclosing such texts in stitched-up leather, as in Qumran, is attested to by the fourth-century B.C.E. poet Anaxilas, who refers to "carrying about the excellent Ephesian letters in little stitched hides."[153] The Ephesian letters were com-

---

151. See David Frankfurter, "Narrating Power: The Theory and Practice of the Magical Historiola in Ritual Spells," in *Ancient Magic and Ritual Power*, ed. Marvin Meyer and Paul Mirecki (Leiden: Brill, 1995), 457–76. See also Jan Assman, "Magic and Theology in Ancient Egypt," in *Envisioning Magic: A Princeton Seminar and Symposium*, ed. Peter Schaefer and Hans G. Kippenberg (Leiden: Brill, 1997), 1–18.

152. It should be noted that the incorporation of constitutive "instruction" verses was not an indiscriminate feature of Jewish ritual. Thus, for example, one of the constitutive verses for the practice of *tsitsit* (Deut 22:12) does not seem, from rabbinic evidence, to have ever been incorporated into its ritual practice.

153. Fragment 18 in T. Kock, *Comicorum Atticorum Fragmenta* (Leipzig: Teubner, 1880–1888), 2:268.

monly used in ancient ritual, both defensively and aggressively, and their practice included their inscription as text.[154]

More specifically, when compared with early Egyptian, Carthaginian and Kushite practice, the *tefillin* cases bear a typological resemblance to one form of Greco-Roman amulet practice. Whereas the latter style involved attaching the housing by a cord or strap that lay along one of its sides (much like *tefillin*), the attachment for the former style was linked to a single loop on the amulet-case, or to loops on two of its sides. The feature encountered in the above Greco-Roman type is also found for Buddhist amulet containers, and it has been surmised that Alexander's soldiers brought back this type from India.[155] (With regard to physical characteristics, another parallel with Hellenistic practice is to be found in the numerous folds in Qumran *tefillin* slips, as well as the Nash Papyrus. Many of the inscribed Greek amulets that have been discovered were also folded, presumably to make them small enough to wear conveniently.[156])

In the quest for correct observance (a characteristic, it is to be noted, of antique rituals having magical effects, as well as of halakah) there seems to have been some uncertainty as to whether correct performance entailed placing the various *tefillin* texts into discrete cells inside the housings. Several one-cell and four-cell containers were found, as well as two of a three-cell type, as mentioned above. In the two instances where decipherable fragments were found inside their housings, the latter were the multicell type, and no more than one constitutive verse was present in any one cell.[157]

In fact, it looks, from the very limited evidence, as though multiple cells were designed to keep the four constitutive verses separate, rather than to keep biblical passages apart. This is because sections from different biblical passages might share a cell in a multicell housing, as evidenced by XQPhyl 1 and 3. The cells that contained 4QPhyl D, E, and F also look to have also been designed to keep constitutive verses separate, as they split up the Exodus passage into two. Indeed, it seems possible that the multiple-cell practice originated with a need to make two distinct passages out of the extended Exodus one, so as to highlight the fact that it contained two constitutive verses. As suggested above, the inclusion of an

---

154. See McCown, "The Ephesia Grammata in Popular Belief," 128–40; Kotansky, "Incantations and Prayers for Salvation," 111; Gager, *Curse Tablets and Binding Spells from the Ancient World*, 5–6.

155. Peter W. Schienerl, "Der Ursprung und die Entwicklung von Amulettbehaeltnissen in der antiken Welt," *Antike Welt* (1984): 49–53.

156. See Kotansky, "Incantations and Prayers for Salvation," 111–12, 15. For an imaginative interpretation of the folds exhibited by one set of Qumran *tefillin* slips, see Genot-Bismuth, "Les Tefilim de Qumran: pour une approche anthropologique."

157. XQPhyl 1–3 and 4QPhyl D,E,F; see Yadin, *Tefillin from Qumran (XQPhyl 1–4)*, 8–15; Milik, "Tefillin, Mezuzot et Targums," 35 and 55–57.

Exodus pericope in *tefillin* is likely to have revolved around its constitutive elements, which might explain an interest in stressing that it included two such verses.

The Qumran "Mezuzot"

I have suggested above that all the texts identified as *mezuzot* in DJD may just as well have been *tefillin*. It is important to note, however, that if my claim for the significance of Deut 11:18–21 is correct, then a fortiori the same protective power should have been ascribed to a *mezuzah* practice described in Deut 11:20 (and 6:9) as to the *tefillin* practice derived from 11:18. More specifically, I have adduced an omission in Table 5 in a so-called *mezuzah*— 4QMez C—that is similar to those observed in *tefillin*. Having interpreted such omissions, I would now argue that if 4QMez C is, in fact, a *tefillin* parchment, then it strengthens my claims; and if it is a *mezuzah*, the omission provides confirming evidence that these were amulets similar to *tefillin*.

The Traditional View

Along different lines, which are similar to the traditional Jewish understanding of why *tefillin* were practiced, E. P. Sanders has asserted that Jews were simply fulfilling a biblical requirement, grounded in Deut 6:4–9, to bear the laws of God in mind.[158] He based his views on the centrality of the *Shema* to Jewish life and worship, but it would be circular for this purpose to argue that the findings of *tefillin* support the idea of the *Shema's* centrality. Here, the strongest evidence seems to be that of the *Letter of Aristeas* and Philo, which suggest the importance of Deut 6:6–9 (and/or 11:18–20) as a group of verses. While this might explain a *mezuzah* practice of some kind, it does not account for the nature of the *tefillin* practice demonstrated by the archaeological findings. In particular, it does not satisfactorily explain the inclusion of Exodus verses, the multiple-cell housings, the inclusion of Deuteronomy 32, or the omissions. All of these are better accounted for by understanding the ritual as a magical practice. While a halakah of *tefillin* practice might, conceivably, explain the Exodus verses, and the attention paid to the housings, I have argued above that the Qumran *tefillin* do not support the idea. Nor would such detailed halakah fit the Common Judaism that Sanders describes.

---

158. See E. P. Sanders, *Judaism: Practice and Belief 63 B.C.E.–66 C.E.* (London: SCM, 1992), 195–97.

A Popular Model for *Tefillin* Practice

If, as argued above, the Qumran *tefillin* were not written according to a fixed set of rules, and if they are not sectarian exemplars, then they most probably represent some form of popular practice.[159] If they were amulets, as has also been argued here, then it seems even more likely that they were part of the religion of the common people.[160]

Major threats with which such religion concerns itself have been outlined by J. Z. Smith, who gives prominence to extinction of the family and dislocation.[161] These are precisely the subjects of Deut 11:21, whose importance was discussed above, which reinforces the idea that *tefillin* would have held appeal as a popular ritual. The physical form of the Qumran *tefillin* lends credence to this idea; the parchment shapes, to the extent they can be determined, show that scraps were often used,[162] and the housings were of very simple construction. They evoke Smith's comment that the artifacts of domestic religion tend to fill up museum basements rather than display cases. (The first *tefillin* housing to be published was, in fact, listed together with findings of olive and date stones.[163])

Although *tefillin* ritual would have had many points of contact with Greek amuletic ritual known from the larger Hellenistic world, it would also have exhibited important differences from it. In the first place, the characteristically Jewish, biblical basis of *tefillin* would have set them apart from any Greek counterpart. An amulet that promised length of days to an entire group of wearers would also have departed in significant measure from inscribed Hellenistic amulets, which often (although not always) had very specific functions, and named individuals whom they were designed to protect.[164] It is noteworthy, however, that the seventh/sixth century B.C.E. Hebrew silver amulets, described in chapter 2, also seem to have functioned in a very general way (and, interestingly, were connected to a formula that became "scriptural"). Moreover, these silver amulets similarly contained no reference to malevolent forces, angels, or oaths. Until beyond the period covered by this book, Jews are not known to have had any practices that incorporated such features.

---

159. See Milik, who in explaining the variety exhibited by the Qumran *tefillin* characterized the practice as "private and semi-sacred" ("Tefillin, Mezuzot et Targums," 47).

160. For a useful discussion of this aspect of ancient religion, see Karel van der Toorn, *Family Religion in Babylonia, Syria and Israel* (Leiden: Brill, 1996), 1–4.

161. Jonathan Z. Smith, "Here, There and Anywhere," in *Relating Religion* (Chicago: University of Chicago Press, 2004), 325–28. Smith prefers the term "domestic religion" to "popular religion."

162. Cf. Kuhn, *Phylakterien aus Höhle 4 von Qumran*, 31; Tov, *Scribal Practices and Approaches*, 256–58.

163. See Harding, "The Archaeological Finds," 7

164. See Kotansky, "Incantations and Prayers for Salvation."

Tefillin and the *Shema*

Finally, as was observed when discussing the Nash Papyrus and the literary evidence, some of the possible evidence for *tefillin* seems overdetermined. This is because it might be evidence instead for the significance of the *Shema* (traditionally, in its entirety, Deut 6:4–9; Deut 11:13–21; Num 15:37–41). The *Letter of Aristeas* and Philo, as earlier discussed, might be taken to suggest that *Shema* liturgy was an important feature of Egyptian Jewish ritual, even if *tefillin* were not. It thus seems worth trying to establish the nature of the relationship between the two practices.

Baumgarten has argued for the institution of *Shema* recital in the Temple during the Maccabean era,[165] and there is possibly a reference to the *Shema* in the Qumran Community Rule (1QS 10:10–10:14a).[166] My hypothesis for the origins of the *tefillin* ritual does nothing to make things clearer on its own, as Deut 6:7 and 11:19 would also have been associated with Deut 11:21, and could well have been taken to call for a *recital* of relevant "words" as a way to achieve length of days. It is to be noted, however, that these verses, while traditionally understood to refer to *Shema* recital, are most simply interpreted as calling for discussion of the "words" rather than their recital. This seems worth stressing, because an obligation to recite *Shema* as a precise formula calls for a highly literalist interpretation of the Torah, as has similarly been suggested for *tefillin* (whereas this is not quite the case for either *tsitsit* or *mezuzah*).

Here it is to be noted that verbal charms or incantations (*epodai*), no less than amulets, were a feature of Hellenistic ritual. Pedro Lain-Entralgo observed that "magic formulas have passed through the following phases: at first they were sung; then they were recited; finally they were written upon a material object worn in some cases as an amulet."[167] Nevertheless, it is improbable that the *tefillin* ritual followed on as a development of an earlier "magical" *Shema* ritual; an incantation that actually mentions amulets, but is nevertheless practiced without them, seems less likely than the alternative. In other words, if *Shema* recital originally had a magical component, then its initial practice is

---

165. Baumgarten, "Invented Traditions of the Maccabean Era," 202–7.

166. See Talmon, "The 'Manual of Benedictions' of the Sect of the Judaean Desert," 488–90; Lawrence H. Schiffman, *Reclaiming the Dead Sea Scrolls* (Philadelphia: Jewish Publication Society, 1994), 293; D. K. Falk, "Qumran Prayer Texts and the Temple," in *Sapiential, Liturgical and Poetical Texts from Qumran*, ed. D. K. Falk, Florentino García Martínez, and Eileen M. Schuller (Leiden: Brill, 2000), 114–18. Scholars have viewed the Community Rule here as an allusion to *Shema* recital, but it is in fact merely a likely allusion to Deut 6:7/11:19, and the significance of these verses to the community does not necessarily imply a recital practice.

167. Lain-Entralgo, *The Therapy of the Word in Classical Antiquity*, 45.

unlikely to have existed independently of the *tefillin* ritual; and the *Letter of Aristeas* and Philo may well have originated in a milieu where *tefillin* practice was well known.

It is, of course, possible that *Shema* recital had no such magical associations, although this would call for some explanation of why the relevant verses were seen to call for a formulaic recital. Baumgarten argued that *Shema* recital in the Temple was a tradition invented by the Maccabees, designed to remind Jews of the essentials of their faith.[168]

I would like to make an alternative proposal, which reinforces the idea of a magical connection between *tefillin, mezuzah, tsitsit,* and *Shema* recital. Here, the latter's inclusion of Num 15:37–41, which focuses on *tsitsit* but is unrelated to Deut 6:7 or 11:19, may shed light on the possible dependence of the rituals on each other. Although an in-depth discussion of *tsitsit* is beyond the scope of this work, it is worth remarking that protecting the wearer (from sin) is their explicit function according to Num 15:39, and their ritual power is accordingly apparent. It is thus intriguing to speculate that all these passages were recited in the Temple precisely in order to consecrate objects considered to have ritual power, or to act as an incantation that accompanied their performance. It is to be noted that amulets, in cultures as distinct as the Hellenistic world[169] and modern Thailand, are taken by their owners to a temple or priest, for their power to be activated.[170] In 2 Maccabees, amulets "had been consecrated to the idols of Jamnia," and instructions in the Greek Magical Papyri for manufacture of inscribed phylacteries include the ending, "and when you have consecrated it, wear it."[171] If *mezuzot* were similarly taken to the Temple, or simply to a priest, for consecration/activation, then the development of a portable scrolled *mezuzah* can well be understood as having been preferable to a more literal interpretation of Deut 6:9 and 11:20, calling for text to be inscribed on doorposts and gates.

---

168. Baumgarten, "Invented Traditions of the Maccabean Era," 207. For the likely historical value of *M. Tamid* 5:1, see also Tzvee Zahavy, "Political and Social Dimensions in the Formation of Early Jewish Prayer: The Case of the Shema" (paper presented at the Tenth World Conference of Jewish Studies, Jerusalem, 1989).

169. See Andrea Becker, "Phylakterion," in *Brill's New Pauly (Encyclopedia of the Ancient World)* (Leiden: Brill, 2007).

170. Activation is also accomplished by other means. See, for example, the reference to activating a clay inscribed amulet by firing it, in Philip S. Alexander, "Incantations and Books of Magic," in *The History of the Jewish People in the Age of Jesus Christ (175 B.C.–A.D. 135) by Emil Schürer, (Revised Version),* volume 3, part 1, ed. Geza Vermes, Fergus Millar, and Martin Goodman (Edinburgh: T. & T. Clark, 1986), 355.

171. See, for example, PGM VII 579–90 in Hans Dieter Betz, *The Greek Magical Papyri in Translation, Including the Demotic Spells,* 2nd ed. (Chicago: University of Chicago Press, 1992), 134. These particular instructions are for manufacturing "a phylactery, a bodyguard against daimons, against phantasms, against every sickness and suffering."

While the idea that *Shema* recital evolved as I am suggesting has some explanatory force, it is a radical departure from previous scholarship. This has tended to view the inclusion of the Numbers passage in the *Shema*, in line with rabbinic literature, as primarily related to its last verse, which (in a close parallel to the first verse of the Decalogue) mentions the exodus from Egypt.[172] Naomi Cohen has, however, also suggested, although along entirely different lines to mine, that *Shema* recital and *tefillin* were originally related.[173]

---

172. See the discussion in Cohen, *Philo Judaeus*, 167–76.
173. See ibid., 173.

4

The Tanna'itic Era
(70 C.E. to the Third Century)

This chapter will assess evidence that relates to *tefillin* practice in the period between the destruction of the Jerusalem temple and the late third century C.E. I will discuss the make-up of *tefillin* and who wore them, as well as when, where, and how they were worn. Other issues to be investigated include sanctity, scribal matters, and purity concerns. A specific focus on the meaning of the ritual will be left to the final section of the book.

The periodization reflects the fact that the most significant pre–70 data arose from archaeological findings (which here too will be discussed first), whereas the evidence most important to this chapter will be of a literary nature. In chapter 1, I provided my background observations on tanna'itic literature. I should again stress that the early rabbinic legacy does not deal with *tefillin* in a purposefully comprehensive manner. Mishnah and Tosefta mention them quite often, but only in passing. The motivation of Midreshei Halakah in discussing *tefillin* is not so much to list attendant halakot as to correlate these with relevant biblical texts. Reading between the lines will therefore be an essential component of my analysis.

The Archaeological Evidence

When compared to the late–Second Temple period (see chapter 3), the findings for this period have been very limited. Six parchment *tefillin* slips have been identified (as well as an indecipherable one identified as a *mezuzah* or *tefillin* slip[1]), and one empty four-cell housing similar to those

---

1. Although DJD 2 classified it as a *mezuzah*, a subsequent paper found it equally likely to be *tefillin*. See Hartmut Stegemann and Jürgen Becker, "Zum Text von Fragment 5 aus Wadi Murabba'at," *Revue de Qumran* 3, no. 11 (1961): 443–48.

known from Qumran. All were from the Judean Desert, where two of these *tefillin* slips as well as the housing were found *in situ* in the caves of Nahal Se'elim and Wadi Murabba'at respectively.[2]

Varying reasons for dating these slips to the first or second century C.E. were provided by the publishers. It is to be noted that all three locations identified—Murabba'at, Se'elim, and Hever—had caves whose contents could be dated to the Bar-Kokhba period. Predestruction dates cannot, however, be ruled out (this is to be contrasted with the Qumran finds, where post-destruction dates *can* more readily be ruled out,[3] although there too many slips were not found *in situ*). When compared to many fragments from Qumran, all six slips were well preserved and appear to have been similarly written on irregularly shaped scraps of parchment.

The following table provides the texts, as reconstructed by their publishers, who reasonably presumed that the identification of part of a verse was evidence for the original presence of the entire verse. As in chapter 3, I use the designations provided in the "name" columns in DJD 39, in which all *tefillin* slips are given a Phyl suffix.[4] These names reflect the three above-mentioned locations in abbreviated form. Mur refers to Murabba'at, and the designation 34Se identifies Cave 34 at Nahal Se'elim, also known as the "Cave of the Scrolls." The designation XHev/Se was constructed to reflect uncertainty as to whether the documents concerned were found in Nahal Hever or in Nahal Se'elim (Wadi Seiyal). It arose because although

---

2. The final volume of the DJD series lists only three such *tefillin*, which it categorizes as being from sites other than Qumran, but each of these consisted of two slips. See Emanuel Tov, "Categorized List of the 'Biblical Texts': Appendix—Phylacteries (Tefillin) and Mezuzot," in *Discoveries in the Judaean Desert*, vol. 39 (Oxford: Oxford University Press, 2002), 182–83. As in chap. 3, I use "found" or "discovered" for all items discussed; see the discussion of the less certain provenance of those slips that were purchased.

References for the official publications are as follows:

J. T. Milik, "Textes littéraires," in *Discoveries in the Judaean Desert*, vol. 2* *(Texte)* (Oxford: Oxford University Press, 1961), 80–86. See also vol. 2** *(Planches)*, XXII-XXIV.

Y. Aharoni, "The Expedition to the Judean Desert, 1960, Expedition B," *Israel Exploration Journal* 11 (1961): 22–23.

M. Morgenstern and M. Segal, "XHev/SePhylactery," in *Discoveries in the Judaean Desert*, vol. 38 (Oxford: Oxford University Press, 2000), 183–91. See also plate XXX.

The above-mentioned housing is described in R. de Vaux, "Archéologie: la période Romaine," in *Discoveries in the Judaean Desert*, vol. 2* *(Texte)* (Oxford: Oxford University Press, 1961), 44. See also vol. 2** *(Planches)*, XIV.4.

3. Here I am following Milik's dating of the Qumran *tefillin* on palaeographic grounds combined with the view of most scholars that the contents of the Qumran caves do not postdate the Temple's destruction. See J. T. Milik, "Tefillin, Mezuzot et Targums," in *Discoveries in the Judaean Desert*, vol. 6 (Oxford: Oxford University Press, 1977), 37; Adam S. van der Woude, "Fifty Years of Qumran Research," in *The Dead Sea Scrolls after Fifty Years*, vol. 1, ed. Peter W. Flint and James C. VanderKam (Leiden: Brill, 1998), 2–3.

4. I have, however, expanded MurPhyl and XHev/SePhyl to reflect the two slips in each of these sets.

the Bedouin who sold these finds in the 1950s claimed that they originated in Wadi Seiyal, which seems to have been bisected at the time by the Jordan/Israel border, some of their finds actually originated in Nahal Hever, which was on the Israel side.[5] (This is certain because in the case of some of the XHev/Se documents, although apparently not the *tefillin*, Yigael Yadin's team that excavated Nahal Hever found residual fragments *in situ*.)

Table 1. The Reconstructed Inscriptions

MurPhyl (identified as originating in one set of slips):

MurPhyl 1	Exod 13:1–16; Deut 11:13–21
MurPhyl 2	Deut 6:4–9

XHev/SePhyl (identified as originating in one set of slips):

XHev/SePhyl 1	Exod 13:1–16; Deut 6:4–9; Deut 11:13–17a
XHev/SePhyl 2	Deut 11:17b–21
34SePhyl A	Exod 13:2–10
34SePhyl B	Exod 13:11–16

Are the Post-Destruction Tefillin Rabbinically Conforming?

No text identified on any of the slips was outside the rabbinically approved textual limits for *tefillin* parchments, although XHev/SePhyl, in particular, includes a large number of variants with the MT, which some consider as a marker for rabbinic conformity, and 34SePhyl A may begin a verse later than rabbinic *tefillin* do. In addition, both MurPhyl and XHev/SePhyl were sets, each consisting of two slips, for which there is no apparent sanction in tanna'itic halakah (where arm *tefillin* are written on a single parchment and head *tefillin* on four).[6] With that in mind, it is noteworthy that both of those sets add up to the exact contents of rabbinic *tefillin*, and that Mur-Phyl conforms to the MT. J. T. Milik, following K. G. Kuhn,[7] saw these

---

5. See Stephen J. Pfann, "Sites in the Judean Desert Where Texts Have Been Found," in *The Dead Sea Scrolls on Microfiche: Companion Volume*, ed. Emanuel Tov and Stephen J. Pfann (Leiden: Brill, 1993), 118. See also Jonas C. Greenfield, "The Texts from Nahal Se'elim (Wadi Seiyal)," in *The Madrid Qumran Congress*, ed. Julio Trebolle Barrera and Luis Vegas Montaner (Leiden: Brill, 1992), 661–65; H. M. Cotton and A. Yardeni, "General Introduction," in *Discoveries in the Judaean Desert*, vol. 27 (Oxford: Oxford University Press, 1997).

6. Although DJD 39 also lists 34SePhyl as a single finding, it is not clear whether (or why) the publisher thought that the two slips might originally have been part of a set. Slip B has a larger letter size than slip A.

7. K. G. Kuhn, *Phylakterien aus Höhle 4 von Qumran* (Heidelberg: Abhandlungen der heidelberger Akademie der Wissenschaften, Phil.-Hist. Klasse 1, 1957), 30–31.

features as evidence for the uniformity of Jewish religious life after the "Council" of Jamnia,[8] although similar texts were subsequently published from Qumran.[9]

Milik also found significance in the choice of Deut 11:13–21 rather than Deut 6:4–9 to follow the Exodus passage on MurPhyl 1, and traced a medieval rabbinic dispute to the difference between this sequence and the differing order exhibited by XHev/Se Phyl.[10] While it is, of course, possible that the MurPhyl scribe viewed its order as halakically correct, it seems more likely that correctness had nothing to do with it, and that the choice of Deuteronomy pericope to round out MurPhyl 1 was dictated by the relative size of the scraps of parchment to hand. Deuteronomy 13:11–21, containing about 2.5 times the number of words of Deut 6:4–9, would simply not have fit onto the MurPhyl 2 slip.[11]

In any event, there is no evidence that second-century Judean Desert *tefillin* included text that differed materially from rabbinic prescriptions. It is probably reasonable to view the following comments by Hannah Cotton, on marriage documents of this period, as applying equally to these *tefillin*: "Rabbinic law itself acquired its shape in the same environment: that it reflects the documents is only to be expected. We would be wrong, though, to assume without compelling proof that the documents reflect the . . . *halacha*."[12]

Who Wore *Tefillin*, and Who Did Not?

I argued in the previous chapter that *tefillin* were part of the religion of the common people, in line with Sanders's assertion that they were a constituent of "common Judaism" (albeit for reasons different from his).[13] Here

---

8. See Geza Vermes and Fergus Millar, *The History of the Jewish People in the Age of Jesus Christ (175 B.C.–A.D. 135) by Emil Schürer, (Revised Version), volume 1* (Edinburgh: T. & T. Clark, 1973), 525–26.

9. 4QPhyl C and 8QPhyl I.

10. While XHev/Se Phyl was not published until 2000, it was already discussed some forty years earlier in Milik, "Textes littéraires," 81.

11. The phenomenon of writing on such a tiny piece of parchment is actually documented in *M. Shabbat* 8:3, which mentions "(enough) parchment for writing on it the small pericope in *tefillin*, which is 'Hear Israel.'" For a fuller discussion of Milik's claim, see my article "Rabbenu Tam's Tefillin: An Ancient Tradition or the Product of Medieval Exegesis?," *Jewish Studies Quarterly* 14, no. 4 (2007): 319–27.

12. H. M. Cotton, "The Rabbis and the Documents," in *Jews in a Graeco-Roman World*, ed. Martin Goodman (Oxford: Clarendon, 1998), 179. For a diametrically opposite approach from within the conventions of rabbinic writing rather than academic scholarship, see Shlomo Goren, "Hatefillin Mimidbar Yehudah Le'or Hahalakhah," in *Torat Hamo'adim* (Tel Aviv: Avraham Tzi'oni, 1964), 496–511 (in Hebrew).

13. See E. P. Sanders, *Judaism: Practice and Belief 63 B.C.E–66 C.E.* (London: SCM, 1992), 195–97.

I will investigate whether the same can be said of the tanna'itic era.[14] It is to be noted that the archaeological evidence for *tefillin* supports the idea of a continuous and widespread practice; they were found among groups as presumably diverse as the users of the Qumran caves, on the one hand, and the caves whose findings are dated to the second century C.E., on the other.

There are other reasons to imagine widespread *tefillin* practice: for one thing, the unusual status awarded to *tefillin* in Mishnah and Tosefta, where they are taken entirely for granted, as ritual objects whose practice requires no elaboration. This certainly cannot have been due to their insignificance, as on numerous occasions the Mishnah and Tosefta single out *tefillin*, among a few other practices, as representative of an entire class of religious observance. Thus *T. Berakhot* 6:10 employs *tefillin*, together with *sukkah, lulav,* and *tsitsit*, to epitomize items that would have been assembled for the performance of *mitsvot*. The Mekhiltot use the same list, as examples of a duty to create beautiful objects whose purpose is the worship of God.[15] *Sukkah, lulav,* and *tefillin* are similarly used in paradigmatic fashion in *M. Nedarim* 2:2; *T. Nedarim* 1:5; and *M. Shevu'ot* 3:8; as well as in *T. Kiddushin* 1:10, where these three are adduced as parade examples that illuminate a technical term. In like manner, *M. Sanhedrin* 11:3 uses *tefillin* to illustrate a general principle (that in certain respects the "words of the scribes" were to be taken more seriously than the words of the Torah itself), and in *M. Shevu'ot* 3:11 *tefillin* practice seems to be representative of actions in general, and not merely *mitsvot*, along with the act of eating: "One adjured by others is culpable. How so? One said 'I did not eat today and/or I did not put on *tefillin*,' (and the other said) 'I put you to an oath (to attest to that).' . . ."[16]

Much as *tefillin* are used as a proxy for an entire class of practices, they can be used analogically to provide a general principle of law. Thus, the wholesale exemption of women from time-engendered obligations is derived, according to *Mekhilta Derabbi Shimon bar Yohai*, from the fact that women are exempt from *tefillin* (where the ruling is itself derived from independent considerations).[17] All in all, it seems reasonable to infer, from

---

14. For a discussion of extending Sanders's term to the Talmudic era, and refining it as "complex common Judaism," see Stuart S. Miller, *Sages and Commoners in Late-Antique Erez Israel* (Tübingen: Mohr Siebeck, 2006), 21–28.

15. H-R p. 127 lines 5–6, and E-M p. 78 line 13–p. 79 line 16 (to Exod 15:2).

16. It may similarly be worth noting that, according to some variants of *M. Berakhot* 3:1, a mourner who had not yet buried his dead would have been exempt from all commandments, and not merely *Shema* recital and *tefillin*, which the mishnah first singled-out. This would then be yet another example of *tefillin* being employed paradigmatically. The variant is, however, absent in the better witnesses. See *Mishnah Zera'im Im Shinuye Nusha'ot*, vol. 1 (Jerusalem: Makhon Hatalmud Hayisre'eli Hashalem, 1971), 25 (in Hebrew).

17. E-M p. 41 lines 8–10 (to Exod 13:9).

the above selection of discourse, that the practice was of some significance to the tanna'im. The fact that its details seem to be taken for granted
in Mishnah and Tosefta accordingly points to an extremely well-known
practice—an implication similar to one drawn by Maimonides.[18]

There is also more direct evidence that suggests widespread *tefillin*
practice. *M. Megillah* 4:8 implicitly has the practice observed in some fashion by unspecified heretics and "outsiders," as well as by the Mishnah's
own audience, since it is critical of the former for their way of wearing
tefillin. *T. Bikkurim* 2:15 talks of "scroll, *tefillin* and *mezuzot* scribes, as well
as the merchants to whom they sell and the merchants to whom those
merchants sell," seeming to indicate an active market for these ritual
objects that would be incompatible with a tiny group of users. The same
is suggested by *T. Avodah Zarah* 3:8, which refers to resellers with bundles
of *tefillin* at their disposal. *M. Eruvin* 10:1–2 discuss the Shabbat rules for
someone who happens to find multiple sets of *tefillin* lying around in a
public space, and unless these mishnayot represent a purely scholastic
exercise, they also seem to hint at a widespread practice.

The idea that *tefillin* practice was not restricted to rabbis and their followers is buttressed by the Mishnah's and Tosefta's regulation of *tefillin*
wearing on Shabbat (to be discussed below). As the Midreshei Halakah
are of one voice in ruling out such practice, it seems quite likely that these
rulings were designed for practitioners other than the rabbis themselves.
Similarly, as will be discussed in chapter 5, *T. Berakhot* 2:20 is aware of certain *tefillin* practices that, "it goes without saying" but nevertheless seems
necessary to declare, are rabbinically proscribed. Here too, then, the
tanna'im allude to *tefillin* wearers from outside their immediate circle.

Consideration of the following reference, in Josephus's *Antiquities*
book 4, may also shed light on the extent of *tefillin* practice:

212. Twice each day, both at its beginning and when the time comes for
turning to sleep, bear witness to God of the gifts that He granted them
when they were delivered from the land of the Egyptians, since grati-
tude is proper by nature: it is given in return for those things that have
already occurred and as a stimulus for what will be.

213. They shall also inscribe on their doorways the greatest of the benefits that God has bestowed upon them, and each shall display them on
his arms; and as many things as are able to show forth the power of God
and His good will towards them let them display on the head and the

---

18. In his commentary on the Mishnah, the twelfth-century scholar commented on
the absence of any special section devoted to the laws of *tsitsit*, *tefillin*, and *mezuzah*, stating
that these had been so well known, even by the masses, as to render their inclusion unwar-
ranted; see *Mishnah with the Commentary of Moses Ben Maimon (Judeo-Arabic with Hebrew
Translation)*, trans. Yosef Kapah (Jerusalem: Mossad Harav Kook, 1963), 122.

arm, so that the favor of God with regard to them may be readily visible from all sides.[19]

The immediate context for this passage begins at paragraph 196, where Josephus claims that he will describe, in full, the constitution that was Moses' departing gift to the Israelites. After a range of other topics, the text proceeds to a likely allusion to reciting the *Shema* prayer, followed by apparent references to *mezuzah* and *tefillin*.[20] While Josephus is basing himself on Deut 6:8/11:18 (in paragraph 213) the reference is more than a paraphrase of the Torah; it is noteworthy that he refers to the arm and head, rather than the "hand" and "between/before the eyes" as in the Torah/Septuagint verses, thus demonstrating familiarity with an actual practice, of the kind that the rabbis discuss. It is precisely because Josephus deviates from scripture in this way that it seems most likely that he is referring to a known ritual (in contrast perhaps to the *Letter of Aristeas* and Philo, both of which were analyzed in chapter 3).

It is unclear why Josephus would have chosen to incorporate *tefillin* practice in his list of laws. David Altshuler has observed that over six hundred verses in biblical laws have no parallel in the *Antiquities*, despite Josephus's claim of completeness.[21] Although one might surmise that he included the practice as a common one, it is also possible that the *Shema* verses as a whole were of particular significance to him, and that *tefillin* (and *mezuzah*) were included as a result. In any event, as Josephus does not suggest any sectarian element to the practice, he is to be taken most simply as regarding it as widespread.

Another source that calls for consideration is Matthew 23:5, which has provided the English language with its word for *tefillin* and has been subject to a variety of interpretations: "They do all their deeds to be seen by others; for they make their phylacteries broad, and their fringes long."

The context of the above verse is Matthew's report of Jesus' speaking to the crowd and his disciples and accusing the scribes and Pharisees of various kinds of ostentation in religious practice. (It thus purports to be reporting events in the early first century c.e., preceding the period under consideration here. However, in light of evidence that Matthew rewrote the life of Jesus to reflect his own time and community, the above reference is best understood as a reflection of the latter.[22])

---

19. Translation taken from Louis H. Feldman, *Judean Antiquities 1–4: Translation and Commentary* (Leiden: Brill, 2000).

20. Cf. Geza Vermes and Fergus Millar, *The History of the Jewish People in the Age of Jesus Christ (175 B.C.–A.D. 135) by Emil Schürer, (Revised Version)*, volume 2 (Edinburgh: T. & T. Clark, 1979), 455 n. 153; Feldman, *Judean Antiquities 1–4*, 406-8.

21. David Altshuler, "On the Classification of Judaic Laws in the Antiquities of Josephus and the Temple Scroll of Qumran," *AJS Review* (1982–1983): 5.

22. The literature on Matthew is vast. See, for example, T. W. Manson, *The Sayings of*

The word *phylakterion* (derived from the verb *phylassein*) refers to a means of protection, and this is its first attested use in reference to Jewish practice. As was seen in chapter 3, earlier writers in Greek describe the objects periphrastically, if indeed they are describing them at all, thus providing no indication as to which noun they might have used to refer to *tefillin*. It is accordingly to be noted that one might argue that Matthew is not referring to *tefillin* but is actually referring to something else as a *phylakterion*, so that those who see him as talking about *tefillin* misunderstand him.[23] The old-Syriac translation, however, reinforces the generally accepted understanding that Matthew is referring to *tefillin*.[24] The citation is *umaften arqa deteflehon*, to be rendered as "and they widen the thongs of their *tefillin*" (or perhaps simply "their amulets," in line with the etymology that will be discussed in chapter 5).[25]

The idea that *tefillin* were means of protection is important support for the argument in the previous chapter. It is particularly noteworthy that

---

Jesus as Recorded in the Gospels According to St. Matthew and St. Luke (London: SCM, 1949); Robert H. Gundry, *Matthew: A Commentary on His Literary and Theological Art* (Grand Rapids: Eerdmans, 1982), 599–609; W. D. Davies and Dale C. Allison, *The Gospel According to Saint Matthew*, vol. 1, International Critical Commentary (Edinburgh: T. & T. Clark, 1988), Introduction; John P. Meier, "Matthew, Gospel of," in *Anchor Bible Dictionary*, vol. 4, ed. David Noel Freedman (New York: Doubleday, 1992); Anthony J. Saldarini, *Matthew's Christian-Jewish Community* (Chicago: University of Chicago Press, 1994); Dale C. Allison, "Matthew," in *The Oxford Bible Commentary*, ed. John Barton and John Muddiman (Oxford: Oxford University Press, 2001).

23. E. R. Goodenough in particular promoted this view, following the fourth- or early-fifth-century commentary found in the Anekaphalaiosis to Epiphanius's *Panarion*, which understands the *phylakteria* here as "purple stripes" on a garment, that is, a *tallit*, whose fringes are also mentioned in Matt 23:5. See *Panarion* 15.1.3–7; E. R. Goodenough, *Jewish Symbols in the Graeco-Roman Period*, vol. 2 (New York: Pantheon, 1953), 209–10; E. R. Goodenough, *Jewish Symbols in the Graeco-Roman Period*, vol. 9 (New York: Pantheon, 1964), 171–72. H. F. Stander suggests that Epiphanius was denying that the *phylakteria* in Matt 23:5 were *tefillin* so as to disabuse his readers of a notion that Jesus might not have condemned all amulets, but only ostentatious ones; see H. F. Stander, "Amulets and the Church Fathers," *Ekklesiastikos Pharos* 75, no. 2 (1993): 57. (Brock doubts that the Anekaphalaiosis goes back to Epiphanius, a fourth-century patristic writer, but observes that it was used by Augustine in 428 and must therefore have been attached to the *Panarion* at an early stage. See Sebastian Brock, "Some Syriac Accounts of the Jewish Sects," in *A Tribute to Arthur Voobus*, ed. R. H. Fischer [Chicago: Lutheran School of Theology at Chicago, 1977], 272.) For another suggestion as to the identity of these *phylakteria*, see Gundry, *Matthew*, 456.

24. See Jeffrey H. Tigay, "On the Term Phylacteries (Matt 23:5)," *Harvard Theological Review* 72, nos. 1–2 (1979): 45–53. The old-Syriac work may date to the early third century c.e.; see Francis Crawford Burkitt, ed., *Evangelion Da-Mepharreshe: The Curetonian Version of the Four Gospels, with the Readings of the Sinai Palimpsest* (Cambridge: Cambridge University Press, 1904), 5–6; Sebastian Brock and David G. K. Taylor, *The Hidden Pearl: The Syrian Orthodox Church and Its Ancient Aramaic Heritage*, vol. 3 (Rome: Trans World Film, 2001), 223.

25. See Burkitt, ed., *Evangelion Da-Mepharreshe*, 135–37. Burkitt translated *deteflehon* as "of their frontlets," in line with the King James Version's translation of *totafot*, in turn rendered as *tefillin* in Targumim Onkelos, Ps.-Jonathan, and Neofiti.

Matthew also mentions fringes (*kraspeda*), as Jesus himself is depicted as wearing fringes in Matt 9:20 and 14:36.[26] Just as in the case of fringes, the most plausible explanation of the *tefillin* reference is that other Jews also wore them, although the Pharisees are described as wearing longer fringes and broader *tefillin* than others. It seems that *tefillin* practice, while prevalent among Pharisees, was not restricted to them, at any rate not in the late-first-century Matthean imagination of early-first-century Jewish life.[27]

As was discussed in chapter 1, several scholars have claimed on the basis of rabbinic literature that *tefillin* were not a widespread practice, but the evidence for such a position is slim, to say the least. A. Buechler cited a story in *T. Demai* 2:17 (which is to be discussed in more detail in the next chapter) as evidence that *tefillin* were worn by the particularly pious *haverim* only but were not worn by *ame ha'arets*.[28] The story tells of a *haver* and a customs collector who had been married to the same woman; whereas the wife had bound her *haver* husband in *tefillin*, she tied customs seals to the hand of his successor. Buechler's claim does not seem, however, to be borne out by his evidence. The story does not contrast the *haver* with an *am ha'arets*,[29] but with a customs collector, and logically can no more be taken to suggest that so-called *ame ha'arets* did not wear *tefillin* than to suggest that all of them were customs collectors! Perhaps the figure imagined by this tosefta did not wear *tefillin*, but that would seem irrelevant to gauging the extent of the practice. The customs collector was a much-reviled Jewish figure,[30] and in the rabbinic imagination could hardly be expected to perform *mitsvot*. The text can anyway be understood as referring to a *haver* who was engaged in preparing *tefillin* for the use of others, and would, in that case, shed no light on who else might have worn them.[31]

---

26. See Dale C. Allison, *Matthew* (London: T. & T. Clark, 2004), 388–89; Joel B. Itzkowitz, "Jews, Indians, Phylacteries: Jerome on Matthew 23:5," *Journal of Early Christian Studies* 15, no. 4 (2007): 564.

27. An astonishing idea that *tefillin* were actually a Pharisaic *privilege* is asserted, without any evidence, in Hermann L. Strack and Paul Billerbeck, "Die Tephillin (Gebetsriemen)," in *Kommentar zum neuen Testament aus Talmud und Midrasch*, vol. 4, part 1 (Munich: C.H. Beck'sche, 1928), 264.

28. A. Buechler, *Der galilaeische 'Am-ha'Ares des zweiten Jahrhunderts* (Vienna, 1906), 22–25. Here Buechler expressed sharp disagreement with Schürer, whose views are summarized in chap. 1.

29. Throughout *Massekhet Demai* and elsewhere, in both Mishnah and Tosefta, the *haver* observes tithing rules rigorously, while the *am ha'arets* does not, but the precise identity of the *haver* is otherwise obscure. See Catherine Hezser, *The Social Structure of the Rabbinic Movement in Roman Palestine* (Tübingen: Mohr Siebeck, 1997), 74–75. For an alternative view, whereby the *haver* here (and elsewhere) refers to a tithe collector, see Solomon J. Spiro, "Who Was the Haber?," *Journal for the Study of Judaism* 11, no. 2 (1980): 186–216.

30. See Martin Goodman, *State and Society in Roman Galilee* (Totowa, N.J.: Rowman & Allanheld, 1983; reprint, 2000), 131.

31. Saul Lieberman, *Tosefta Ki-Fshutah*, vol. 1, 2nd augmented ed. (Jerusalem: Jewish Theological Seminary of America, 1992), 218.

Equally inconclusive, as an indicator of whether the practice was widespread, is a statement, attributed to the tanna R. Yehoshu'a in *B. Bera-khot* 47b,[32] that identifies an *am ha'arets* as "anyone who does not wear *tefil-lin*," and is cited by some scholars as evidence that *ame ha'arets* did not.[33] No such definition is attested in Palestinian sources[34]; in fact, *T. Avodah Zarah* 3:8, which mentions selling *tefillin* to *ame ha'arets*,[35] suggests that the latter *did* wear *tefillin*. Even at face value, the discussion in the Bavli concerns a tanna'itic dispute regarding the demarcation of the rabbinically constructed *am ha'arets* category, with different tanna'im suggesting different markers. R. Yehoshu'a circumscribed this group of ill-defined "others" by excluding from it those people who engaged in *tefillin* practice, which is hardly evidence for the idea that observance of the practice was restricted to a narrow elite. Indeed, it has recently been demonstrated that the Talmudic figure of the *am ha'arets* is anyway not to be simplistically identified with the Jewish "commoner."[36]

The tanna'im did not view their actions in performing *mitsvot* in general to be those of an elite, as evidenced for *tefillin* in particular by *T. Berakhot* 6:25, which presents an idealized picture of widespread *tefillin* observance, with there being "no man in Israel who is not surrounded by *mitsvot*. The *tefillin* on his head, the *tefillin* on his arm, the *mezuzah* at his entrance and the four *tsitsit* surround him." Although this tosefta might be taken to imply universal Jewish *tefillin* observance, it seems more likely that it is simply a depiction of an ideal "Israel." (This is borne out by the end clause of the preceding tosefta, which asserts inter alia that there is no man in Israel who does not pray three times each day.)

All in all, however, it seems plausible that *tefillin* were a rather common ritual and that many adult males in Palestine wore them (women and children, as well as the Diaspora, will be discussed below). Of course though, even if many Jews did see *tefillin* as fulfillment of a Torah prescription, the practice may have been a contested one. *M. Sanhedrin* 11:3, in referring to "one who says there are no *tefillin*, to contravene the words of the Torah," may be mentioning a familiar figure.[37] Alternative explana-

32. In the parallel in *B. Sotah* 22a this view is attributed to the Sages. A similar inference can be drawn from a statement attributed to the tanna R. Shimon ben Elazar in *B. Shabbat* 130a.

33. In addition to Buechler, see A. M. Habermann, "The Phylacteries in Antiquity," *Eretz Israel* 3 (1954): 175 (in Hebrew); Aharon Oppenheimer, *The 'Am Ha-Aretz*, trans. I. H. Levine (Leiden: Brill, 1977), 224–27.

34. See also chap. 1, for general reservations about using ostensibly tanna'itic material found in amora'ic sources. I adduce it here only to address the claims made by other scholars.

35. According to the Erfurt manuscript and *editio princeps*.

36. See Miller, *Sages and Commoners in Late-Antique Erez Israel*, 301–38.

37. Cf. A. R. S. Kennedy, "Phylacteries," in *A Dictionary of the Bible*, ed. James Hastings

tions for the enigmatic *tefillin* verses are entirely possible, as was discussed in chapter 2, and may have had certain currency.[38] Some people may, in any case, have cared little for the Torah's instructions, although they may have worn *tefillin* nonetheless, as a traditional amuletic practice.

The above has related entirely to the presumptive subject of much tanna'itic discourse, namely, the practices of the free adult Jewish male. According to *M. Berakhot* 3:3, however, "Women, slaves and minors are exempt from *Shema* recital and *tefillin*, but obligated with respect to prayer, *mezuzah* and grace after meals." Although this mishnah mentions the three groups in one breath, there is good reason, as will be demonstrated, to imagine distinctions between them with respect to *tefillin* practice. The discussion that follows will accordingly distinguish between women and minors (and include what little evidence there is for slaves). Other subsections will discuss the evidence for the practice in the Diaspora, and among Samaritans and gentiles.

Women

T. Qiddushin 1:10 provides an ostensible rationale for a man/woman distinction with respect to *tefillin* practice (and others): "Which positive obligations are time-engendered? Examples are *sukkah*, *lulav* and *tefillin*. Which positive obligations are not time-engendered? Examples are (returning) a lost object, sending away (a mother bird from) the nest, a roof railing and *tsitsit*.[39] R. Shimon exempts women from *tsitsit*, considering it to be a positive obligation that is time engendered." This tosefta is an apparent comment on *M. Qiddushin* 1:7, which mentions that women are exempt (*patur*) from those positive obligations that are engendered by the onset of a particular time designated for their observance.[40] The requirements of *sukkah* and *lulav*, for example, are engendered by the Sukkot festival, but do not apply at other times. The *tefillin* obligation, as will be discussed below, is not applicable at night according to the tanna'im, and can thus

---

(New York/Edinburgh: Charles Scribner's Sons/T. & T. Clark, 1903), 873; Jeffrey H. Tigay, "Tefillin," in *Encyclopaedia Biblica* (Jerusalem: Mosad Bi'alik, 1982), 8:890 (in Hebrew).

38. It has, however, been demonstrated that it is impossible on the basis of rabbinic texts to identify groups who did not subscribe to the practice; see David Rothstein, "From Bible to Murabba'at: Studies in the Literary, Textual and Scribal Features of Phylacteries and Mezuzot in Ancient Israel and Early Judaism" (Ph.D. diss., UCLA, 1992), 157–80.

39. These four appear, in the order presented here, in Deuteronomy 22.

40. See Jay Rovner, "Rhetorical Strategy and Dialectical Necessity in the Babylonian Talmud: The Case of Kiddushin 34a–35a," *Hebrew Union College Annual* 65 (1994): 200 n. 48. This seems the simplest way of looking at the meaning of the principle; for further discussion, see the bibliography in Elizabeth Shanks Alexander, "From Whence the Phrase "Timebound, Positive Commandments"?," *Jewish Quarterly Review* 97, no. 3 (2007): n. 2.

be considered as engendered by daybreak. The rabbinic construct in the tosefta, whereby women are excluded from any *tefillin* obligation, begs the question of whether women wore *tefillin* or not. Did the above ruling merely reflect a preexisting situation in which women's *tefillin* practice had been largely unknown, or were the tanna'im looking to curtail (or at any rate downplay) women's *tefillin* practice, which was perhaps widespread beyond rabbinic circles?

In the first place, it is rather unlikely that the principle articulated in *M. Qiddushin* 1:7 was designed to change women's behavior. The word *patur* means "exempt," not "precluded" (and *T. Sotah* 2:8 further implies that the general principle governs an exemption, in stating that women are not held liable for failure to observe such commandments as are engendered by time). It is additionally quite probable that discussions of time-engenderment are merely an instance of rabbis using women "to think with,"[41] so that *T. Qiddushin* 1:10 is simply asserting as a theoretical matter that women's *tefillin* practice is not mandatory,[42] and is not to be interpreted as a reaction to such practice.

T. Qiddushin 1:10 is to be compared to the ruling in *M. Berakhot* 3:3, where women, along with slaves and minors, are exempted from *tefillin* without reference to the above principle (or any other, for that matter).[43] It is also worth noting that considerations of time-engenderment are absent from the *Mekhilta Derabbi Yishma'el*'s discussion of women and the *tefillin* exemption.[44] Indeed, the *Mekhilta Derabbi Shimon bar Yohai*, which seems to know many of the Mishnah and Tosefta's *tefillin* traditions, asserts that it was consideration of women's *tefillin* exemption that led to the formulation of the time-engenderment ruling, and not the other way around: "just as women are exempt from *tefillin*, which have the characteristic of being a positive commandment engendered by time, so (too) women are exempt

---

41. See Peter Brown, *The Body and Society: Men, Women and Sexual Renunciation in Early Christianity* (Columbia University Press, 1988), 153. Brown talks of the "deeply ingrained tendency of all men in the ancient world to use women 'to think with'" (attributing the expression to Lévi-Strauss). For the rhetorical nature of the construct of time-engenderment, see Marjorie Lehman, "The Gendered Rhetoric of Sukkah Observance," *Jewish Quarterly Review* 96, no. 3 (2006): 309–35; Alexander, "From Whence the Phrase," 317–46. It is also to be noted that the principle of time-engenderment as a determining factor is apparently contradicted by *T. Berakhot* 6:18, which asserts (although possibly in the name of R. Yehudah only) that women are not obligated with respect to *any* commandment.

42. See above for the way in which *tefillin* are frequently used by the tanna'im in paradigmatic fashion.

43. For the contention that *M. Berakhot* 3:3 disagrees with the principle of women's exemption from time-engendered *mitsvot*, see Judith Hauptman, *Rereading the Rabbis: A Woman's Voice* (Boulder/Oxford: Westview Press, 1998), 226–29.

44. H-R p. 68 lines 1–6 (to Exod 13:9). There may, however, be a connection between the reasoning employed there and the principle; see Alexander, "From Whence the Phrase," 335–39.

from all positive commandments engendered by time."[45] The characteristic of time-engenderment, therefore, seems highly unlikely even to have *generated* the rabbinic exemption of women from *tefillin* practice; nor is any midrashic derivation likely to have created such a halakah out of whole cloth.[46] Accordingly, the exemption is probably one that the rabbis inherited, in the form of previous customary practice, rather than created.[47]

Thus, a general absence of women's *tefillin* practice seems more likely than not, with rabbinic halakah following popular practice. Other Mishnah and Tosefta references in which the practice of women is implicit or incidental also support the notion that tanna'itic declarations of women's exemption from *tefillin* practice arose out of a social reality in which women simply did not wear them.[48] Thus, *M. Shabbat* 6:2 lists *tefillin* along with weaponry as men's items in a section in which these are contrasted with women's items. *T. Eruvin* 8:15 spells out that when it comes to wearing *tefillin* found outdoors on Shabbat (so as to bring them back without contravening Shabbat rules for transporting objects) even women ought to wear them, just like men.[49]

Mekhilta Derabbi Yishma'el does, however, mention a woman who wore *tefillin*, so that the practice was not entirely unknown: "There is a teaching to say, 'so that God's Torah may be in your mouth.'[50] I only said (that) about one who is obliged with regard to Torah learning. From here they said: all are obliged with regard to *tefillin* other than women and slaves. Mikhal daughter of Kushi would put on *tefillin*, the wife of Jonah would go up for festivals, Tevi the slave of Rabban Gamliel would put on *tefillin*."[51]

These traditions regarding Mikhal and Tevi were presumably preserved, if my above analysis is correct, because of the highly unusual

---

45. E-M p.41 lines 8–10 (to Exod 13:9).

46. I subscribe to the view that midrash halakah was generally "supportive" of pre-existing halakah. A view that it always was is famously associated with Ya'akov Nahum Halevi Epstein, *Introduction to Tannaitic Literature* (Jerusalem: Magnes Press, Hebrew University, 1957), 511–12 (in Hebrew). For a summary of opposing views, see Moshe Halbertal, *Interpretative Revolutions in the Making: Values as Interpretative Considerations in Midrashei Halakhah* (Jerusalem: Magnes Press, Hebrew University, 1997), 14–15 (in Hebrew).

47. The time-engenderment rule itself is, however, a summary of the results of exegetical practice rather than of prevalent social practice, according to Alexander, "From Whence the Phrase."

48. See S. Safrai, "The Mitzva Obligation of Women in Tannaitic Thought," *Annual of Bar-Ilan University, Studies in Judaica and the Humanities* 26/27 (1995): 227–36 (in Hebrew).

49. See Tal Ilan, *Jewish Women in Greco-Roman Palestine* (Peabody, Mass.: Hendrickson, 1996), 179. Ilan observes, "The historical reality, as opposed to ideal set forth in the halakah, can be partly drawn out by examining those places in which the sources, involved in a discussion of some other matter, incidentally mention women's participation in the commandments."

50. A citation from Exod 13:9.

51. H-R p. 68 lines 3–6 (to Exod 13:9).

nature of their behavior[52] (there is, however, no suggestion that it would have been problematic[53]). Possible reasons for women's avoidance of the ritual will be discussed in the concluding chapter.

It is also worth noting the speculative possibility that women had an alternative but parallel practice. The *Testament of Job* talks of Job giving cords to each of his three daughters prior to his death, telling them: "gird them round you, that they may keep you safe all the days of your life and fill you with every good thing."[54] Job goes on to say that the Lord had given the cords to him, that they had cured him of worms and disease, and given him strength (*T. Job* 47:5–7), and that they will protect his daughters from the enemy (Satan), because it is a *"phylakterion tou patros"* (*T. Job* 47:10), an expression that should probably be understood as "given by your heavenly father" (the phylactery had earlier been described as God-given).[55] The first daughter to wind her cord around herself says a hymn to God, and "the Spirit let the hymns she uttered be recorded on her robe (*T. Job* 48:3)." In the imagination of the author, therefore, Jewish women might bind uninscribed amulets, having certain points of contact with *tefillin*:

1. they are worn in order that they may provide safety all the days of the wearers' lives (see Deut 11:18, 21)

2. they were given by God (as in the understanding of scripture as referring to *tefillin*)

---

52. However, See Tal Ilan, *Mine and Yours Are Hers: Retrieving Women's History from Rabbinic Literature* (Leiden: Brill, 1997), 186–89.

53. Only in later recensions of these traditions is Mikhal's action problematized. See *Y. Berakhot* 2:3 (4c); *Y. Eruvin* 10:1 (26a); *B. Eruvin* 96a.

54. *T. Job* 46:9. All translation are taken from R. Thornhill, "The Testament of Job," in *The Apocryphal Old Testament*, ed. H. F. D. Sparks (Oxford: Clarendon, 1984). Some have dated the work to the first century c.e., but dates between 100 b.c.e. and 200 c.e. have also been proposed, and there is a consensus that it was originally written in Greek. See B. Schaller, *Das Testament Hiob* (Gütersloh: Gerd Mohn, 1979); Geza Vermes, Fergus Millar, and Martin Goodman, eds., *The History of the Jewish People in the Age of Jesus Christ (175 B.C.–A.D. 135) by Emil Schürer, (Revised Version)*, volume 3, part 1 (Edinburgh: T. & T. Clark, 1986), 552–55; R. P. Spittler, "The Testament of Job: A History of Research and Interpretation," in *Studies on the Testament of Job*, ed. Pieter Van der Horst (Cambridge: Cambridge University Press, 1989), 7–32. The work has generated considerable scholarly attention, and is generally regarded as a Jewish composition (although the end of the book in particular, where the reference that is relevant for our purposes occurs, has also been associated with some degree of Christian influence). The *Testament of Job* is of particular importance for women's studies in early Judaism, with a remarkably high proportion of the work dealing with women, who play a dominant role in chaps. 46–53; see Michael A. Knibb and Pieter Van der Horst, *Studies on the Testament of Job* (Cambridge: Cambridge University Press, 1989), 1–6; Pieter Van der Horst, "Images of Women in the Testament of Job," in *Studies on the Testament of Job*, ed. Michael A. Knibb and Pieter Van der Horst (Cambridge: Cambridge University Press, 1989), 93–116.

55. See Van der Horst, "Images of Women in the Testament of Job," 102.

3. they are described in Greek as *phylakteria* (see Matt 23:5)
4. they relate to an inscription that is worn and consists of a hymn to God (as in *tefillin* and the *Shema*)

It is also noteworthy that *M. Shabbat* 6:1 and 6:5[56] talk of women's *totafot*. "What may a woman go out wearing (on Shabbat), and what may she not go out wearing? A woman may not go out to a public space wearing wool threads . . . nor a *totefet* nor ribbons at a time when they are not sewn (on). . . . A woman may go out (on Shabbat) wearing . . . a *totefet* or ribbons at a time when they are sewn on. . . . "

These mishnayot and adjacent ones list objects that may/may not be worn out to a public space on Shabbat, including women's *totafot* (as well as men's *tefillin*, and a certain kind of men's amulet). The former object could apparently be sewn onto a garment, although it could be tied on as well, and in that respect was similar to ribbons. This *totefet* is usually interpreted as a mere ornament and, following later amora'ic literature, as having no religious significance.[57] It certainly seems possible, however, that the word had no particular meaning during the tanna'itic period beyond its association with biblical verses. The pairs "woman/*totafot*" and "man/*tefillin*," suggested by *M. Shabbat* 6:1–5, might thus fall into place as parallel rituals, with the women's ritual involving an uninscribed amulet of some kind.[58] Presumably many amulets had a supplementary ornamental function, and the mention of an amuletic *totefet* would easily fit in with the other women's objects described in these mishnayot.

There is also some Mandaean evidence that imagines the *totifta* as a Jewish women's ritual object.[59] In the *Book of John* (*Drasha d-Yahya*) the

---

56. As well as a parallel at *T. Shabbat* 4:6.

57. See Hanokh Albeck, *Shishah Sidrei Mishnah, Seder Mo'ed* (Jerusalem: Mosad Bi'alik and D'vir, 1958), 30; Abraham Goldberg, *Commentary to the Mishna, Shabbat* (Jerusalem: Jewish Theological Seminary of America, 1976), 99 (in Hebrew). It has also been suggested that both women and men initially wore an inscribed ornamental amulet in fulfillment of the scriptural *totafot*, that men had developed an alternative ritual that became known as *tefillin*, and that the women's ritual had eventually been abandoned; see Michael L. Rodkinson, *History of Amulets, Charms and Talismans* (New York, 1893), 11–13 and n. 23. There is, however, no reason to imagine that the Mishnah's *totefet* was an inscribed object.

58. The word *totafot* was *not* used by the tanna'im to describe *tefillin*, although in midrashic contexts it can refer to parchment cells/text sections; see F p. 63 line 14 (to Deut 6:8), H-R p. 66 line 16 (to Exod 13:9) and p. 74 line 9 (to Exod 13:16).

59. It is extremely difficult to date Mandaean texts, because few contain any allusion to history, or are referred to in other sources. Parts of the literature are known from Manichaean parallels to have existed in the third century c.e., and others have been related to second-century-c.e. Christian texts. Mandaean script has been dated to a similar era; see E. S. Drower, *The Mandaeans of Iraq and Iran* (Leiden: Brill, 1962), 21; Kurt Rudolph, *Mandaeism* (Leiden: Brill, 1978), 3. The most likely location for the written redaction of the stories about Miriai has been identified as Caliphate Baghdad, although the traditions themselves may be earlier, and can be related to Christian legends about Mary; see J. J. Buckley, "The Man-

defiant female convert from Judaism, Miriai, "has abandoned Judaism and gone to love her Lord . . . abandoned the *totifta* and gone to love the man with the *burzinqa*"[60] [the Mandaean ritual turban[61]]. In the Canonical Prayerbook, Miriai "hates the *totifta* and loves the fresh wreath; on the Sabbath she carries on work, on Sunday she keeps her hand from it."[62] The word *totifta* is otherwise unattested in Mandaic, or in other non-Jewish Aramaic, and seems to relate to a women's practice of the kind hypothesized above.[63] (It is to be noted that amora'ic literature seems to know nothing of women's *totafot* beyond the above-mentioned mishnayot, so that any such practice would seem to have died out by the time of the amora'im. This makes it more likely that the Mandaean evidence stems from our period, if it indeed refers to a real Jewish practice.)

Children

A distinction between the theoretical and the practical may be at the root of some inconsistency in the sources with regard to *tefillin* practice by children, other than the very youngest. Despite an exemption for minors (in *M. Berakhot* 3:3), *T. Hagigah* 1:2 seems to state that a father would be responsible for providing *tefillin* to a child old enough to look after them: "A child . . . once he knows how to shake is obligated with respect to *lulav*; once he knows how to wrap himself is obligated with respect to *tsitsit*; once he knows how to talk—his father teaches him *Shema* and Torah and the sacred tongue, and if not it were better that he had not come into the world; once he knows how to look after his *tefillin—aviv loqe'ah tefillin elav*."

The words left in Hebrew in the above citation are, however, unclear. There are variants in the Tosefta manuscripts, with the text provided here being that of the Vienna manuscript.[64] In the Erfurt manuscript and the *editio princeps* the word *elav* is missing, and the additional word *lo*

---

daean Appropriation of Jesus' Mother Miriai," *Novum Testamentum* 35, no. 2 (1993): 181–95; Edmondo Lupieri, *The Mandaeans: The Last Gnostics*, trans. Charles Hindley (Grand Rapids: Eerdmans, 2002), 153.

60. Mark Lidzbarski, *Das Johannesbuch der Mandaeer* (Giessen: Alfred Töpelmann, 1915), 129.

61. Rudolph, *Mandaeism*, 6.

62. E. S. Drower, *The Canonical Prayerbook of the Mandaeans* (Leiden: Brill, 1959), prayer 149, 30.

63. It has been suggested that the references, in presuming women's *tefillin* practice, were revealing ignorance of Jewish tradition; see Lidzbarski, *Das Johannesbuch der Mandaeer*, 129 n. 1. This is not at all compelling, as it seems unlikely that one would know of *tefillin* ritual, yet be unaware that women did not practice it (if indeed they did not).

64. See Saul Lieberman, *The Tosefta According to Codex Vienna, with Variants from Codices Erfurt, London, Genizah Mss. and Editio Princeps (Venice 1521)*, 2nd ed. (Jerusalem: Jewish Theological Seminary of America, 1992), 375.

appears after *loqe'ah*, with the effect of making the best translation of the final clause "who knows how to look after his *tefillin*—his father buys him *tefillin*." While the root *lqh* usually connotes "purchase" in rabbinic literature, it is, however, to be noted that in the case of *lulav* and *tsitsit* the tosefta make no reference to a father buying such objects. Indeed, extreme disdain is exhibited for *tefillin* resellers in *T. Bikkurim* 2:15, so that an explicit call for *tefillin* purchase actually seems quite unlikely unless it was deemed particularly important for the wearer of *tefillin* to own them. While at first sight it is unclear why the father's role as a purchaser would be singled out in the case of *tefillin*, this actually fits in very well with their being treated as an apotropaic amulet, where ownership is known to have been an important feature of practice.[65] Even so, the text is problematic, because the *tefillin* ruling—unlike the others in this tosefta—does not refer to a child's physical ability to perform an adult obligation, which calls into question the traditional view that it is simply describing duties incumbent on a father as part of his child's education.[66]

The *lectio difficilior* is that of the Vienna and London[67] manuscripts, with *lqh el* an otherwise unknown construction in Mishnaic/Toseftan Hebrew. In biblical Hebrew *lqh* means "take," and *lqh el* can mean "take to," as in Num 23:27 and 2 Kgs 13:15.[68] There is thus an alternate possibility, that the expression has a meaning here that is similar to the biblical one and refers to taking *tefillin* to one's child.[69] I would suggest, as a possible interpretation, that when a child knows how to look after *tefillin*—that is, treat them respectfully—even before being able to tie them on, its father *may* take *tefillin* and put them on him (or her?). Such an idea would be suggestive of an anticipated apotropaic effect.[70] Thus, whether *lqh* here means "purchase," in line with its common rabbinic usage, or instead means "take to," this tosefta could well be referring to an apotropaic practice that was considered optional rather than mandatory by the rabbis. Mishnaic and Toseftan Hebrew do not, however, consistently distinguish

---

65. See Campbell Bonner, *Studies in Magical Amulets, Chiefly Graeco-Egyptian* (Ann Arbor: University of Michigan Press, 1950), 2.

66. See Saul Lieberman, *Tosefta Ki-Fshutah*, 2nd ed. (Jerusalem: Jewish Theological Seminary of America, 1992), 5:1269.

67. The London manuscript reads *loqe'ah lo tefillin elav*.

68. For a discussion of the earliest evidence for the change in standard meaning reflected by Mishnaic Hebrew, see Azzan Yadin, "A Greek Witness to the Semantic Shift 'Lqh'—'Buy,'" *Hebrew Studies* 43 (2002): 31–37.

69. Such a meaning for *lqh*, while rare, is not unknown in rabbinic Hebrew; see, for example, *M. Rosh Hashanah* 1:9. However, see G. Sarfatti, "Semantics of Mishnaic Hebrew and Interpretation of the Bible by the Tanna'im," *Lesonenu* 30 (1965–66): 34–35.

70. A practice of placing *tefillin* on a sick or startled child having difficulty sleeping, presumably for a soothing effect, is attested to in *Y. Shabbat* 6:2 (8b) and *Y. Eruvin* 10:11 (26c), and in both instances the practice is proscribed.

between obligation and optional practice,[71] so that one's precise understanding of the context is often (as here) a critical element in making the
distinction. At any rate, this tosefta can readily be reconciled with the
exemption of minors in *M. Berakhot* 3:3, if it is describing a sanctioned-but-
optional practice, rather than a mandatory one.

T. Hagigah 1:2 is also to be compared with the *Mekhilta Derabbi Yishma'el*,
which seems to know a somewhat similar tradition: "'And you shall guard
(*veshamarta*) this statute at its appointed time'[72]; I only said that of one who
knows how to look after (*lishmor*) his *tefillin*. It is from here that they said:
a minor, (if he is) one who knows how to look after *tefillin*, then he makes
him *tefillin*."[73] As making *tefillin* cannot have been a common skill, it seems
possible that the *Mekhilta* reflects an amendment to the Toseftan tradition, whereby *loqe'ah lo* was transformed into *oseh lo*. Earlier, the *Mekhilta*
had excluded women and slaves, but not children, from *tefillin* practice,
and stated that all others who were obliged to study Torah were obligated
with respect to the practice.[74] Here, then, it seems to classify children's
observance of the ritual as mandatory, provided they are old enough to
look after them, in diametric opposition to *M. Berakhot* 3:3.

The *Mekhilta Derabbi Shimon bar Yohai*, on Exod 13:10,[75] is unambiguous in deriving from that verse that even an infant (*tinoq*) is obligated
with respect to *tefillin*, provided it knows how to look after them, and
the *Sifre Zuta* on Num 15:38 is similar. It seems quite likely that these are
later developments of the traditions articulated in the Tosefta and *Mekhilta Derabbi Yishma'el*.[76]

All in all, it looks plausible to infer from the above texts that children,
other than the very youngest, routinely wore *tefillin*, despite the exemption to which *M. Berakhot* 3:3 refers. Since Deut 11:21, suggested in chapter
3 as the initial link between *tefillin* and their apotropaic power, makes
specific reference to the length of children's lives, it would actually be surprising if *tefillin* were viewed as protective but not given to children. To
the extent that the rabbis saw this as mandatory, they may well have been
taking common practice and turning it into a virtue, even though another
strand of rabbinic lore, represented by *M. Berakhot* 3:3, saw no virtue to

---

71. See, for example, *M. Pesahim* 1:4, where in the space of a few words the present
tense is used in both senses.

72. A citation from Exod 13:10.

73. H-R p. 68 lines 9–13 (to Exod 13:10). The *Mekhilta* here is playing on the root *shmr*,
meaning both "to guard" and "to look after."

74. H-R p. 68 lines 1–5 (to Exod 13:10).

75. E-M p. 41 lines 12–15 (to Exod 13:10).

76. For a book-length treatment of the precedence of a large section in *Mekhilta Derabbi
Yishma'el* over the corresponding part of *Mekhilta Derabbi Shimon bar Yohai*, see Menahem
Kahana, *Hamekhiltot Lepharashat Amaleq* (Jerusalem: Magnes Press, Hebrew University,
1999, in Hebrew).

it. Clearly, the idea that unwitting infants might not treat *tefillin* properly played some role in rabbinic deliberations on the subject.

The Diaspora

In the light of Deut 11:21, which linked *tefillin* practice to length of days on the promised land, it seems possible that the ritual was slower to develop in the Diaspora than in Palestine. *Sifre Devarim,* perhaps for that reason, points out that *tefillin* were to be worn even outside the land of Israel.[77] This does not, of course, mean that they were. Josephus, although writing in the Diaspora in the late first century C.E., cannot be considered evidence for Diaspora practice; in the above-mentioned reference, he is paraphrasing scripture and putting a gloss on it, and the result cannot be expected to clarify this particular point.

Further evidence from outside Palestine, however, is provided by the following passage in Justin's *Dialogue with Trypho:*

> 46:5 You are aware that on account of the hardness of the heart of your people God enjoined on you by Moses all such precepts, in order that by these many means you should always, and in every action, have God before your eyes, and not begin to commit injustice or impiety. For He also enjoined you to wear the scarlet dye, in order that by its means forgetfulness of God should not come upon you; and He commanded you to gird yourselves with a phylactery of certain letters written on very thin parchments, which we assuredly consider holy, by these means pressing you ever to hold God in mind, and at the same time to have a sense of sin in your hearts.[78]

Although located in a discourse about observance of the commandments, the above passage, within this context, seems something of a non sequitur to the preceding elements of the discussion. The idea that Jews were given positive commandments to remind them of God, and/or that their essential nature required this special treatment, is however found elsewhere in the *Dialogue with Trypho.* This is evident both for specific laws, such as Shabbat and *kashrut* rules, as well as in a form covering positive obligations in general.[79]

It is not clear why *tefillin* would have been singled out for mention. The commandment "to wear the scarlet dye" seems to refer to *tsitsit* in some

---

77. F p. 103 lines 1–7 (to Deut 11:18).
78. Translation taken from A. Lukyn Williams, *Justin Martyr: The Dialogue with Trypho* (London: Macmillan, 1930).
79. See *Dialogue with Trypho,* 19:5–6; 20:1; 20:4; 45:3.

way,[80] and the practice of *tefillin*, as another worn object, may have been included by way of comparison. *Tsitsit* itself can be viewed as a parade example of Justin's ideas on the commandments, as the rationale provided by Num 15:39 for that practice bears a remarkable resemblance to his own above-mentioned views. Accordingly, he may well have mentioned *tsitsit* precisely because of his predilection for their scriptural rationale.

More significantly, for our purposes, Justin seems to have known about *tefillin* as actually practiced by his second-century-c.e. contemporaries; he presumes that Trypho, a Jew in Asia Minor (who is probably not to be regarded as rabbinic[81]), would be familiar with *tefillin* as scripturally ordained. Justin's knowledge of *tefillin* practice has several components, including their being written on thin parchment and containing scriptural text[82] (as evidenced by "a phylactery of certain letters written on very thin parchments, which we assuredly consider holy"). He could neither have derived such information from the Septuagint, nor from the Gospel of Matthew. In addition, one can discount the possibility that Justin's knowledge of *tefillin* arose solely from familiarity with Jewish exegesis of relevant scriptural passages. For one thing, the earlier scholarly consensus that Justin was familiar with rabbinic traditions has lately been undermined. As David Rokéah has demonstrated, there is in fact little reason to imagine that Justin was knowledgeable about rabbinic midrash.[83] In addition, there is no hint in rabbinic literature of a requirement for *tefillin* parchment to be thin.

The *Dialogue* cannot, however, be considered solid evidence for *tefillin* practice in the Diaspora, as it is possible that Justin's familiarity with *tefillin* arose from his origins in Samaria, and not from Diaspora Jews in his later surroundings. Trypho, while expected to know about them, is depicted as a Judean, and cannot be regarded as typical of Diaspora Jews.

---

80. The reference is far from clear-cut, referring as it does to a scarlet dye, whereas *tsitsit* are generally seen as a blue thread. Emil Schürer emended the Greek *bamma* here to *ramma* (thread). See Emil Schürer, *Geschichte des jüdischen Volkes im Zeitalter Jesu Christi*, fourth ed. (Leipzig, 1901–1909), 2:566. This still leaves the issue of the scarlet color, which P. R. Weis explained away as a reflection of Samaritan practice. See P. R. Weis, "Some Samaritanisms of Justin Martyr," *Journal of Theological Studies* 45 (1944): 199–205. See also Phillip Sigal, "An Inquiry into Aspects of Judaism in Justin's Dialogue with Trypho," *Abr-Nahrain* 18 (1978/79): 88–90.

81. See Timothy Horner, *Listening to Trypho* (Leuven: Peeters, 2001).

82. Cf. Judith M. Lieu, *Image and Reality: The Jews in the World of the Christians in the Second Century* (Edinburgh: T. & T. Clark, 1996), 125.

83. See *Justin Martyr, Dialogue with Trypho the Jew*, trans. David Rokéah (Jerusalem: Hebrew University Magnes Press, 2004), 16–20 (in Hebrew). The earlier consensus had already been questioned in Marc Hirshman, "Polemic Literary Units in the Classical Midrashim and Justin Martyr's Dialogue with Trypho," *Jewish Quarterly Review* 83, nos. 3–4 (1993): 369–84. However, see Lieu, *Image and Reality*, 144 and 81.

Similarly, while the above-mentioned reference in Matt 23:5 might reflect a Diaspora milieu, the work is possibly of Palestinian provenance, and is in any event transmitting a tradition about Jesus. Nor can the old-Syriac version, with its use of *deteflehon*, be viewed as conclusive evidence for familiarity with Diaspora practice. The word is known to have been used in Aramaic to denote amulets,[84] and might therefore have been a natural way to render *phylakteria*, whether the translator was familiar with *tefillin* or not.

Nevertheless, Diaspora practice can certainly not be ruled out. Observing that Jews are not identified by their *tefillin* (or *tsitsit*) in Greco-Roman sources, Shaye Cohen has suggested that those coming into contact with outsiders, such as Diaspora Jews, did not wear them in public, if at all.[85] It is, however, to be noted that *tefillin* may well have been inconspicuous (the Judean Desert exemplars are tiny). Thus R. Eli'ezer infers that they are worn high up on the arm from what he sees as the Bible's implication that "it (that is, arm *tefillin*) is a sign for you, but not a sign to others."[86] *M. Megillah* 4:8 links objectionable practices of placing arm *tefillin* over one's sleeve, and wearing gilded ones, with a particular (and small?) group of uncertain identity, and deems heretical a practice of wearing them on one's palm or forehead—all of which might have made them more noticeable than otherwise. If head *tefillin*, as well as arm ones, were generally unremarkable objects that were worn under the cover of clothing, then lack of attention in Greco-Roman sources is hardly surprising.[87] It also bears mentioning that the absence of pagan remarks about Jewish practice is anyway not much of a guide to what Jews were actually doing, as is particularly evident in the case of the synagogue's role in Jewish life.

In conclusion, *tefillin* must have been known in the Diaspora, but awareness of the practice by some highly educated individuals who lived outside Palestine (Josephus and Justin) sheds no light on whether the practice was widespread there. It is to be noted that the third century Dura Europos synagogue findings, in Syria, show no trace of *tefillin* in their depictions, although they do seem to show *tsitsit*.[88] (The Babylonian Talmud, which does provide solid evidence for *tefillin* practice east of Palestine, is not considered here as historically reliable for the period under discussion.)

---

84. See chap. 5 for further discussion of this point.

85. Shaye Cohen, *The Beginnings of Jewishness* (Berkeley: University of California Press, 1999), 33–34.

86. H-R p. 67 lines 1–3 (to Exod 13:9).

87. *T. Eruvin* 8:17 might seem to suggest that head *tefillin* were not customarily covered, but its *mekhasseh et rosho*, while literally to be rendered "covers his head," may simply mean "ought keep his head covered."

88. Carl H. Kraeling, *The Excavations at Dura-Europos: The Synagogue* (New Haven: Yale University Press, 1959), 81 and n. 239.

Gentiles and Samaritans

Finally, *T. Avodah Zarah* 2:4, in specifying that *tefillin* (as well as scrolls and *mezuzot*) ought not be sold to gentiles and Samaritans,[89] may suggest that *tefillin* were in demand outside Jewish circles. In the case of gentiles, at least, this would most likely have been due to the objects' apotropaic function.[90] Matthew and Justin Martyr (and presumably others too) saw them as *phylakteria*, and some gentiles may have been impressed enough by this feature to want to wear them as well. The precise nature of the protection that *tefillin* offered will be discussed in further detail in the concluding chapter.

The Make-Up of *Tefillin*, and How They Were Worn

Much of the evidence for *tefillin* observance, as described here, will present few surprises to a reader familiar with modern-day practice (although there is no tanna'itic reference to one of its most striking aspects, namely, the manner in which *tefillin* are strapped to the arm, hand, and fingers). Indeed, in all likelihood it was precisely the formulation of those rabbinic sources to be discussed that anchored much subsequent *tefillin* tradition. It bears mentioning at the outset that (somewhat uncharacteristically) tanna'itic literature presents no internal disputes of practical import with respect to the above-captioned issues. There is thus no evidence for variety of practice *within* the rabbinic realm. While certain halakot are midrashically derived in different ways by different rabbis, this is without any disagreement as to the final outcome.

Contained Text

The rabbinically approved *tefillin* text is derived by *Mekhilta Derabbi Yishma'el* from the repetition in Exod 13:16 of much of Exod 13:9:

> In four places it mentions the matter of *tefillin*: "Sanctify to me," "And it shall be when he brings you," "Hear," "And it shall be if (you) hearken." It is from here that they said that the *mitsvah* of *tefillin* is four text-

---

89. The clause in question is found in the Erfurt manuscript (but is missing in the Vienna manuscript and the *editio princeps*). The reference to Samaritans is a little ambiguous, as it may refer to the following clause rather than the one that includes *tefillin*.

90. It is to be noted that Chrysostom, although later than our period, states that many Christians turned to Jewish customs in their use of amulets (*De Pseudoprophetis*, PG 59.561); see Stander, "Amulets and the Church Fathers," 59–60.

sections—the hand's being one scroll of four text-sections, the head's being four *totafot*—and these are they: "Sanctify to me," "And it shall be when he brings you," "Hear," "And it shall be if (you) hearken."[91]

Here the *Mekhilta* specifies four pericopes that *tefillin* contain, using keywords from each to identify the sections.[92] The four verses that "mention the matter of *tefillin*" are evident from the Judean Desert findings, as discussed in the previous chapter, and the identity of the keyword verses is unambiguous:

1. "Sanctify to me" refers to Exod 13:2, with the *tefillin* verse being 13:9. The Masoretic text (MT) limits for this passage are 13:1–10.

2. "And it shall be when he brings you" refers to Exod 13:11, with the *tefillin* verse being 13:16. The MT limits for this passage are 13:11–16.

3. "Hear" refers to Deut 6:4, with the *tefillin* verse being 6:8. The MT limits for this passage are 6:4–9.

4. "And it shall be if (you) hearken" refers to Deut 11:13, with the *tefillin* verse being 11:18. The MT limits for this passage are 11:13–21.

It is noteworthy that there were archaeological findings of *tefillin* parchments containing the precise verses associated with the forementioned MT passages, both at Qumran and elsewhere. There is, however, no evidence for *tefillin* slips having included any text from these pericopes after the last relevant MT verse, and it seems highly likely that the endpoint of the four rabbinic passages was the same as that of the MT.

As far as the beginning of the passages is concerned, the keywords in the *Mekhilta* were presumably intended to represent the first verse in the relevant passages, with the exception of Exod 13:2. Here the first verse may well have been Exod 13:1, which introduces the passage; it is also the most commonly repeated verse in the Torah, so it is hardly surprising to find keywords taken from the subsequent verse. That said, it is worth noting that 34SePhyl A, which is dated to the second century c.e., did begin at Exod 13:2.

In any event, while the *Mekhilta* and its parallels in *Sifre Devarim*[93] do not specify the passage limits precisely, it seems plausible that the MT limits were intended. If so, 34SePhyl A (see previous paragraph) would be probable post–70 evidence for minor non-conformity with tanna'itic practice, although the more expanded texts known from Qumran may have also continued in use beyond rabbinic circles. The *Sifre* explicitly

---

91. H-R p. 74 lines 7–10 (to Exod 13:16).
92. M. *Menahot* 3:7 also mentions that *tefillin* contain four text sections.
93. F p. 60 line 14—p. 61 line 4; and p. 63 lines 3–11 (to Deut 6:7–8).

presumes that the Decalogue was not included in *tefillin*, and proceeds to demonstrate midrashically why it was not, which may reflect awareness of a competing practice of including it. (It is also possible, of course, that the *Sifre* is driven by scholastic concerns rather than knowledge of a variant practice.)

The tanna'im, at any rate, did not include the Decalogue in *tefillin*, and generally favored a shorter text than exhibited by many Qumran exemplars. The exclusion of the Decalogue from *tefillin* has been connected by scholars to the Yerushalmi's assertion that it had been eliminated from the liturgy (according to *M. Tamid* 5:1 it had earlier been recited in the Temple) so as to prevent heretics from claiming that its commandments were the only ones to have been given to Moses at Sinai.[94] This might, of course, have had something to do with the choice of rabbinic *tefillin* contents, although it seems far from certain. Perhaps the Decalogue and its initial aftermath were simply dropped from *tefillin* as part of a general trend (not limited to the rabbis) to make them shorter. As noted in the previous chapter, the shorter Deuteronomy passages avoided highlighting some rather stringent prerequisites for achieving length of days in the promised land, which may have seemed like a good idea. Perhaps shorter texts were also thought desirable because they allowed for less chance of error in transcription.

It is additionally to be noted that Josephus apparently saw the contents of *tefillin* as "the greatest of the benefits that God has bestowed upon them (*Antiquities* 4:213)." Conceivably this refers to the Decalogue and/or Deut 10:12–11:12, both found in Qumran *tefillin*.[95] If it does, this might suggest continued variety post–70 c.e., although his information may have been out of date.[96]

---

94. *Y. Berakhot* 1:5 (3c); see also *Bavli Berakhot* 12a. For the Decalogue in liturgy, see E. E. Urbach, "The Role of the Ten Commandments in Jewish Worship," in *The Ten Commandments in History and Tradition*, ed. Ben-Zion Segal and Gershon Levi (Jerusalem: Magnes Press, Hebrew University, 1985), 161–89; Reuven Hammer, "What Did They Bless? A Study of Mishnah Tamid 5:1," *Jewish Quarterly Review* 81, nos. 3–4 (1991): 305–24. Reuven Kimelman finds it unlikely that there had been a historical connection between the *minim*'s claim and the removal of the Decalogue. See Reuven Kimelman, "The Shema and the Amidah: Rabbinic Prayer," in *Prayer from Alexander to Constantine*, ed. Mark Kiley (London: Routledge, 1997), 108–20. For discussion of *tefillin* in this context, see Heinrich Schneider, "Der Dekalog in den Phylakterien von Qumran," *Biblische Zeitschrift* 3 (1959): 18–31; Geza Vermes, "Pre-Mishnaic Jewish Worship and the Phylacteries from the Dead Sea," *Vetus Testamentum* 9 (1959): 65–72.

95. See Feldman, *Judean Antiquities 1–4*, 407 n. 642.

96. It is difficult to know what to make of Josephus's reference (*Antiquities* 4:213) to the display of "as many things as are able to show forth the power of God and His good will towards them," which might anyway not be connected to the contents of *tefillin*. See ibid., 644.

Midrash Tanna'im on Deut 6:9, while referring to *mezuzah*, might actually be related to some variety in *tefillin* practice too, if the Qumran exemplars are any guide. Its comment "And you shall write them; all is in writing, even the instructions" is referring to the self-referential nature of *mezuzah* and, by extension, *tefillin* inscriptions. Even the very instructions to write them are themselves written in them, say the rabbis, and perhaps they stressed this point precisely because it was not universally practiced.

The *Mekhilta Derabbi Shimon bar Yohai* on Exod 13:16 observes that this verse teaches that "*tefillin* were said (i.e. instructed) in memory of the exodus from Egypt."[97] There may have been some awareness, reflected also in *Sifre Devarim*, of the strangeness of the Exodus verses being taken to refer to *tefillin* at all; it is noted in the *Sifre* that "other *mitsvot* precede them."[98] This expression may have evolved from the consideration that Exod 13:9 and 16 look to be talking about Pesah and firsborn redemption rather than about certain "words," as do Deut 6:8 and 11:18.[99] Here, however, there is no reason to imagine a practice that had excluded these passages, as opposed to scholastic concerns. The tanna'im probed the reasoning behind the texts included, as well perhaps—in the case of the Decalogue—one that might have been but was not.

Other Features

The *Mekhilta Derabbi Yishma'el*'s first lines on Exod 13:9 are typical of midrashic engagement with our topic:

> "And it shall be for you as a sign on your hand" [Exod 13:9]: this is one roll, having four text-sections. And it is justified (as follows); since the Torah said "put *tefillin* on the hand, put *tefillin* on the head"[100], (one might think that) just as there are four *totafot* on the head there are four *totafot* on the hand too. There is a teaching to say, "And it shall be for you as a sign on your hand"—one roll having four text-sections.[101]

The *Mekhilta*'s concern here is to justify, by appeal to a Torah verse taken to refer to *tefillin*, in which the noun *ot* (sign) is in the *singular*, a prac-

---

97. E-M p. 44 lines 20–21 (to Exod 13:16).

98. F p. 63 line 6 (to Deut 6:8).

99. Cf. Finkelstein's comment on Pisqa 34 *ad loc.* that the expression simply reflects a belief that the Decalogue was given to Israel before any other commandments, including those in Exodus 13.

100. This is not a quotation, but rather reflects a belief as to what the Torah means. The belief concerned dates back to Qumran, as shown in chap. 3.

101. H-R p. 66 lines 14–16 (to Exod 13:9); cf. F p. 63 lines 12–14 (to Deut 6:8).

tice of having *one* continuous parchment in hand-*tefillin*. Similar methods are then used to justify a practice of having four separate parchments, or cells (which would then require separate parchments) in head *tefillin*, as well as having each of these cells contain only one of the relevant text sections, rather than all four.[102] *T. Kelim Bava Batra* 4:1 also makes it clear that *tefillin shel yad* had one cell, whereas *tefillin shel rosh* had four. Someone with two head types might wear one of them as a hand type, but only after first recovering it with leather, so as to place the four cells inside one cell.[103] (This was, it is to be noted, despite the fact that the contained texts for each type were identical.)

It seems reasonable to imagine that the above distinctions were well established by the time of the tanna'im, and had originally developed out of a desire to differentiate between head and hand *tefillin*, as well as to generally "get things right" by fulfilling highly ambiguous verses in different ways. The Judean Desert housings demonstrate that the latter concern, at least, probably dated back to the first century b.c.e., if not earlier.[104] However, both MurPhyl and XHevSePhyl, mentioned earlier, included the rabbinically approved text on only two slips, and therefore represent clear evidence for variety during our period (as they do not conform, in this respect, with tanna'itic requirements).

Mekhilta Derabbi Yishma'el derives the correct placement of *tefillin* on the body, demonstrating that the so-called hand-*tefillin* are in fact worn on the highest part of the arm[105] (and on the left rather than the right arm), and that head *tefillin* are worn on the highest part of the head rather than between the eyes.[106] The Mishnah and Tosefta provide less information on these rules than Midreshei Halakah but corroborate some of the details in the latter. Thus, *T. Sanhedrin* 4:7 is consistent with *tefillin* being worn on the left side or on the arm.[107] *T. Berakhot* 6:25 has the idealized "man of Israel" wearing *tefillin* on his arm.[108] *M. Miqva'ot* 10:3–4 refers to *tefillin shel zaro'a*. Josephus too apparently knew *tefillin* to be worn on the arm (*Antiquities* 4:213).

---

102. H-R p. 66 lines 16–20 (to Exod 13:9); cf. F p. 63 line 15—p. 64 line 1 (to Deut 6:8).

103. E-M p. 40 lines 14–16 (to Exod 13:9).

104. *T. Kelim Bava Batra* 4:1 implies that the strap was inserted inside the housing, demonstrating congruence of another aspect of the ritual with the Judean Desert findings.

105. "*Al govah shel yad keneged halev.*"

106. H-R p. 66 line 20—p. 67 line 11; and p. 67 lines 14–18 (to Exod 13:9). Similarly F p. 64 lines 1–17 (to Deut 6:8).

107. Depending on textual witnesses.

108. *T. Demai* 2:17 mentions tying them to the hand (*yad*) rather than to the arm, but the word is probably to be understood as simply arising from the scriptural reference. So too for the references to *tefillah/tefillin shel yad* in *M. Menahot* 4:1; *T. Menahot* 6:12; *T. Avodah Zarah* 3:8; and *T. Kelim Bava Batra* 4:1. (However, see Lieberman, *Tosefta Ki-Fshutah*, 1:218. He saw *al yado* in *T. Demai* 2:17 as a figure of speech.)

Another midrashic derivation from Exod 13:9 reads as follows: "'And it shall be for you as a sign on your hand and as *totafot* between your eyes'; whenever the hand one is on the hand wear the head one on the head. It is from here that they said 'The *mitsvah* of *tefillin*—when putting them on one first puts on the hand one, and after that puts on the head one; and when taking them off one first takes off the head one, and after that takes off the hand one.'"[109] While this may have been a rabbinic standardization of procedure, it also seems entirely plausible that prerabbinic midrash looked to the verse for guidance, which led to this particular specification. The entire ritual was based on an understanding of scripture, and people would naturally have looked to scripture so as to determine its correct performance. In any event, the expression "it is from here that they said" suggests a certain antiquity to the described practice.[110]

Similarly, on Exod 13:16: "It is from here that they said: head *tefillin* cannot invalidate the arm type, and the arm type cannot invalidate the head type and if he has but one, then he should put it on."[111] The reference to invalidation is presumably addressing the issue of whether performing the ritual incompletely constituted invalid practice even of the element performed[112] (perhaps some practitioners wore only one of the two types, at least some of the time). If *tefillin* were indeed worn for much of the day, as will be suggested below, then considerations of convenience may have been in play, and the tanna'im might be clarifying that wearing either one would be better than nothing.

The reference to broad phylacteries, in Matt 23:5, seems to relate to some variation in practice regarding the size of housings or *tefillin* straps.[113] In addition, *M. Sanhedrin* 11:3 has been taken by some scholars as similar evidence for variety: "A stricture with regard to the words of the scribes, when compared to the words of the Torah; one who says there are no *tefillin*, to contravene the words of the Torah, is not liable; (how-

109. H-R p. 67 lines 11–14 (to Exod 13:9); cf. F p. 65 lines 1–3 (to Deut 6:8).

110. Wilhelm Bacher made the claim that this introductory formula is a shortened form of *mikan amru hakhamim*, and it is under any circumstances most simply understood as a reference to a prior tradition. See Wilhelm Bacher, *Die exegetische Terminologie der jüdischen Traditionsliteratur* (1899; reprint, Darmstadt: Wissenschaftliche Buchgesellschaft, 1965), part 1, 77; Wilhelm Bacher, *Tradition und Tradenten in Schulen Palaestinas und Babyloniens* (Leipzig, 1914), 171.

111. E-M p. 44 lines 16–20 (to Exod 13:16).

112. Here the *Mekhilta Derabbi Shimon bar Yohai* seems to be attempting to reconcile the conflicting traditions of *M. Menahot* 4:1 and *T. Menahot* 6:12. The latter might have been seen as contradicting itself, in simultaneously stating that the two types invalidate each other, but that someone who has only one of the types ought wear it. The *Mekhilta* reads more smoothly, and can therefore be suspected of harmonizing the tosefta with the idea (taken from *M. Menahot* 4:1) that the two types do not in fact invalidate each other.

113. See Burkitt, ed., *Evangelion Da-Mepharreshe*; Tigay, "On the Term Phylacteries (Matt 23:5)."

ever one who says there ought be) five *totafot*, to add to the words of the scribes, is liable."[114] Jacob Mann viewed *M. Sanhedrin* 11:3 as evidence for an actual practice, deemed deviant by the tanna'im, of having five *tefillin* cells instead of four: "Sanhedrin 11,3 clearly reflects the time when the Tephillin included the Decalogue and hence had five sections. . . . Now what could these five Totafot (viz. five compartments of the phylactery on the head) contain if not the Decalogue?"[115] This looks to be an overreading of the mishnah, which is probably simply employing *tefillin* as a means to illustrate a general principle of law. Nevertheless, the earlier clause in *M. Sanhedrin* 11:3 may indeed reflect variety, in the form of an ongoing debate as to whether *tefillin* were an obligation found in the Torah (prefiguring a later Rabbanite/Karaite debate).

M. Megillah 4:8, with its list of practices of which the rabbis did not approve, provides an outspoken indication of variety in observance: "One who makes his *tefillah* circular; that is a danger and there is no *mitsvah* to it. If he placed it on his forehead or on his palm; that is the way of heresy (*derekh haminut*). If he covered it with gold or placed it on a garment-sleeve;[116] that is the outsiders' way (*derekh hahitsonim*)."

Placing *tefillin* on the forehead or palm would have constituted a more literal interpretation of the Torah than had actually been adopted.[117] The Midreshei Halakah demonstrate that the tanna'im were well aware of that, as can be seen from their repeated characterization of the literal meaning as *kemashma'o*,[118] but such a competing appeal to the literal is nevertheless portrayed as deviant. It is interesting, in that regard, to note that *T. Sanhedrin* 13:5 lumps the *minim* together with "those who depart from the ways of the community." It may be precisely the departure from common practice that would have rendered it *derekh haminut* in the eyes of the rabbis.[119]

---

114. The context of this mishnah is a discussion of the crime and punishment of the rebellious elder, a figure seen as depicted by Deut 17:12. It is unclear where the interest in constructing such a figure came from, given the seemingly tenuous connection between this verse and the mishnaic representation. For a discussion of the rabbinic construct, see Richard Hidary, "Tolerance for Diversity of Halakhic Practice in the Talmud" (Ph.D. diss., New York University, 2008), 307–52. One might also speculate about some connection to the depiction of Jesus in the Gospels.

115. Jacob Mann, "Changes in the Divine Service of the Synagogue Due to Religious Persecutions," *Hebrew Union College Annual* 4 (1927): 289–99. Here he was following Abraham Krochmal, *Iyyun Tefillah* (Lemberg, 1885), 24–37 (in Hebrew).

116. See Daniel Sperber, *Material Culture in Eretz-Israel During the Talmudic Period* (Jerusalem: Yad Izhak Ben-Zvi Press/Bar-Ilan University Press, 1993), 129–30 (in Hebrew). Cf. E-M p. 40 lines 9–11 (to Exod 13:9) for a ruling similar to this mishnah's.

117. The reference to circular *tefillin* will be discussed in detail in the next chapter, but it is already to be noted that the housings found in the Judean Desert were rectangular or squarish in shape (the Midreshei Halakah do not mention the shape of *tefillin* at all.)

118. H-R p. 66 line 20–p. 67 line 5 (to Exod 13:9); F p. 64 lines 1–8 (to Deut 6:8).

119. See the suggestion that the rabbis used the term in a vague way, without necessarily having a particular group in mind, in Martin Goodman, "The Function of Minim

An alternative explanation is suggested by Hanokh Albeck's observation that this mishnah is referring to late–Second Temple era sectarian practices.[120] The text may be associating literalism with Sadducees, and using *derekh haminut* to refer to the latter's ideology.[121] Other possibilities are that *minut* refers to belief in multiple powers[122] or to the heresy exhibited by Jewish followers of Christ,[123] although it is unclear why their adherents might have been more likely than others to adopt a literalist stance toward the verses taken to refer to *tefillin*. Yet another possible referent is professional magicians and their devotees, who might have tried to practice *tefillin* in hypercorrect (that is, hyperliteral) fashion. In any event, it seems plausible that this mishnah relates to knowledge of actual variety in practice, whether still extant at the time of the tanna'im or not.

The final clause of *M. Megillah* 4:8 may be problematizing ostentatious *tefillin* observance, also known from the reference in Matthew, although it seems unlikely that the mishnah here is referring to Pharisees, as Matthew does. Indeed, the identity of the *hitsonim* is unknown. *M. Sanhedrin* 10:1 has R. Aqiva referring to "outsider books," but the word there is an adjective rather than a noun, and possibly refers to works considered extracanonical. Other groups referred to in that mishnah seem to be identifiable as sectarians, followers of Greek philosophy, and practitioners of magic, but the books concerned may have belonged to none of these. The word here may be no more than a pun[124]: wearing *tefillin* on one's sleeve or wearing gold-plated ones might have earned people with overly conspicuous practice the deprecatory nickname "outsiders," in view of their concern for external aspects of the ritual. Nor was tanna'itic disdain for ostentation likely to have been limited to the specific practices described at the end of *M. Megillah* 4:8; *Midrash Tanna'im* interprets part of Deut 17:20, with its general effect being that a king should not lord himself over his brothers, to mean that he ought not have special gold *tefillin* straps. The rabbis seem to have eschewed ornamental *tefillin*, despite ostensible enthusiasm

---

in Early Rabbinic Judaism," in *Geschichte—Tradition—Reflexion,* vol. 1, ed. Peter Schaefer (Tübingen: Mohr Siebeck, 1996), 507.

120. Albeck, *Shishah Sidrei Mishnah, Seder Mo'ed,* 504.

121. See Yaakov Sussmann, "The History of Halakha and the Dead Sea Scrolls—Preliminary Observations on Miqsat Ma'se Ha-Torah (4qmmt)," *Tarbiz* 59, nos. 1–2 (1989/90): 53 n. 176 (in Hebrew). See also B. Z. Luria, "Differences of Opinion About the Form of Tefillin," in *The Hasmonean Kings* (Israel: Karni, 1985), 193–202 (in Hebrew). The *Sitz im Leben* of this mishnah, according to Luria, is sectarian disputes of the Hasmonean era.

122. Cf. *M. Megillah* 4:9.

123. As in *T. Hulin* 2:24, where R. Eli'ezer is apprehended by the authorities on account of מינות.

124. For some discussion of puns in rabbinic literature, see Yonah Fraenkel, *Sippur Ha'aggadah—Ahdut Shel Tokhen Vetzurah* (Tel Aviv: Hakibbutz Hameuchad, 2001), 174–97 (in Hebrew).

expressed for making such objects beautiful[125]; perhaps making them larger (as in Matthew) was the only sanctioned way of doing so.

Finally, it is to be noted that *tefillin* were to be worn on the left arm only.[126] A reason for this ruling will be proposed in chapter 5.

When/Where were *Tefillin* Worn/Not Worn?

According to the tanna'im, *tefillin* were not to be worn in a tannery,[127] nor under certain circumstances at the baths.[128] It accordingly seems plausible to infer a general presumption that they were worn while going about one's daily business. This seems borne out by *Mekhilta Derabbi Yishma'el*'s provision that someone reading Torah was exempt from *tefillin*[129]; apparently those engaged in other activities were not.[130] There is no suggestion in tanna'itic literature that *tefillin* were worn for morning prayers only, as was later to be the case.[131]

T. Sanhedrin 4:7 explicitly envisages a king as wearing *tefillin* more or less all the time while about in the world, which reinforces the idea that this would have been widespread practice among *tefillin*-wearing Jews:

> (When) he goes out to war it (his personal Torah scroll) is with him, (when) he comes in it is with him, (when) he goes out in the court of law it is by his side, (when) he goes into the privy (literally water-house) it waits for him by the door. And thus (King) David says "I have placed the

---

125. H-R p. 127 lines 5–6 and E-M p. 78 line 13—p. 79 line 16 (to Exod 15:2). In an unpublished paper Yinon and Rosen-Zvi suggest that the rabbis in essence view *tefillin* and other practices as ornamenting the male body for God, so that making them decorative to other mortals is problematic. Cf. Steven Fine, *Art and Judaism in the Greco-Roman World* (Cambridge: Cambridge University Press, 2005), 108-9.

126. H-R p. 67 lines 5–11 (to Exod 13:9).

127. F p. 282 lines 1–2 (to Deut 23:15).

128. F p. 282 lines 1–2 (to Deut 23:15); and *T. Berakhot* 2:20.

129. H-R p. 68 lines 6–8 (to Exod 13:9).

130. The Mishnah grants exemptions from *tefillin* observance to mourners who had not buried their dead and the groom/members of a wedding party for seven days of celebration. *M. Berakhot* 3:1 and *T. Berakhot* 2:10, respectively. There may have been a common custom of not wearing *tefillin* under such circumstances.

131. Nor is the practice implied by the Talmudim any different. *Tefillin* were understandably associated with the *Shema*, and might routinely be put on around the time when morning prayers were recited, but that is a somewhat different matter; see *Bavli Berakhot* 14b. For a different understanding to mine see Andreas Lenhardt, "Massekhet Tefillin—Beobachtungen zur literarischen Genese eines kleinen Talmud-Traktates," in *Jewish Studies between the Disciplines*, ed. K. Herrmann, M. Schlueter, and G. Veltri (Leiden and Boston: Brill, 2003).

Lord by me at all times" [Ps 16:8]. R. Yehudah says: a Torah scroll on his right (hand/arm), and *tefillin* on his left.[132]

T. Berakhot 6:10 implies that, as far as the tanna'im were concerned, *tefillin* might be worn throughout the day but ought to be taken off at night: "How early does one put them on? In the morning. Had one not put them on in the morning then one might put them on the entire day." The Midreshei Halakah indeed specify that *tefillin* were not worn at night,[133] and this aspect of the practice will be discussed in further detail in the next chapter; but wearing them until dusk seems to have been unremarkable.[134]

The apparent tanna'itic focus on merely placing *tefillin* or putting them on—the verbs *lehani'ah* or *latet* are used[135]—calls for some comment, although the English "to wear" often seems to be the best translation.[136] A couple of factors may have been in play. In the first place, the ritual was to be performed not simply by wearing *tefillin* but by placing them in such a way that they contravened the literal meaning of scripture, as earlier discussed. The rabbis were, of course, aware of the discrepancy in this regard between scripture and practice, and the language may have functioned to reduce cognitive dissonance. This factor may underlie the specification in *T. Berakhot* 6:10 that the placing of *tefillin* had been commanded by God. In a somewhat similar vein, the word *mezuzah* (doorpost) was used to describe a piece of inscribed parchment attached to a doorpost. Thus the parchment, by taking the place of the Torah's inscribed doorpost, came to be viewed as the *mezuzah* itself. Here, too, the dissonance between practice and scripture would have been reduced by the choice of language. In addition, perhaps, the above usage was a consequence of *tefillin* being considered a supplemental worn item, rather than an article of clothing. This would be consistent with *M. Shabbat* 6:2, where *tefillin* are listed together with, and treated as, other such items.

---

132. Following the Vienna manuscript and the *editio princeps*. The Erfurt manuscript has "on his arm" instead of "on his left."

133. See H-R p. 68 lines 15–18 (to Exod 13:10).

134. See *T. Shabbat* 1:11.

135. For the former, see *T. Berakhot* 6:10; *M. Nedarim* 2:2; *M. Shevu'ot* 3:8 and 3:11; H-R p. 68 lines 3–8 (to Exod 13:9); and for the latter see, inter alia, *T. Berakhot* 2:20; *T. Nedarim* 1:5; H-R p. 68 line 18 (to Exod 13:10); E-M p. 44 lines 16–18 (to Exod 13:16); F p. 63 lines 12–14 (to Deut 6:8); *Midrash Tanna'im* to Deut 6:8.

136. By way of contrast, the scriptural *liqshor* is, surprisingly, never used to describe putting them on (although the Aramaic equivalent *liqkmo'a* does appear once, in *T. Demai* 2:17).

Tefillin and Shabbat

It is clear from Mishnah and Tosefta regulations that *tefillin* might readily have been worn on Shabbat, with the Midreshei Halakah also showing that the tanna'im generally disapproved of such practice. According to *M. Shabbat* 6:2, "A man may not go out (on Shabbat) wearing a nailed sandal . . . nor *tefillin*, nor an amulet at a time when not from an expert, . . . but if he did so he is not required to bring a sin offering." Restrictions on transporting objects pervade the Shabbat rules in rabbinic literature,[137] and this mishnah and adjacent ones list objects that may/may not be worn out to a public space on Shabbat (including women's *totafot*, as discussed above). There would seem to have been no need for the *tefillin* ruling unless some people were likely to have worn them when leaving the home on Shabbat. Exceptions to it are encountered in *M. Eruvin* 10:1–2 and *T. Eruvin* 8:15, which specify that someone who found *tefillin* lying around outdoors on Shabbat was obliged to bring them in, apparently by wearing them. (It should be noted that there would have been no difference, from the standpoint of tanna'itic halakah, between leaving one's home on Shabbat while wearing *tefillin*, and returning to it on Shabbat while wearing them. In either case there would have been the same underlying prohibition—as is clear from *M. Shabbat* 7:2 and *T. Shabbat* 1:3—against transporting objects between domains.[138])

A further demonstration that some Jews wore *tefillin* on Shabbat is provided by *T. Eruvin* 8:17: "One who went out to the public space (on Shabbat), and realized that he had *tefillin* on his head, covers his head[139] until he reaches his home. If there was a study house, then he takes them (off), and puts them in a concealed place." What was one to do, having neglected—perhaps inadvertently—to follow the ruling in *M. Shabbat* 6:2? The question would have been of interest to someone who wore *tefillin* at home on Shabbat but was concerned not to transport them. The tosefta's solution seems to involve repeating the problematic behavior of wearing them while crossing from one domain to another, albeit while dissembling. Covering the head would prevent others seeing that one was transporting *tefillin* on Shabbat, and drawing the incorrect inference that doing so was not problematic. Here, then, is an implicit acknowledgment that rabbinic practice may have been at odds with the practice of others.[140]

---

137. Which is not to say that the rabbis invented them wholesale. See, for example, the discussion of Shabbat rules in Lawrence H. Schiffman, *The Halakhah at Qumran* (Leiden: Brill, 1975).

138. For similar rules at Qumran, see CD 11:7–9; 4Q251; and 4Q265.

139. Or, perhaps, "keeps his head covered."

140. The end of *T. Eruvin* 8:17 is most simply explained as teaching that under these

The mention of a potential sin offering in *M. Shabbat* 6:2 is worthy of note, as it might be taken to suggest traditions of considerable antiquity. In all likelihood, however, the putative sin offering was simply being used as a theoretical marker for classifying Shabbat offenses, even though Temple sacrifice had ceased to be an option after 70 C.E. The exemption from an expiatory sacrifice signifies that wearing the objects listed was considered a misdemeanor rather than a more serious infraction, and *tefillin* wearers may have been addressed leniently precisely because *tefillin* were, in fact, widely worn in public on Shabbat.

In any event, there is no basis, from Mishnah or Tosefta, for imagining that the rabbis disapproved of wearing *tefillin* on Shabbat while indoors. The Midreshei Halakah, however, explicitly exclude any *tefillin* wearing on Shabbat and festivals. Thus, for example, one of many derivations of this exclusion in *Mekhilta Derabbi Yishma'el*: "*Miyamim yamimah*: There are days when you wear (*tefillin*) and there are days when you do not wear (*tefillin*), so Shabbat and festivals were excluded."[141] The *Mekhilta* here takes the statement in Exod 13:10 that a statute is to be observed at its appointed time to be referring to *tefillin*, taken in turn to be the subject of the previous verse. The two introductory words are understood to mean "from day to day," with the midrashic result that *tefillin* are worn on some days but not others, thereby excluding Shabbat and festivals.

There is no trace here of a known practice of wearing *tefillin* on Shabbat, but named tanna'im in the *Mekhilta* are then cited to derive a similar rule in language that is strongly suggestive of conflict between these two aspects of religious life:

> R. Yitzhaq says: Since Shabbat is called a "sign"[142] and *tefillin* are called a "sign,"[143] (is this to say that) one should not place a sign within a sign, or should one place a sign within a sign? You said[144]—Shabbat, which is called a sign and a covenant [Exod 31:16], ought to push aside (*tidheh*) *tefillin*, which are merely called a sign.

---

circumstances one ought take off *tefillin* in a study house, and leave them there, rather than take them home. See Saul Lieberman, *Tosefta Ki-Fshutah*, 2nd ed. (Jerusalem: Jewish Theological Seminary of America, 1992), 3:465.

141. H-R p. 69 lines 4–5 (to Exod 13:10). A similar ruling is derived in several different ways between p. 68 line 18 and p. 69 line 10. *Sifre Devarim*, while deriving the same halakot as the *Mekhilta* on the nature of *tefillin* and how they were to be worn, and even on occasion using an Exodus verse to do so, shows no interest in Shabbat, or nighttime, exclusions.

142. Presumably a reference to Exod 31:13 or 31:17.

143. All four constitutive verses were understood to be referring to *tefillin* in using the word *ot*.

144. The subject of the verb is an anonymous, and presumably imagined, earlier exegete. See Bacher, *Die exegetische Terminologie der jüdischen Traditionsliteratur*, 6; Halbertal, *Interpretative Revolutions in the Making*, 15.

R. Eli'ezer says: Since Shabbat is called a "sign" and *tefillin* are called a "sign," (is this to say that) one should not place a sign within a sign, or should one place a sign within a sign? You said—Shabbat, concerning which one is (potentially) liable to *karet* and death administered by the court, ought push aside *tefillin*, concerning which one is liable neither to *karet* nor to death administered by the court.

The word *tidheh* is revealing. The verb is used in tanna'itic sources when rules conflict, and one rule (or set of rules) must take precedence over another.[145] Implicitly, then, R. Yitzhaq and R. Eli'ezer are not dealing with a blanket Shabbat exclusion; their concern, rather, is to derive the law for those situations where Shabbat and *tefillin* are in conflict. Indeed, R. Eli'ezer, in stating that Shabbat pushes *tefillin* aside, derives his ruling from the severity of the punishments for Shabbat violation. In addition, it is noteworthy that R. Eliezer is explicitly associated with a view that Exod 13:10, used by other tanna'im in both Mekhiltot to derive the blanket exclusion, is not dealing with *tefillin* at all, but with Passover laws.[146]

In light of the above, it seems plausible that there was some development during the tanna'itic period with respect to the rabbinic approach to *tefillin* wearing on Shabbat. Early rabbinic halakah precluded leaving one's home on Shabbat while wearing *tefillin* (thus *M. Shabbat* 6:2), and this was justified in the midrashic framework by the idea that Shabbat rules overrode *tefillin* obligations. It is interesting that the *Mekhilta* names R. Eli'ezer, who is routinely associated with early traditions, in this context.[147] A subsequent concern, that *tefillin* might nevertheless be illicitly transported outside the home, ultimately led the rabbis to abandoning the practice on Shabbat altogether.[148]

This seems particularly likely if, as will be suggested in the concluding chapter, *tefillin* were generally worn outdoors rather than at home. Under such circumstances, *tefillin* and Shabbat would indeed have been in frequent conflict, and there would have been little point in limiting the practice to the home. Some tanna'im proceeded to demonstrate midrashically from Exod 13:10 that *tefillin* were simply not *in effect* on Shabbat and festivals, much as they were not in effect at night.[149] Tradents used vari-

---

145. See, for example, *M. Pesahim* 6:1.

146. E-M p. 41 line 16 (to Exod 13:10).

147. See Yitzhak Gilat, *The Halakhot of R. Eliezer Ben Hyrcanos: A Chapter in the History of the Halakha* (Jerusalem, 1965), 2–20.

148. Mann, who associated *tefillin* with prayer, suggested that permitting them to be worn at home would have made it more likely that they would get transported to the synagogue. See Mann, "Changes in the Divine Service of the Synagogue Due to Religious Persecutions," 290.

149. H-R p. 68 line 15—p. 69 line 5 and E-M p. 41 line 17—p. 42 line 5 (to Exod 13:10).

ous midrashic means to derive the Shabbat/festivals exclusion on the basis of this verse, and all are likely acknowledging that it does in fact look to be related to festival laws (if only by virtue of its inclusion of the word *lemo'adah*). Neither R. Eli'ezer nor R. Yitzhaq, however, mentions a *tefillin* exclusion on festivals; because the strict rules for transporting objects did not apply on festivals but only Shabbat, this omission bears out my earlier suggestion that Shabbat violation of these rules was their only concern.

M. Shabbat 16:1 may be seen as reflecting a scenario in which *tefillin* were not routinely in use on Shabbat: "One saves all writings of sanctity from a conflagration (on Shabbat, even though this entails the violation of rules against moving objects from one domain to another), whether one reads from them or whether one does not read from them. . . . One saves the scroll case as well as the scroll, and a *tefillin* case as well as *tefillin*, even though they contain coins." It is unclear what the mishnah means by the *tiq* ("case"), and the possibilities include the *tefillin* housing[150] as well as some kind of carrying case (whose usage would be analogous to the modern practice of keeping *tefillin* in a bag between uses). The word does not occur elsewhere in tanna'itic literature in connection with *tefillin*; the Mishnah typically uses the word *tefillin* indiscriminately for both parchments and housings[151] (and frequently to refer to the parchment/housing package[152]). In any event, it is conceivable that the *Sitz im Leben* of this mishnah entailed *tefillin* not being worn on Shabbat, which might explain why *tefillin* cases could well be expected to contain coins.[153]

It should be noted, however, that the last clause cited—in view of the plural form *betokhan*—may also refer to scroll cases, which presumably would have been in use on Shabbat as a matter of routine. Perhaps, then, this mishnah reflects nothing of Shabbat practice per se but simply that scroll and *tefillin* cases were occasionally used as safes. This would be an interesting point of contact with *M. Sheqalim* 3:2, which implies that *tefillin* housings could somehow be used to conceal coins:

> In three containers, each three *se'ah* (in volume) they would clear out the (Temple treasury) chamber. . . . The clearer would not enter wearing a bordered cloak, nor shoe, nor sandal, nor *tefillah*,

---

150. Cf. Catherine Hezser, *Jewish Literacy in Roman Palestine* (Tübingen: Mohr Siebeck, 2001), 216.

151. For examples of each of these uses, see *M. Mo'ed Qatan* 3:4 and *M. Megillah* 4:8.

152. See, for example, *M. Arakhin* 6:3.

153. To the rabbis, an injunction against moving objects that contained money on Shabbat constituted an entirely separate issue from general prohibitions against transporting objects between domains on that day. See *M. Kelim* 18:2.

nor amulet—in case he became poor, and they might say that he became poor because of the sin of the (Temple treasury) chamber; or in case he became rich, and they might say that he became rich from clearing out the (Temple treasury) chamber.

Other Aspects of *Tefillin* Ritual

Sanctity and Respect

As far as the tanna'im were concerned, *tefillin* were similar to Torah scrolls with regard to their sanctity. *M. Shabbat* 16:1, discussed above, includes *tefillin* under *kitve haqodesh*, which were to be saved from a conflagration on Shabbat, even when doing so compromised other Shabbat rules. Similar leniency with regard to *tefillin*, exhibited in *M. Eruvin* 10:1–2, was also presumably owing to consideration of the respect due to sacred objects: "One who finds *tefillin* (on Shabbat) brings them in one pair at a time, Rabban Gamliel says—two at a time. . . . One who found them in (many) sets, or bundled, stays with them until nightfall (the end of Shabbat) and brings them back, but when in danger covers them and departs." Rather than leaving found *tefillin* lying around, one was obliged to bring them in, apparently by wearing them, even though *tefillin* were generally not to be transported between domains on Shabbat, even when worn.

The above reference to danger might simply be taken as counseling against lingering in any questionable neighborhood until nightfall, even though leaving it entailed abandoning *tefillin* there. If, however, as seems possible, the *Sitz im Leben* for this section is Jews fleeing Roman antagonists, then the danger could be connected to that antagonism. The Bar-Kokhba revolt and its aftermath seem one possible point of reference,[154] although Rabban Gamliel of Yavneh's death presumably preceded those events. *T. Eruvin* 8:15, however, reporting a somewhat different tradition, also mentions a different tanna[155]: "One who finds *tefillin* (on Shabbat) brings them in one pair at a time, R. Yehudah says—two at a time." R. Yehudah is presumably R. Yehudah bar Ila'i of Usha, who would be a likely candidate for discussing the implications of the Bar-Kokhba revolt. While this tosefta does not address the "danger" in connection with *tefillin*, the following one poignantly tackles a similar issue: "One who finds a scroll (on Shabbat), in a field, sits and guards it, and stays with it until nightfall, and takes it and returns on his way, but when in danger leaves it and goes on his way. If it was raining then he wraps himself in skin and returns and covers it."

---

154. See Peter Schaefer, *Der Bar Kokhba-Aufstand: Studien zum zweiten jüdischen Krieg gegen Rom* (Tübingen: Mohr Siebeck, 1981), 196.

155. According to the Vienna manuscript.

According to *M. Gittin* 4:6, "One does not redeem captives for more than their worth, in order to improve the world . . . nor does one purchase scrolls and *tefillin* and *mezuzot* from gentiles for more than their worth, in order to improve the world." The issue at stake here is one of public policy, but why anyone would have been interested in purchasing these products at above-market value is unclear. It does, however, seem possible that such "redemption" could have followed on from a period of persecution (much as Jews have been known to buy Torah scrolls and Judaica in Eastern Europe since the Shoah). If so, the sanctity of the objects would likely have been the driving force.[156] According to one variant of *T. Avodah Zarah* 2:4 one ought not sell *tefillin* to gentiles, and all these texts may reflect a concern that the latter (particularly if they had persecuted Jews) would treat such objects in sacrilegious fashion.

In *T. Hagigah* 1:2, the child too small for *tefillin* is one who does not yet know how to look after them, and here too considerations of respect would seem to be in play. The rabbis endorsed a practice of providing children with *tefillin*, but only where the child could be expected to look after them respectfully. In a similar vein, the rabbinic views regarding *tefillin* in the bathhouse (to be discussed in more detail in the next chapter) clearly relate to a conflict between sanctity and nakedness.[157]

Indeed, *tefillin* could apparently backfire in some way if treated sacrilegiously. *Sifre Devarim* derives a rule from Deut 23:15 that one does not recite the *Shema* by a launderer's vat, nor enter a bathhouse or tannery with scrolls or *tefillin* in hand.[158] The verse describes God as walking in the camp of Israel to save them and defeat their enemies, but specifies that the camp must be holy, lest God depart from it.

Purity

A concern for purity, even among those who were not priests, was a major trend in Judaism by the second century B.C.E.,[159] and occasioned sectarian dispute.[160] It is difficult to reconstruct how some of the relevant laws came into being, and consistency over time cannot be presumed. Although the

---

156. Albeck asserts that the reason for this mishnah's ban is to avoid giving gentiles an incentive to steal these objects from Jews. This seems unlikely, as the mishnah does not exclude purchase per se but merely purchase for amounts in excess of the objects' true value. It is indeed implicit here that it *was* deemed acceptable in the ordinary course of commerce to purchase scrolls, *tefillin,* and *mezuzot* from gentiles. See Hanokh Albeck, *Shishah Sidrei Mishnah, Seder Nashim* (Jerusalem: Mosad Bi'alik and D'vir, 1958), 283.

157. *T. Berakhot* 2:20.

158. F p. 282 lines 1–2 (to Deut 23:15).

159. See Eyal Regev, "Non-Priestly Purity and Its Religious Aspects," in *Purity and Holiness,* ed. M. J. H. M. Poorthuis and J. Schwartz (Leiden: Brill, 2000), 223–44.

160. See, for example, the Qumran scroll 4QMMT, and *M. Yadayim* 4:6–7.

details of purity halakah are beyond the scope of this work, some light
may be shed on *tefillin* practices by reference to purity issues, particularly
in view of the fact that *tefillin* were worn on the body.

In the first place, the practice of sewing *tefillin* shut is evidenced by
the Judean Desert exemplars. *M. Miqva'ot* 10:2 reinforces the idea that this
would have kept their parchment texts from pollution:

> A round cushion, ball, and last, and amulet, and *tefillah*; these do
> not need water to go inside them (when immersed in a *miqveh* to
> render them pure). This is the principle: All that do not ordinarily
> let (anything) in or out, one immerses when closed.

The housings were another matter. There were complex tannaitic
rules for purifying a head-*tefillin* housing removed from a corpse, as its
four individual receptacles involved particular challenges from a purity
perspective.[161] To the extent that *tefillin* were worn for protection they
would doubtless have been worn on the deathbed,[162] so that the issue was
probably of more than theoretical interest. Perhaps they were frequently
recycled after an owner's death; no less a figure than the venerable Sham-
mai is said to have worn his grandfather's *tefillin*.[163]

Purity considerations were also entailed by *tefillin*'s status as *kitve
haqodesh* (discussed above). Rabbinic Jews followed the Pharisees in viewing the hands as becoming defiled by touching holy scripture,[164] and
M. Yadayim 3:3 specifies, "*Tefillin* straps as well as *tefillin* defile the hands.
R. Shimon says: *Tefillin* straps do not defile the hands."[165]

It would, of course, have been rather inconvenient for the straps or
housings to defile the hands (for those concerned about such impurity).

---

161. *M. Kelim* 18:8. See also *T. Kelim Bava Batra* 1:4

162. It is noteworthy that *tefillin* are worn on the deathbed in talmudic stories about
two of the most famous tanna'itic figures—R. Eli'ezer (see *Y. Shabbat* 2:7 [5b] and *B. Sanhedrin* 68a), and Rabbi Judah the Prince (see *B. Ketubot* 103b/104a).

163. H-R p. 69 lines 13–14 (to Exod 13:10).

164. The origin of the tanna'itic halakah of "defilement of the hands" is unclear. See
Martin Goodman, "Sacred Scripture and 'Defiling the Hands,'" *Journal of Theological Studies*
n.s. 41, no. 1 (1990): 99–107; Shamma Friedman, "The Holy Scriptures Defile the Hands—the
Transformation of a Biblical Concept in Rabbinic Theology," in *Minhah Le-Nahum*, ed. Marc
Brettler and Michael Fishbane (Sheffield: JSOT Press, 1993), 117–32; Menahem Haran, *The
Biblical Collection*, vol. 1 (Jerusalem: Bialik Institute, 1996), 201–76 (in Hebrew). For a sharp
critique of Haran's views, see Chaim Milikowsky, "Reflections on Hand-Washing, Hand-
Purity and Holy Scripture in Rabbinical Literature," in *Purity and Holiness*, ed. M. J. H. M.
Poorthuis and J. Schwartz (Leiden: Brill, 2000), 149–62.

165. It is worth noting that other paraphernalia connected with holy scripture, and
not merely *tefillin* housings or straps, could have the same halakic status as scripture itself,
according to *T. Yadayim* 2:12 and *M. Shabbat* 16:1. According to both *M. Yadayim* 4:6 and *T.
Yadayim* 2:19 the holy writings defile "because they are precious," and associated paraphernalia seem to have been deemed precious as well.

While according to one opinion in *M. Yadayim* 3:3 the straps nevertheless defiled, *T. Yadayim* 2:9 specifies that only by touching the parchment, or possibly the parchment-cell, would one become defiled[166]; cells were the immediate containers for *tefillin* parchments and may therefore have been considered more holy than the rest of the housing. Indeed, a practice of manufacturing *tefillin* so as to create such discrete cells, leaving a part of the housing beyond the cells, might have originated with a concern for holding them in an appropriate fashion.

The laws of defiling the hands, which according to *M. Yadayim* 4:6 are part of Second Temple halakah, may also have been connected to the origins of the practice of wearing *tefillin* on the arm rather than the hand. Here it is interesting to note the Sadducean disdain for the hand-defilement rules,[167] which may be the source of the claim in *M. Megillah* 4:8 that wearing *tefillin* on the hand is the "way of *minut*" (*minim/minut* are sometimes used as a codeword for Sadducees[168]). It is also possible that wearing *tefillin* on the forehead, another "way of *minut*" according to this mishnah, was more likely to lead to touching them than wearing them higher on the head, where the effects of gravity would not be constantly calling for their adjustment. Even in the absence of purity considerations, however, wearing *tefillin* on the hand or between the eyes, in a literal understanding of scripture, might have been inordinately inconvenient.

Finally, there is a tradition in the *Mekhilta Derabbi Shimon bar Yohai* that *tefillin* were written on the hides of clean animals only.[169] The reference is, presumably, to those animals considered clean by Leviticus.

Scribes and Scribal Practice

In the scribal context, as in others, *tefillin* are frequently mentioned together with *sefarim* (presumably Torah scrolls) and *mezuzot*. Writing these was considered vital work by the tanna'im, to the extent that, according to some opinions in *T. Berakhot* 2:6, such scribes ought not interrupt their writing for assigned prayers and perhaps not even for *Shema* recital. Presumably, such interruptions were deemed too distracting (the halakah concludes with a report about Rabban Gamli'el and his court, who dealt with community needs without pause, so as not to be distracted).

---

166. This is according to the Vienna manuscript; the Erfurt manuscript, which specifies that only by touching the straps might one defile the hands, makes little sense. See Saul Lieberman, *Tosefeth Rishonim, Seder Tohoroth* (New York and Jerusalem: Jewish Theological Seminary of America, 1939; reprint, 1999), 155.

167. See *M. Yadayim* 4:6.

168. See Sussmann, "The History of Halakha and the Dead Sea Scrolls," 53 n. 176.

169. E-M p. 41 lines 11–12 (to Exod 13:9).

T. Berakhot 6:10 mentions people who made *tefillin* for themselves, as though this were a common occurrence. At first sight this seems a little strange, as their manufacture involved scribal skills that would presumably have been rare. The ruling may, however, have been a theoretical one, as *sukkah* and *lulav* are mentioned in the same halakah, and these three were frequently ruled on together. (As previously observed, the word *tefillin* could be used in tanna'itic parlance to refer to the housing, whose manufacture might have been a more common skill than writing its parchments, so that *T. Berakhot* 6:10 might in any case be referring to one who made his own housings, rather than one who wrote parchments for himself.)

If anything, scribal skill looks to have been in short supply. According to *T. Bikkurim* 2:15, "Scroll, *tefillin*, and *mezuzot* scribes, as well as the merchants to whom they sell and the merchants to whom those merchants sell, and all who deal for the sake of the exalted one; none will ever see any sign of blessing. If they deal for the sake of heaven then they are included for blessing."[170] The resentment toward some scribes is clear and suggests a lack of rabbinic influence over much-needed service providers.[171] This may also be inferred from the lack of systematic tanna'itic attention to scribal practice; it would have made little sense to try to impose standards in this area, unless those supposed to adhere to them had some interest in following them (much the same case can be made to explain the general absence of the synagogue from the Mishnah's regulatory framework). An additional implication of this halakah is a high cost for *tefillin*, which could, of course, go some way to explaining a tendency toward recycling, mentioned earlier. Expert scribes may have charged a heavy price for their skills.

One clue as to scribal practice may be adduced from *M. Megillah* 1:8: "There is no difference between scrolls, and *tefillin* and *mezuzot*, other than that scrolls are written in any language, whereas *tefillin* and *mezuzot* are only written in *Ashurit*. Rabban Shimon ben Gamli'el says—even for scrolls they permitted writing in Greek only."[172] The reference to *Ashurit* is to the Hebrew language, written in the Aramaic characters that were standard Hebrew script.[173] It is noteworthy that not only are the Judean Desert *tefillin* written in Hebrew in Aramaic script, but so too is the Nash Papy-

---

170. The distinction between the undesirable *leshem gavo'ah* and commendable *leshem shamayim* is unclear, and the *editio princeps* of the tosefta has "not for the sake of heaven," instead of "for the sake of the exalted one."

171. For the competition between scribes and rabbis, see Hezser, *The Social Structure of the Rabbinic Movement*, 467–75.

172. The context is a list of "the only (halakic) difference" between a variety of comparable things, triggered by a similar analysis of the two months of Adar, in *M. Megillah* 1:4.

173. See Tosefta *Sanhedrin* 4:7, where it is clear that the rabbis concerned viewed this script as more authentic than paleo-Hebrew.

rus.[174] "Scrolls" from Egypt were, however, written in Greek, as evidenced by the Septuagint. The Mishnah also reinforces the idea that, as exemplified by the Judean Desert findings, *tefillin* were written on parchment (in Palestine, if not perhaps in Egypt).[175] *M. Shabbat* 8:3 talks of "(enough) parchment for writing on it the small pericope in *tefillin*, which is 'hear Israel.'"[176]

T. Avodah Zarah 3:6–7 specifies as follows: "One buys scrolls, *tefillin*, and *mezuzot* from a gentile, but only when they are written properly. And there was an instance of one gentile, who was writing scrolls in Tyre, and the instance came before the sages and they said, 'It is permitted to buy from him.'" The story may suggest that this was hardly a common occurrence, which would not be surprising. Although "proper" writing is not defined, it seems reasonable to imagine that it refers to the contained text being faithful to scripture.[177] *M. Menahot* 3:7 spells that out: "The two sections of the *mezuzah* can each invalidate the other, even one character renders them invalid; the four sections of the *tefillin* can each invalidate the other, even one character renders them invalid."

As the reference to purchase in *T. Avodah Zarah* 3:6–7 seems to include *tefillin* etc. *written* by gentiles (and not merely bought and sold by them) it is possible that its ruling was designed to break the monopoly of Jewish scribes over a much-needed service; recall the harsh resentment toward some scribes mentioned earlier. *Midrash Tanna'im*, however, excludes non-practitioners from writing scrolls, *tefillin*, and *mezuzot*, explicitly mentioning gentiles and Samaritans,[178] and *T. Avodah Zarah* 3:6–7 may represent a different stage in the evolution of halakah.

Some scribes were clearly more scrupulous about their writing than others. Although initially precluding buying *tefillin* from anyone other than an expert (possibly to discourage *tagarim*, middlemen who were not themselves scribes[179]), *T. Avodah Zarah* 3:8 proceeds to demonstrate how to buy them from someone who was apparently a reseller: "If one did buy from one who is not an expert and found two or three bundles of *tefillin* in

---

174. See Rothstein, "From Bible to Murabba'at," 377–84.

175. The exact type of parchment used is a subject of later rabbinic concern.

176. This mishnah is part of a long list of limit cases (*shi'urim*), a typical subject of rabbinic concern. *M. Shabbat* 7:2–3 had asserted a proscription against taking objects from one kind of space to another on Shabbat, as well as a principle for determining the liability of a hypothetical transgressor to bring a hypothetical sin offering. *M. Shabbat* 7:4–8:7 then provides the threshold, for a variety of objects, which is deemed to reflect this principle. In the case of *qelaf* (a type of parchment), the limit case is provided by the smallest *tefillin* pericope, Deut 6:4–9.

177. It is also possible that "proper" writing refers to adherence to certain other scribal rules, although tanna'itic evidence for the existence of these is restricted to *baraitot*. For an extensive discussion, see Rothstein, "From Bible to Murabba'at," 181–427.

178. *Midrash Tanna'im* to Deut 6:9.

179. See *T. Bikkurim* 2:15.

his possession, then he checks one hand or head *tefillin* of his in the first bundle, and so too in the second, and so too in the third, and so too in the fourth." Apparently the rabbis felt that one might presume the reliability of certain scribes, without checking their work exhaustively.

Finally, *Sifre Devarim* seems to attest to some *mezuzah* practices viewed as aberrant by the rabbis that could equally have applied to *tefillin*. It seems quite likely, after all, that practices for writing *tefillin* and *mezuzah* resembled each other, even if the rabbis articulated their disapproval only in the case of *mezuzah* (where a verse that explicitly referred to writing allowed for a suitable *derashah*). The aberrant practices included writing the names of God in gold, and writing "a song like it."[180] The latter is obscure, and may refer to writing a text that was an embellishment of the scriptural passages, or perhaps to a particular format. Alternatively, it refers to a practice of writing the Song of Moses, known from the evidence of 4QPhyl N. There is, however, no instance of special writing used for the Tetragrammaton (such as gold writing, or paleo-Hebrew characters) for any Judean Desert *tefillin* or *mezuzot*, although a similar phenomenon is known from other scrolls.[181]

The Evidence for Change Post–70 C.E.

Owing to the nature of the available evidence, it is difficult to assess the extent to which many elements of *tefillin* practice changed, if at all, during the period under discussion. There is simply no baseline for many aspects of the ritual; evidence for the late–Second Temple era did not, for example, enable an assessment (of the kind made in this chapter) of who had worn *tefillin* during that period, and when/how they had been worn. To put this differently, there is no good reason to imagine that *tefillin* practice had, in many respects, been any different in the earlier period than its depiction in this chapter. (With respect to the contents of *tefillin*, while archaeological evidence is consistent with less variety post–70 C.E. than was observed at Qumran, the abbreviated textual limits observed for the later period had already been noted on some Qumran slips).

The rabbinic evidence discussed earlier shows some indication of changes within rabbinic circles during the period under discussion, in particular with respect to *tefillin* wearing on Shabbat and festivals, as well as in the attitude taken toward children's practice. With regard to possible change in the meaning of the *tefillin* ritual there is some additional post–70 C.E. evidence, as will be discussed in the next chapter.

---

180. F p. 66 lines 1–2 (to Deut 6:9).
181. See Fine, *Art and Judaism in the Greco-Roman World*, 108.

5

In Conclusion, the Meaning
of *Tefillin* Ritual

The discussion thus far can be summarized as follows with respect to some of its major implications. *Tefillin* are to be considered a part of "complex common Judaism"[1] rather than a minority or sectarian ritual, and as a widely observed practice for Jewish men and children. They originated in all likelihood after the Jewish encounter with Hellenism, when some rather obscure verses in Deuteronomy, which seem to mention amulets (if only as a metaphor), began to be read in a new light. The prevalence of inscribed amulets in the Hellenistic world, and particularly perhaps of the widespread and formulaic *ephesia grammata*[2] (which we know to have been carried around in little stitched hides[3]), and of Homeric verses as amulet contents,[4] led to a change in the horizon of expectations with which Jews approached this biblical text.[5] Henceforth, many understood it

---

1. Stuart S. Miller is responsible for the expression "complex common Judaism"; see Miller, *Sages and Commoners in Late-Antique Erez Israel* (Tübingen: Mohr Siebeck, 2006), 21–28.

2. See Chester McCown, "The Ephesia Grammata in Popular Belief," *Transactions and Proceedings of the American Philological Association* 54 (1923): 128–40; Roy Kotansky, "Incantations and Prayers for Salvation on Inscribed Greek Amulets," in *Magika Hiera: Ancient Greek Magic and Religion,* ed. Christopher A. Faraone and Dirk Obbink (New York: Oxford University Press, 1991), 111; John G. Gager, *Curse Tablets and Binding Spells from the Ancient World* (New York/Oxford: Oxford University Press, 1992), 5–6.

3. See Fragment 18 in T. Kock, *Comicorum Atticorum Fragmenta* (Leipzig: Teubner, 1880–1888), 2:268.

4. See, for example, PGM IV 2145–49 in Hans Dieter Betz, *The Greek Magical Papyri in Translation, Including the Demotic Spells,* 2nd ed. (Chicago: University of Chicago Press, 1992), 76.

5. For an elaboration of the horizon of expectations and its significance for the reception of texts, see Hans Robert Jauss, "Literary History as a Challenge to Literary Theory," *New Literary History* 2 (1970–71), 19–37; Susan R. Suleiman, "Introduction: Varieties of Audience-Oriented Criticism," in *The Reader in the Text,* ed. Susan R. Suleiman and Inge Crosman (Princeton: Princeton University Press, 1980), 36.

both as calling for, and as demonstrating the effectiveness of, a length-of-days amulet that was linked to the *Shema* liturgy (and may have played a role in its inception). In view of the promise of Deut 11:21, *tefillin* were not simply an all-purpose amulet for long life but were specifically associated with survival of the family and persistence on the land, two characteristic outcomes of domestic religious ritual.[6] Although taken to be a scripturally endorsed amulet, *tefillin* can be seen as an invented tradition, an adaptation to Greek life whose form was enabled by the centrality of Torah to Jewish life,[7] and an example of how (in Erich Gruen's general formulation) the Jews' "adjustment to the Hellenistic world expressed itself not as accommodation but as reaffirmation of their own lustrous legacy."[8]

The archaeological evidence, while providing the grounds for the above hypothesis, does not allow us to say more about the meaning of the ritual, and literary evidence prior to 70 c.e. does little more than paraphrase the biblical text. Rabbinic literature and other isolated references from the late first century on are more forthcoming in their own way, and enabled the analysis in the previous chapter of many aspects of the practice. The remainder of this chapter will take this study to its final stage and attempt to evaluate what *tefillin* meant, by the later period, to the people who practiced the ritual.

Etymology of the Word *Tefillin,*
and Its Implications

The word *tefillah*, meaning "prayer," is found frequently in the Bible and rabbinic literature and is known from the Mishnah as the singular form of the word *tefillin*.[9] Some scholars have accordingly imagined a link between the word *tefillin* and prayer service, with Jacob Mann in particular asserting that it derived from the practice of wearing such objects while at prayer.[10] The lexicographer Jacob Levy had earlier denied that derivation on the grounds that *tefillin* had originally been worn throughout the day, but did not suggest an alternative.[11]

---

6. See Jonathan Z. Smith, "Here, There and Anywhere," in *Relating Religion* (Chicago: University of Chicago Press, 2004), 323–39.

7. See Martha Himmelfarb, "The Torah between Athens and Jerusalem: Jewish Difference in Antiquity," in *Ancient Judaism in Its Hellenistic Context*, ed. Carol Bakhos (Leiden/Boston: Brill, 2005), 113–29.

8. Erich S. Gruen, *Heritage and Hellenism: The Reinvention of Jewish Tradition* (Berkeley: University of California Press, 1998), 246.

9. See, for example, *M. Menahot* 4:1.

10. Jacob Mann, "Changes in the Divine Service of the Synagogue Due to Religious Persecutions," *Hebrew Union College Annual* 4 (1927): 289–90.

11. Jacob Levy, *Chaldäisches Wörterbuch* (Leipzig, 1881), 551.

The first attested use of *tefillah* in either Hebrew or Aramaic to describe a material object is in an Egyptian document that mentions ten *"tefillah* of silver."[12] This papyrus was dated to the third century B.C.E., and classified as a record of sales, income, and inventory of a private household. The reference to *tefillah* as a material object is clear, and suggests an amulet, surely the most likely candidate for a prayer in material form.[13] I am unaware of any other use of the word in early Aramaic, and the many Hebrew names in this papyrus—including one Jonathan, in whose possession these objects are to be found—make the use of a Hebrew word seem plausible here.[14] Moreover, silver amulets are known to have been a feature of Jewish life, albeit a few hundred years earlier, as shown in chapter 2. This expansion of the original meaning of *tefillah* to describe objects that *functioned* as prayers, can be analogized to the one experienced by the English word "charm," which developed from its original meaning of "spell" to include a subsidiary meaning as "amulet," whereby the function of the object came to be used to refer to the object itself.[15]

While the later plural form *tefillin* or *tefillim*[16] is unattested before the Mishnah,[17] another Hebrew noun, also formed from a *pe/ayin/ayin* root

---

12. The relevant lines read, "In the hand of Jonathan: 6 string(s) of beads, *tefillah* of silver, 10; 2 . . . of silver." For the use of singular nouns here, in conjunction with numbers greater than one, see H. L. Ginsberg, "Aramaic Dialect Problems," *The American Journal of Semitic Languages and Literature* 52, no. 2 (1936): n. 26. For the full text, see C3.28 in Bezalel Porten and Ada Yardeni, *Textbook of Aramaic Documents from Ancient Egypt*, vol. 3: *Literature, Accounts, Lists* (Jerusalem: Hebrew University, 1993), 260, column 9, lines 104–5. For the same document, see also papyrus number 81 in A. Cowley, *Aramaic Papyri of the 5th Century B.C.* (Oxford: Clarendon, 1923). Despite the title of the book, Cowley dates a few of the texts, including this one, to around 300 B.C.E. The editio princeps was H. Sayce and A. Cowley, "An Aramaic Papyrus of the Ptolemaic Age from Egypt," *Proceedings of the Society of Biblical Archaeology* 29 (1907): 260–72. Sayce had purchased it in Luxor.

13. For an example of a Greek prayer-amulet, see PGM LXXI in Betz, *The Greek Magical Papyri*, 298. Here a papyrus, categorized in its own title as a *phylakterion*, seems to be little more than a Greek prayer to the Jewish God IAO, requesting protection from evil.

14. In the only other usage in a Northwest Semitic inscription—a Punic one from the second half of the second century B.C.E.—the word is also taken to refer to prayer. See H. Donner and W. Röllig, *Kanaanäische und aramäische Inschriften*, vol. 1 (Wiesbaden: Otto Harrassowitz, 1962), 30; H. Donner and W. Röllig, *Kanaanäische und aramäische Inschriften*, vol. 2 (Wiesbaden: Otto Harrassowitz, 1964), 152; J. Hoftijzer and K. Jongeling, *Dictionary of the North-West Semitic Inscriptions*, vol. 2 (Leiden: Brill, 1995), 1225–26.

15. See Oxford English Dictionary, s.v. "Charm." Quite independently of my argument, Jacqueline Genot-Bismuth has also understood the word *tefillin* as reflecting its function as a prayer for long life, which she analogized to Hezekiah's prayer and its outcome, in 2 Kgs 20:1–5. See Jacqueline Genot-Bismuth, "Les Tefilim de Qumran: pour une approche anthropologique" (paper presented at the 10th World Congress of Jewish Studies, 1989), 241–42.

16. The plural form *tefillim*, as opposed to *tefillin*, is attested in the highly regarded Kaufman manuscript of the Mishnah (see, for example, *Shabbat* 8:3), and elsewhere.

17. The use in the old-Syriac version of Matthew may date to more or less the same

with a preceding *tav* and subsequent *he*, exhibits a similar plural form in the Qumran text 11QPs[a], where the word *tehillim* appears as the plural of *tehillah*.[18] This scroll is dated to the first half of the first century C.E., and it thus seems entirely possible that the corresponding plural form of *tefillah* was already in use during the late–Second Temple period. In any event, the word *tefillin* is, in light of the Aramaic papyrus, best translated as "amulets," and its usage by the rabbis to designate the objects under discussion (which I have argued were commonplace) suggests that they had continued to be seen as such. The word had, however, become dedicated to scripturally ordained amulets that contained biblical text from the *Shema* prayer; *qame'a* was used for other amulets, ones that did not include sacred writing or were simply not inscribed at all.

Greek sources (Matthew and Justin Martyr, as discussed in the previous chapter) use *phylakterion* to describe *tefillin*, buttressing the idea that these were regarded as amulets. It is interesting to note that the Greek word bore structural similarity to the Hebrew/Aramaic *tefillin*, similarly identifying such items by their function. (Here I disagree with Jeffrey Tigay, who argued that *phylakterion* in Matthew was itself a rendering of *qame'a*.[19] The latter connotes a tied-on object, so that either of the more common Greek words for amulet—*periapton* or *periammon*—would seem to have been a better translation.) An alternative possibility, that *phylakterion* was used by Matthew to express the writer's contempt for (or ignorance of) a Jewish practice,[20] is improbable in light of Matthew's likely Jewish-Christian provenance.[21] There is, in addition, no hint of contempt in a subsequent use of the word by Justin Martyr, who views *tefillin* as a scripturally endorsed means of protection. Thus, both the Hebrew/Aramaic and the Greek suggest that *tefillin* were seen as amulets, and whenever the word was used in tanna'itic literature it likely carried this connotation.[22]

---

time as the Mishnah's redaction. Here it is worth noting that its *umaften arqa deteflehon*, in Matt 23:5, might simply mean, "and they widen the thongs of their amulets" rather than ". . . the thongs of their *tefillin*," in view of the etymology suggested here.

18. See J. A. Sanders, *Discoveries in the Judaean Desert of Jordan*, vol. 4: *The Psalms Scroll of Qumran Cave 11* (Oxford: Clarendon, 1965), 48. (Elsewhere in this scroll the words *tehillah* and *tefillah* seem to have been used interchangeably: the opening word of Psalm 145, *tehillah* in other witnesses, is here *tefillah*. See Sanders, *Discoveries in the Judaean Desert of Jordan*, vol. 4: *The Psalms Scroll of Qumran Cave 11*, 37.)

19. Jeffrey H. Tigay, "On the Term Phylacteries (Matt 23:5)," *Harvard Theological Review* 72, nos. 1–2 (1979).

20. As claimed in G. George Fox, "The Matthean Misrepresentation of Tephillin," *Journal of Near Eastern Studies* 1 (1942).

21. See W. D. Davies and Dale C. Allison, *The Gospel According to Saint Matthew*, vol. 1, International Critical Commentary (Edinburgh: T. & T. Clark, 1988), 17–19.

22. Othmar Keel's assertion that Jews avoided the use of *phylakterion* when describing *tefillin* in order to avoid any association with an amuletic function is accordingly problematic; it seems as though the word *tefillin* had precisely that connotation. See Othmar Keel,

A Commanded/Obligatory Practice

Ostensibly however, as far as the tanna'im were concerned, these amulets were first and foremost an obligation (*hovah*) or commandment (*mitsvah*). While the word *hayyav* is never used in Mishnah or Tosefta to characterize the *tefillin* obligation, several references in these works serve to make it apparent that they were viewed as an obligatory practice. *T. Berakhot* 6:10 is the most explicit statement of obligation to be found there, although in context it is merely an elaboration of a general discussion about reciting blessings when preparing for, or performing, *mitsvot*: "When putting them on (one says), 'Blessed is the one who sanctified us with his commandments and commanded us to put on *tefillin*.'" In a similar vein, *T. Berakhot* 6:10, 25; *M. Nedarim* 2:2; *T. Nedarim* 1:5; *T. Kiddushin* 1:10; and *M. Shevu'ot* 3:8 all refer to *tefillin* as a commandment. *M. Megillah* 4:8 qualifies incorrect or deviant *tefillin* performance by observing that there is no *mitsvah* to it, and *M. Menahot* 4:1 implies that arm and head *tefillin* are distinct *mitsvot*. The *Mekhilta Derabbi Yishma'el* addresses the issue more directly; all are *hayyav* with respect to *tefillin*, except for women and slaves.[23] Males, excluding the very youngest (as discussed in the previous chapter), were simply obligated by the Torah to wear *tefillin*, although nowhere do tanna'im spell out the precise extent of the obligation.

That the Torah was the source of the *tefillin* obligation is evidenced not only by Midreshei Halakah but also by *M. Sanhedrin* 11:3: "one who says there are no *tefillin*, to contravene the words of the Torah, is not liable; (however one who says there ought be) five *totafot*, to add to the words of the scribes, is liable." Here, however, a particular element of the practice, its four cells (or perhaps four discrete passages[24]), is attributed by the mishnah to the "words of the scribes," best understood as representing a conception of long-standing laws, firmly established by this time, whose promulgation had followed that of the divinely ordained Torah. (Some views as to the possible identity of these scribes are based on the idea that rabbinic literature on the subject constitutes meaningful historiography,[25] but even if it does not, the four-cell practice was clearly a long-standing one, being known from Qumran.)

"Zeichen der Verbundenheit," in *Mélanges Dominique Barthélemy*, ed. Pierre Casetti, Othmar Keel, and Adrian Schenker (Fribourg: Editions Universitaires, 1981), 172. Cf. André Pelletier, *Lettre d'Aristée à Philocrate* (Paris: Les éditions du Cerf, 1962), 178 n. 2.

23. H-R p. 68 lines 4–5 (to Exod 13:9).

24. See F p. 63 line 14 (to Deut 6:8), which mentions "one roll having four *totafot*."

25. See Ya'akov Nahum Halevi Epstein, *Introduction to Tannaitic Literature* (Jerusalem: Magnes Press, Hebrew University, 1957), 503–5 (in Hebrew); Hugo Mantel, *The Men of the Great Synagogue* (Israel: Dvir, 1983), 146–65 (in Hebrew).

It was precisely the perceived command to write *tefillin* texts that elevated the status of its parchments over other passages excerpted from the Torah. While *tefillin* were to be saved from a fire on Shabbat as sacred writings,[26] other such excerpts from the Torah were not. According to *T. Shabbat* 13:4: "Blessings, even though they contain letters from the (divine) name and many matters of the Torah, are not saved but are burned in their place (that is, they are not removed from the scene of a fire on Shabbat, when their removal would violate Shabbat rules). From here they said—those who write down blessings are like those who burn the Torah." It seems rather likely that the "blessings" here would have had a theurgic function and that the text reflects rabbinic disapproval of using the Torah for such purposes, in the absence of a commandment to do so.[27] The mention of God's written name in *T. Shabbat* 13:4 is particularly striking, because a tanna'itic belief in the power of God's name seems to have been at the root of the apotropaic nature of *mezuzah*, as will be discussed below.

Both Josephus and Justin saw *tefillin* (similarly to the rabbis) as a commanded practice, and others, too, presumably related them to Torah verses. To the extent that people recited the *Shema*, the two Deuteronomy "*tefillin* verses" (Deut 6:8 and 11:18), would have been well known, and this context could only have reinforced the understanding that they were to be regarded as an obligation. In addition, the *Shema* may have been taken as reflecting the desirability of reciting the Torah's words at just about any time—Deut 6:7 and 11:19 can readily be understood that way— which would have been harder to perform than *tefillin*, especially for the unschooled. Thus, a tradition cited in *Mekhilta Derabbi Yishma'el* to the effect that someone who wears *tefillin* is like someone who reads Torah[28] may also have contributed to observance of the ritual.

Within the framework of obligation, *tefillin* are on one occasion associated by the rabbis with the exodus from Egypt—the *Mekhilta Derabbi Shimon bar Yohai* remarks that Exod 13:16 "teaches that *tefillin* were said [that is, mandated] in memory of the exodus from Egypt."[29] (There is also a possible indication by Josephus that he viewed *tefillin* as commemorating the exodus [*Antiquities* 4:212–13].)

---

26. *M. Shabbat* 16:1.

27. See Catherine Hezser, *Jewish Literacy in Roman Palestine* (Tübingen: Mohr Siebeck, 2001), 222. Indeed, a parallel to this tosefta in *B. Shabbat* 115b mentions amulets as well as blessings. For the idea that these blessings were simply parts of the liturgy, see Saul Lieberman, *Tosefta Ki-Fshutah*, 2nd ed. (Jerusalem: Jewish Theological Seminary of America, 1992), 3:207–8. In any event, one can presume that Torah texts used for theurgic purposes would have been viewed no more favorably.

28. H-R p. 68 lines 6–8 (to Exod 13:9). It is prefaced by *mikan amru*, which in this instance may mean that it was proverbial.

29. E-M p. 44 lines 20–21 (to Exod 13:16).

Tanna'itic Evidence for a Magical/
Protective Function

Several texts, to be discussed below, strongly suggest *tefillin*'s magical function, which in some cases is the key to understanding an otherwise difficult passage.[30] While the first examples relate to practices of which the rabbis disapproved, others do not. Here and in the balance of this chapter I will be adducing texts that refer to *mezuzah* (as well as ones referring to *tefillin*). Although not my primary topic, *mezuzah* is, by virtue of its scriptural referents and contained texts,[31] a close parallel to *tefillin*. In addition, my hypothesis for the development of *tefillin* practice, revolving as it does around the significance of Deut 11:21 and immediately prior verses, would apply just as readily to *mezuzah*.

Dangerous Tefillin and Mezuzot

M. Megillah 4:8

> One who makes his *tefillah* circular; that is a danger and there is no *mitsvah* to it (*sakkanah ve'en bah mitsvah*).

T. Megillah 3:30

> One who suspends his *mezuzah* inside his doorway; that is a danger and there is no mitsvah to it. If one placed it in a stick and suspended it behind the door; that is a danger and there is no *mitsvah* to it. Those of the house of Adiabene (*Munbaz*) would do so at inns.

Modern scholars,[32] following the twelfth-century Tosafist R. Jacob Tam, have interpreted the above passages as referring to a period when Jews were persecuted for adherence to their religious rites.[33] The percep-

---

30. Here I am disagreeing with Blau's claim that "there is not a single passage in the old literature to show that they were identified with magic." See Ludwig Blau, "Phylacteries—Historical View," in *The Jewish Encyclopedia* (New York and London: Funk & Wagnalls, 1905), 10:27.

31. Deuteronomy 6:9 and 11:20 are identical verses, understood to refer to a *mezuzah* practice whose components were Deut 6:4–9 and 11:13–21. (The Qumran evidence has been interpreted as showing that *mezuzot* also included Exodus passages similar to those in *tefillin*, as discussed in chap. 3).

32. See A. M. Habermann, "The Phylacteries in Antiquity," *Eretz Israel* 3 (1954): 174–77 (in Hebrew); Hanokh Albeck, *Shishah Sidrei Mishnah, Seder Mo'ed* (Jerusalem: Mosad Bi'alik and D'vir, 1958), 367, 504 (in Hebrew); Saul Lieberman, *Tosefta Ki-Fshutah*, 2nd ed. (Jerusalem: Jewish Theological Seminary of America, 1992), 5:1212.

33. See *B. Megillah* 24b. R. Tam connects the passage to a story in *B. Shabbat* 49a about

tion has these texts counseling against practices that would have been followed in order to trick those who persecuted Jews for observing *tefillin* and *mezuzah* into thinking that they were not in fact doing so. The reference to danger is based on these ruses being risky, because unlikely to work.

The above interpretation is problematic. In the first place, there are no other instances of something characterized as *sakkanah ve'en bah mitsvah*. If indeed these texts refer to a time when many Jewish practices were outlawed and ruses were used to mislead Roman oppressors, then it would be surprising to find *mezuzah* as the only parallel to *tefillin*. After all, such expedients would presumably have been created to deal with the entire gamut of outlawed practices. It therefore seems more likely that the danger relates to a common characteristic shared in particular by *mezuzah* and *tefillin*.

In any event, scholars now consider it highly doubtful that the Romans suppressed any Jewish practices, other than circumcision.[34] In addition, these texts say nothing about a period of persecution. They do not refer to "a time of danger"[35] but rather characterize making *tefillin* circular or placing *mezuzot* incorrectly as *constituting* a danger. To suggest that this also refers to a time of danger seems to be reading too much into the texts. Finally, *M. Megillah* 4:8 is dealing with heterodox practices, both before and after the clause about circular *tefillin*. Accordingly it seems likely that the problematic clause also refers to such a practice rather than to an attempt at modifying orthodox practice to account for adverse circumstances.

A far more plausible interpretation for *M. Megillah* 4:8 is that circular *tefillin* were simply ones worn like common amulets, which were often

---

a Roman ban on wearing *tefillin*. The Bavli itself makes no such claim in interpreting *M. Megillah* 4:8; the only explanation it offers for the *sakkanah* is that "circular" actually means shaped like a nut, which might dig into the skull and thus cause harm.

34. See Ra'anan Abusch, "Negotiating Difference: Genital Mutilation in Roman Slave Law and the History of the Bar Kokhba Revolt," in *The Bar Kokhba War Reconsidered*, ed. Peter Schaefer (Tübingen: Mohr Siebeck, 2003), 71–91; Benjamin Isaac, "Roman Religious Policy and the Bar Kokhba War," in *The Bar Kokhba War Reconsidered*, ed. Peter Schaefer (Tübingen: Mohr Siebeck, 2003), 37–54. There is, for example, no clear suggestion until later rabbinic works (the Bavli and *Vayikra Rabbah*) that *tefillin* had ever been outlawed; see Saul Lieberman, "Redifat Dat Yisra'el," in *Sefer Hayovel Likhvod Shalom Baron*, ed. Saul Lieberman and Arthur Hyman (Jerusalem: American Academy for Jewish Research, 1974), 215 (in Hebrew). Cf. Peter Schaefer, *Der Bar Kokhba-Aufstand: Studien zum zweiten jüdischen Krieg gegen Rom* (Tübingen: Mohr Siebeck, 1981), 194–235.

35. As in *M. Eruvin* 10:1 and *T. Eruvin* 8:16, which address a situation where *tefillin* and Torah scrolls are found lying around unclaimed. It indeed seems quite possible that the original *Sitz im Leben* for those rulings was Roman persecution, which would be consistent with their reference to a time or state of danger. However, while the brutal Roman suppression of Jewish revolt is unquestioned, it is not to be confused with later rabbinic ideas as to Roman suppression of Jewish religious ritual.

rolled up and placed in tubes.[36] *Tefillin* found in the Judean Desert, however, had roughly rectangular containers for their parchment slips, and later rabbinic sources (that are possibly tanna'itic) also insist on rectangular or square *tefillin*.[37] This explanation would account for the assertion that there was no *mitsvah* to the practice, as the latter needed to be executed in adherence to its traditional form, which served to distinguish *tefillin*'s status as a commanded practice from optional amulets having no scriptural foundation. The parallel reference to *mezuzah* is likewise related to objects that were considered optional house-amulets,[38] rather than the commanded Deuteronomic *mezuzot* in traditional form, which the tanna'im wished to promote.

Why might these *tefillin* and *mezuzot* have been dangerous? I suggest that the tannai'm were simply asserting that once these were made to resemble common amulets they became ineffective in securing the protection that the scripturally ordained objects provided, even if their contained texts seemed to render them equivalent to *tefillin* and *mezuzot*. The word *sakkanah* in these texts is to be linked to the dangers that amulets averted.[39] Not only did tubular *tefillin* not fulfill the *mitsvah*; they were actually dangerously unreliable. Incorrectly placing a *mezuzah*, much as wearing an incorrectly constructed *tefillin* housing, was deemed dangerously negligent with respect to the object's protective function. As far as the tanna'im were concerned, any such function was inextricably tied in with correct performance, itself an idea that is common to magical rituals across cultures. The idea that incorrectly placed *mezuzot* were dangerous because of their failure to provide protection can in fact be traced to Rashi's interpretation of a parallel to our tosefta text (in *B. Menahot* 32b).[40]

---

36. See Yigael Yadin, "Tefillin (Phylacteries) from Qumran (XQPhyl 1–4)," *Eretz Israel* 9 (1969): 61 n. 13 (in Hebrew); Kotansky, "Incantations and Prayers for Salvation on Inscribed Greek Amulets," 107–37. For examples of tubular amulet containers, see Peter W. Schienerl, "A Historical Survey of Tubular Charm-Cases up to the 7th Century A.D.," *Ornament* 4, no. 4 (1980): 10–14; Roy Kotansky, *Greek Magical Amulets: The Inscribed Gold, Silver, Copper, and Bronze Lamellae* (Opladen: Westdeutscher Verlag, 1994), 93.

37. See *baraita* in *B. Megillah* 24b.

38. For house amulets in the ancient world, see E. Reiner, "Plague Amulets and House Blessings," *Journal of Near Eastern Studies* 19 (1960): 148–55; Christopher A. Faraone, *Talismans and Trojan Horses: Guardian Statues in Ancient Greek Myth and Ritual* (New York/Oxford: Oxford University Press, 1992).

39. Cf. the use of the word *sakkanah* in *T. Shabbat* 4:9.

40. Rashi's view is discounted as (mere?) Geonic tradition by Lieberman, *Tosefta Ki-Fshutah*, 5:1212. Here it seems fair to point out that Lieberman generally played down any connection between magic/mysticism and "normative" Judaism. (He famously remarked, in introducing a lecture series on *Merkabah Mysticism* by Gershom Scholem, that "Nonsense is nonsense, but the history of nonsense is a very important science.") For a critique of the view expressed by Lieberman on magic, in his *Hellenism in Jewish Palestine*, see Ithamar Gruenwald, "Hamagiyah Vehamitos—Hamehqar Vehametsi'ut Hahistorit," in *Myth*

Other clauses in *M. Megillah* 4:8 deal with incorrect ways of placing *tefillin*, and placement may also have been an issue with respect to the circular ones, as it is with respect to the *mezuzot* in the tosefta. Tubular amulets were worn in a convenient fashion, often suspended around the neck, but head *tefillin*, then as now, could not have been convenient to wear all day long as a protective device. The temptation to wear them in an easier fashion may have been considerable, and the Mishnah could well be reflecting a common nonrabbinic practice.[41]

Tefillin at the Baths

T. Berakhot 2:20[42]

> One who goes into the bathhouse; in the part where people stand clothed there may be recital[43] and prayer and, it goes without saying, one may greet one's fellow. One may put on *tefillin* and, it goes without saying, need not remove them. In the part where people stand naked there may be no greeting of one's fellow and, it goes without saying, neither recital nor prayer; one must remove *tefillin* and, it goes without saying, may not put them on. In the part where some stand naked and some clothed there may be greeting of one's fellow, but neither recital nor prayer. One need not remove *tefillin*, but nor may one put them on there.[44]

The text seems highly stylized, and the assertion of things that "go without saying" invites the suspicion that these might not be that obvious after all. The statements about *tefillin*, incidentally, look as though they reflect a practice of wearing them at just about any time. This tosefta is (inter alia) instructing those who care to take notice that whatever other Jews are doing, it is improper to wear *tefillin* while naked and to put on *tefillin* while in the presence of naked people.[45] The latter point may be related

---

in *Judaism*, ed. Havivah Pedayah (Beer-Sheva: Ben-Gurion University of the Negev Press, 1996), 24–27 (in Hebrew).

41. Understanding the words *al nafshekhem* in Deut 11:21 to mean "around your neck" would in fact have been consistent with biblical usage of the word *nefesh*; see Jonah 2:6; Prov 3:22; and Ps 69:2.

42. The translation provided here follows the Vienna manuscript. The passage is cast in a somewhat different order in the Erfurt Tosefta ms. and the *editio princeps*, as well as in the Bavli.

43. In *B. Shabbat* 10a, Rashi interpreted *miqra* in this context to refer to *Shema* recital.

44. For the idea that the threefold division of space in this halakah reflects the functions of different rooms in the Roman bathhouse, see Yaron Z. Eliav, "The Roman Bath as a Jewish Institution," *Journal for the Study of Judaism* 31, no. 4 (2000): 429.

45. According to Stefanie Hoss, it is likely that someone wearing nothing but a loin-

to the requirement to utter an attendant blessing,[46] and both clauses are clearly connected to the nexus of holiness and nakedness.[47]

It is interesting to note that the tosefta implies that wearing *tefillin* among naked people in a bathhouse, while clothed oneself, was thought to be a reasonable practice, even in rabbinic circles,[48] and that some non-rabbinic Jews were in the habit of wearing *tefillin* even while naked at the baths. Pagans might well have been engaged in cultic ritual (often associated with healing) at the same baths as frequented by Jews, and this may have encouraged the latter to bring their own rituals to play in the bathhouse setting.[49]

If *tefillin* were viewed as protecting life, as I have claimed, then wearing them at the baths would, of course, have been entirely sensible; demons were widely believed to reside there, and flames, extreme heat, and the potential for slipping posed more mundane dangers.[50] Indeed, *T. Berakhot* 6:17 describes a blessing, to be recited before entering the baths, that expressly mentions the fear of dying there as a result of an accident: "and if God forbid some accident befall me, then may my death be atonement for all my sins,"[51] as well as a blessing on leaving the baths, in which the bather thanks God for having been able to leave *beshalom* (and expresses the wish to return home in similar fashion).

The Indispensability of Individual Ownership

T. Hagigah 1:2

> (A child) once he knows how to look after his *tefillin*—his father buys him *tefillin*.

---

cloth would have been considered naked; for her analysis of nakedness at the baths see Stefanie Hoss, *The Culture of Bathing and the Baths and Thermae in Palestine from the Hasmoneans to the Moslem Conquest* (Oxford: BAR, 2005), 12–13 and 74–76.

46. *T. Berakhot* 6:10.

47. For this characterization, see Michael Satlow, "Jewish Constructions of Nakedness in Late Antiquity," *Journal of Biblical Literature* 116, no. 3 (1997): 429–54. For notions of sanctity and respect, in connection with *tefillin*, see the previous chapter.

48. For the idea that the tosefta would not have entertained *tefillin* wearing while naked people were actually present, and was merely referring to a space where naked people sometimes congregated, see Saul Lieberman, *Tosefta Ki-Fshutah*, 2nd augmented ed. (Jerusalem: Jewish Theological Seminary of America, 1992), 1:26.

49. See Eliav, "The Roman Bath as a Jewish Institution," 430–33.

50. See Katherine Dunbabin, "Baiarum Grata Voluptas—Pleasures and Dangers of the Baths," *Papers of the British School at Rome* 57 (1989): 35–39.

51. A parallel in *Y. Berakhot* 9:4 (14b) refers specifically to burning by fire, damage from hot water, and structural collapse.

M. Arakhin 6:4

> One who sanctifies (all) his possessions (thereby rendering them Temple property) *ma'alin lo et tefillav.*[52]

As discussed in the previous chapter (see pp. 118–19), the above rendering of *T. Hagigah* 1:2 is one of two possibilities, both of which would imply that *tefillin* were treated as amulets when it came to providing them to children. The stress on purchase in this translation makes little sense unless ownership were considered an important feature of practice, as would have been characteristic of amulets in general.[53] In a similar vein the last clause of *M. Arakhin* 6:4 rules that someone who had given everything he owned to the Temple would have been obligated to pay the assessed value of his *tefillin* in lieu of forfeiting them; alternatively, that it was presumed he had intended to exclude *tefillin* from the blanket offering of his effects.[54] In either event, *tefillin* were singled out as the one object for which ownership was indispensable, even for those who had foresworn personal possessions.

The previous mishnah, dealing with a slightly different case, has much the same import.[55]

> Even though they said, "They seize (as a pledge) the possessions of those who undertake to pay their worth (to the Temple treasury)"[56] they give him [that is, leave him with[57]] food for thirty days, and twelve months clothing, a spread bed, his sandals, and his *tefillin.*

Tefillin included no text of a personal nature, unlike many Greco-Roman inscribed amulets as well as later Jewish ones. Nevertheless, it appears inconceivable that an individual might dispense with his personal *tefillin*, whatever the circumstances. The mishnayot in *Arakhin,* like *T. Hagigah* 1:2, strongly suggest a magical function.

---

52. Or, according to the Kaufman manuscript, *ma'alin et tefillav.*

53. See Campbell Bonner, *Studies in Magical Amulets, Chiefly Graeco-Egyptian* (Ann Arbor: University of Michigan Press, 1950), 2.

54. See Hanokh Albeck, *Shishah Sidrei Mishnah, Seder Qodashim* (Jerusalem: Mosad Bi'alik and D'vir, 1959), 209, 404.

55. As does *T. Arakhin* 4:6, which is a parallel to it.

56. See Leviticus 27 for the origins of such an undertaking.

57. See Albeck, *Shishah Sidrei Mishnah, Seder Qodashim,* 208.

The (Short) Story about Tefillin and the Haver's Wife

T. Demai 2:17

> A *haver's* daughter who married an *am ha'arets*, (or) *haver's* wife who mar-
> ried an *am ha'arets*, (or) *haver's* slave who was sold to an *am ha'arets*—
> they maintain their status (of being presumed to fulfill tithing rules)
> until they fall under suspicion (of failing to do so). R. Shimon ben Elazar
> says: They must first affirm (to their practice of tithing). And so would
> R. Shimon ben Lazar say in the name of R. Me'ir: There is a story about
> a woman who married a *haver*, and would bind *tefillin* to his hand.[58]
> (Then) she married a customs collector, and would tie customs seals to
> his hands.[59]

The moral of the closing story is that one must be careful not to presume too much of women, merely because of their prior history. It is told
to justify the view that a woman cannot simply be trusted to continue
tithing practices learned from earlier exposure to the household of a *haver*
(a place where the rabbis deemed such practice to be meticulous).

This story is to be related, from interconnected perspectives, to an
apotropaic function for *tefillin*, and I will differentiate these as (a) the literary, (b) the folkloristic, (c) the philological, and (d) the stereotypical.

a. From a literary standpoint the story has maximum impact if the
    woman is seen as so devoted to her husband's well-being that she
    took charge of ensuring that he was protected (by *tefillin*). Her
    subsequent behavior, superficially similar but now devoted to the
    reviled occupation of her second husband, then becomes all the
    more ironic.

b. Viewed in this light, the story then conforms to standard folkloristic
    patterns.[60] In particular, it shows strong affiliation with the wide-
    spread Matron of Ephesus (Vidua) folktale, wherein extreme devo-
    tion to a husband is followed by fickle behavior upon his death.[61]

---

58. For the idea that the *haver* in the above story was preparing *tefillin* for the use of
others, and that his wife was helping him do so, see Lieberman, *Tosefta Ki-Fshutah*, 1:218.

59. See p. 111 above for my earlier comments on this halakah.

60. A theoretical justification for using this perspective in evaluating such stories is
provided by Galit Hasan-Rokem, "Narratives in Dialogue: A Folk Literary Perspective on
Interreligious Contacts in the Holy Land in Rabbinic Literature of Late Antiquity," in *Sharing the Sacred: Religious Contacts and Conflicts in the Holy Land*, ed. Arieh Kofsky and Guy G.
Stroumsa (Jerusalem: Yad Ben-Zvi, 1998), 109–29.

61. The Matron of Ephesus folktale is classified in secondary literature as Aa-Th Narrative type 1510; see A. Aarne and S. Thompson, *The Types of the Folktale: A Classification and
Bibliography* (Helsinki: Suomalainen Tiedeakatemia, 1961), 430. For an overview of Jewish
stories about female fickleness, including other narrative types, see Haim Schwarzbaum,

In addition, it corresponds to a standard model whereby the folk legend chooses a supposedly "superior" woman (here the wife of a *haver*) to make the point about women's fickleness.[62]

c.   In the Hebrew the possibility of an apotropaic function is made more striking by the word *qoma'at*, rendered above as "bind." The cognate *qame'a* occurs on several occasions in Mishnah and Tosefta, where it means amulet (the etymology being similar to the Greek *periammon/periapton*, connoting tied-on objects).[63] It bears spelling out that this use, suggestive of amuletic practice, would not have been designed to negate the status of *tefillin* as a religious obligation; indeed, it is none other than the devout *haver* who wears them, unlike the customs collector.

d.   Certain apotropaic practices were considered illicit magic,[64] so that the role of the woman in this story may be seen as a stereotypical one. The link between women and magic is a dominant one in rabbinic, including tanna'itic, literature.[65] In addition, as Michael Satlow has pointed out with respect to Palestinian rabbinic stories in general, "real women are not to be found . . . only essentialized Woman."[66]

Encompassed by Mitsvot

T. Berakhot 6:25

There is no man in Israel who is not surrounded by *mitsvot*. The *tefillin* on his head, the *tefillin* on his arm, the *mezuzah* at his entrance and the four *tsitsit* surround him. . . . Going into the bath (house) his circumcision is on his body . . . and it says "The angel of God camps around those who fear him and rescues them [Ps 34:8]."

The proof text is to be understood as referring to the encompassing *mitsvot* of the tosefta's first clause, namely, *tefillin*, *tsitsit*, and *mezuzah*—all

"Female Fickleness in Jewish Folklore," in *Jewish Folklore between East and West*, ed. Eli Yassif (Beer-Sheva: Ben-Gurion University of the Negev Press, 1989), 173–96.

62. See Haim Schwarzbaum, "International Folklore Motifs in Joseph Ibn Zabara's 'Sepher Sha'shu'im,'" in *Studies in Aggadah and Jewish Folklore*, vol. 7, ed. Issachar Ben-Ami and Joseph Dan (Jerusalem: Magnes Press, Hebrew University, 1983), 68.

63. The verb form appears on only one other occasion in the Tosefta (*Kelim Bava Metsi'a* 6:1), where it refers to tying on a sandal, and not at all in the Mishnah.

64. See, for example, *T. Shabbat* 6:1, where tying a red thread on one's finger is categorized as one of the proscribed "Ways of the Emorite."

65. See Michael Satlow, "Fictional Women: A Study in Stereotypes," in *The Talmud Yerushalmi and Graeco-Roman Culture*, vol. 3, ed. Peter Schaefer (Tübingen: Mohr Siebeck, 2002), 227; Yuval Harari, "The Sages and the Occult," in *The Literature of the Sages, Part 2*, ed. S. Safrai et al. (Assen: Royal Van Gorcum and Fortress, 2006).

66. Satlow, "Fictional Women: A Study in Stereotypes," 243.

of these represent God's angel, who rescues their practitioners.[67] In mentioning both *tefillin* and the bathhouse, *T. Berakhot* 6:25 can be seen (in the light of *T. Berakhot* 2:20, discussed above) as pointing to a time when *tefillin* were not worn by rabbinic Jews,[68] and providing reassurance that protection would nevertheless be present, as provided by the circumcised penis.[69]

A parallel to this text, in *Sifre Devarim*, omits the above proof text but alludes to a protective function in a different way: God is compared to a king, who tells his wife to wear all her jewelry so as to be desirable to him.[70] It is in much the same way, states the *Sifre*, that God told Israel, "My children, mark yourselves with *mitsvot* so as to be desirable to me." The word *ratsuy* (rendered here as "desirable") also connotes placation, so that one observing these "jewelry-wearing" commandments looks to be placating God in the process.

It is noteworthy that according to Josephus *tefillin* are worn "so that the favor of God with regard to them (that is, the Jews) may be readily visible from all sides" (*Antiquities* 4:213), an idea that evokes the encompassing *tefillin* of *T. Berakhot* 6:25 and the *Sifre*, as well as the *Sifre*'s assertion that *tefillin* make Israel desirable to God. In view of the work's generally apologetic nature one cannot infer from this brief reference, embedded as it is in a paraphrase of scripture, what Josephus actually thought the function of *tefillin* to be.

Tefillin at the Sea of Reeds

A belief that *tefillin* and *mezuzah* were efficacious in protecting those committed to them is demonstrated in the midrashic version of the parting of the Sea of Reeds. In Exod 14:22, "the water was like a wall for them, at their left and at their right."[71] The *Mekhilta* explains, "He made them a kind of wall at their right and at their left; at their right, that is Torah, and at their left, that is *tefillin*. Another thing [that is, alternatively], at

---

67. It is also to be noted that the named tanna here is R. Me'ir, a figure associated in other sources with mystical speculation. See G. Scholem, *Jewish Gnosticism, Merkabah Mysticism and Talmudic Tradition* (New York: Jewish Theological Seminary of America, 1960), 28.

68. See also F p. 282 lines 1–2 (to Deut 23:15).

69. A tanna'itic belief in the protective power of circumcision is made explicitly in *T. Berakhot* 6:13. See D. Flusser and S. Safrai, "'Who Sanctified the Beloved from the Womb,'" in *Judaism of the Second Temple Period*, ed. Serge Ruzer (Jerusalem: Magnes, 2002), 183–90 (in Hebrew). The rabbis do not seem to have viewed a circumcised penis as a *lack*, partly perhaps because the procedure was seen as reversible. See Nisan Rubin, "The Stretching of the Foreskin and the Enactment of 'Peri'ah,'" *Zion* 54 (1989): 105–17 (in Hebrew).

70. F p. 67 line 12—p. 68 line 7 (to Deut 6:9).

71. The identical words also appear in Exod 14:29.

their right, that is *mezuzah*, at their left, that is *tefillin*."[72] The text suggests that God designed *tefillin* and *mezuzah* (but also for that matter the entire Torah) as protective walls. In a somewhat similar midrash (to Exod 14:29) the sea seems to have a demonic nature,[73] so that the Children of Israel need the protection of *tefillin/mezuzah* from it rather than by it.[74]

Correctness and Efficacy

Extraordinary care was needed to ensure that the *tefillin* ritual was performed correctly. This can be seen, in particular, from references to the correctness of their inscriptions, which can be contrasted with more lenient rules (or the absence of similar rules) for Torah scrolls. Thus, for example, one letter improperly written could render *tefillin/mezuzot* invalid; and while Torah scrolls might be written in Greek, *tefillin* (and *mezuzot*) not only had to be written in Hebrew but also in Aramaic characters only.[75] The latter script was seen as the original Hebrew script in which the Torah had been written,[76] and the requirement for slavish adherence to the original text is comparable to Origen's observation that spells needed to be in their native language in order to be effective (*Contra Celsum* 1.25). According to Bet Hillel, one was required to check *tefillin* every twelve months; opening them to check the integrity of their texts seems the most likely referent.[77] The *Mekhilta* further states that *tefillin* could only be used if written in scriptural sequence.[78]

Prescriptions for how *tefillin* were to be worn, derived from Midreshei Halakah, were discussed in the previous chapter. While the attention to detail reflected there is characteristic of halakah in general, the scope of *tefillin* rulings calls for explanation, particularly if (as is probable) midrash was generally used to support preexisting ritual.[79] Here too it seems quite likely that considerations of efficacy were in play, making it particularly noteworthy that *tefillin* were to be worn on the left arm. Both the Maori

---

72. H-R p. 107 lines 5–6 (to Exod 14:22).

73. For which see Jonathan Z. Smith, "Towards Interpreting Demonic Powers in Hellenistic and Roman Antiquity," in *Aufstieg und Niedergang der römischen Welt* (Berlin: de Gruyter, 1978), 425–39.

74. See H-R p. 111 line 17–p. 112 line 4 (to Exod 14:29).

75. *M. Menahot* 3:7 and *M. Megillah* 1:8.

76. See *T. Sanhedrin* 4:7–8.

77. H-R p. 69 lines 10–13 (to Exod 13:10).

78. H-R p. 74 line 10 (to Exod 13:16).

79. See Epstein, *Introduction to Tannaitic Literature*, 511–12. For a summary of the debate on this issue, see Moshe Halbertal, *Interpretative Revolutions in the Making: Values as Interpretative Considerations in Midrashei Halakhah* (Jerusalem: Magnes Press, Hebrew University, 1997), 14–15 (in Hebrew).

custom of wearing amulets on the left side and the European habit of wearing rings on the left hand have been connected to beliefs regarding the particular weakness/exposure associated with the left side of the body, and its consequent need for protective reinforcement.[80] In addition, the efficacy of the left hand in magical procedures is evident from both the Tosefta and Pliny.[81]

Tanna'itic Disregard for the Magical Function

In general, however, the tanna'im prefer to view the practice of *tefillin* as fulfillment of a *mitsvah*, as was discussed above, rather than the use of magical devices. It is accordingly important to investigate possible tanna'itic reticence regarding a magical function for *tefillin*, which I will argue is only to be expected. I should reiterate, however, that the very use of the word *tefillin* likely signified such a function, so that the reticence may not be as marked as a surface reading would suggest.

In the first place, as will now be demonstrated, tanna'itic theology demonstrates aversion to the idea that mechanical theurgic processes, even when explicitly commanded as such by God, provided protection (much less guaranteed it). The position thus negated was considered problematic, presumably because it might serve to weaken the focus on God's own power, as well as on the need to live a righteous life. Instead, protection was to be seen as flowing from ignoring this aspect of God's commands, and focusing instead on belief in the One who had commanded them. *Mekhilta Derabbi Yishma'el* illustrates this dramatically:[82]

> "And the Lord said unto Moses: 'Make thee a fiery serpent,'" [Num 21:8] etc. Now, could that serpent kill or revive? It merely means this: When Moses did so, the Israelites would look at him [that is, the serpent] and believe in him who commanded Moses to do so; then God would send them healing.

---

80. Robert Hertz, *Death and the Right Hand*, trans. R. and C. Needham (Aberdeen: Cohen & West, 1960), 101.

81. Tosefta *Shabbat* 6:17; Pliny, *Naturalis Historia* 21.83 and 143. See G. Veltri, "The 'Other' Physicians: The Amorites of the Rabbis and the Magi of Pliny," *Korot* 13 (1998–99): 37–54.

82. H-R p. 179 line 19–p. 180 line 4 (to Exod 17:11). There are parallels in *M. Rosh Hashanah* 3:8 and the *Mekhilta Derabbi Shimon bar Yohai*. For a discussion of the difference between the parallels, see Marc Hirshman, "Polemic Literary Units in the Classical Midrashim and Justin Martyr's Dialogue with Trypho," *Jewish Quarterly Review* 83, nos. 3–4 (1993): 373–77. The rendering here is taken from Jacob Z. Lauterbach, *Mekilta De-Rabbi Ishmael* (Philadelphia: Jewish Publication Society, 1933), 2:143–44.

The citation addresses Num 21:4–9, in which God tells Moses to make a serpent and place it on a standard, so that victims of snake bite would survive by virtue of looking at it. According to the *Mekhilta*, however, the copper snake that Moses made was instrumental only because it focused the people's attention on God, who had commanded its manufacture. The tanna'im here valorize a focus on God and his commands, and away from instruments that are merely a part of the material world.[83]

In somewhat similar fashion, tanna'im decry the apotropaic utterance of a divine promise from the Torah. R. Aqiba's list of those who have no share in the world to come, in *M. Sanhedrin* 10:1, includes, "One who whispers over a wound and recites 'any illness that I placed in Egypt I will not place among you, for I am the Lord who heals you.'" Here, focusing on God's promise not only minimizes the importance of living a righteous life, on which the scriptural promise in this verse (Exod 15:26) was contingent, but presumably is a challenge to him as well. Much the same would have been true for any apotropaic procedure associated with a promise made by God, and the challenge would only have been magnified if God had actually commanded the procedure. (If amulets did not work, then perhaps they had not been manufactured with sufficient expertise. There was, however, no such subjective element to the correct performance of *tefillin*, whose details had been commanded.[84]) In addition, while *tefillin* may have been viewed as protective because of the promise implied by Deut 11:21, the rabbis knew well that the larger passage (vv. 13–21) was first and foremost about observing the *mitsvot*; and a focus on the former could only divert attention from the latter.

The above texts seem important for understanding why the tanna'im might have known of, and indeed believed in, a magical function for tefillin, but chose not to highlight it.[85] Mere theurgy, when connected to scripture, was something to be denied.[86] Perhaps, too, there was some anxiety about the Torah being deemed as in any way similar to gentiles' law codes, which some rabbis imagined as codifications of magical practices. (This can be seen from the *Sifra's* comments on Lev 18:3: "And why the teaching

---

83. See David Flusser, *Judaism and the Origins of Christianity* (Jerusalem: Magnes Press, Hebrew University, 1988), 549.

84. See Hezser, *Jewish Literacy in Roman Palestine*, 482.

85. For an interesting discussion in the medieval and early-modern context of Jewish "strategies that enable the mutual coexistence of magic and its limitation," see Avriel Bar-Levav, "Death and the (Blurred) Boundaries of Magic: Strategies of Coexistence," *Kabbalah: Journal for the Study of Jewish Mystical Texts* 7 (2002): 51–64.

86. For negation as a symptom of defense against its opposite, see Sigmund Freud, "Negation," in *The Standard Edition of the Complete Psychological Works of Sigmund Freud*, ed. James Strachey (London: Hogarth Press and Institute of Psycho-Analysis, 1961; reprint, 1995), 235–39. (Freud's translator Strachey acknowledges avoiding the simpler "denial" so as to distinguish between the German words that he rendered as "disavowal" and "negation.")

to say 'And you shall not proceed according to their statutes' [Lev 18:3]?—that you not proceed according to their *nomoi*, according to those things legislated for them. . . . R. Me'ir says, these [that is, these statutes] are the ways of the Emorite, which the sages enumerated."[87] An enumeration of "ways of the Emorite" is provided in *T. Shabbat* 6 and 7, and consists of magical practices.) In short, if I am correct that *tefillin* and *mezuzot* were seen as magical, then the tanna'itic reticence in discussing this function overtly can be viewed as noise rather than signal.

As an alternative position to the above, one might suggest that the tanna'im simply did not believe in the power of protective magic. Clearly, however, this was not the case, as can be demonstrated most usefully here by considering the status of the amulet (*qame'a*).[88] The literature treats the amulet as a part of life in matter-of-fact fashion.[89] They are generally mentioned in the same breath as *tefillin*[90]; presumably the two objects had similar physical characteristics and were subject to similar considerations for the purposes of Shabbat and purity halakot, as both were worn on the body. Both inscribed amulets and ones made of roots were potentially efficacious.[91]

While *M. Shabbat* 6:2 permits transporting amulets from the home on Shabbat, provided they originated with an expert, it demonstrates no such leniency toward transporting *tefillin*.[92] I would suggest that the Mishnah's ruling is best understood in the spirit of its tendency to downplay a magi-

---

87. For a fuller discussion of this passage, see G. Veltri, "Defining Forbidden Foreign Customs: Some Remarks on the Rabbinic Halakhah of Magic" (paper presented at the Eleventh World Congress of Jewish Studies, Jerusalem, 1994); G. Veltri, "The Rabbis and Pliny the Elder: Jewish and Greco Roman Attitudes toward Magic and Empirical Knowledge," *Poetics Today* 19, no. 1 (1998): 66–68.

88. It is, however, beyond the scope of this work to analyze tanna'itic attitudes to magic in detail. For a large, and growing, bibliography on Jewish magic see the following Web sites: http://faculty.washington.edu/snoegel/jmbtoc.htm and http://faculty.biu.ac.il/~barilm/bibmagic.html. The greater part deals with texts that must be considered post-tanna'itic, although there have been studies of the tanna'itic *Darkhei Ha'emori* material. See also Giuseppe Veltri, *Magie und Halakha* (Tübingen: Mohr, 1997); Harari, "The Sages and the Occult," 521–64. For a survey of earlier material, as well as much that may in part be earlier, see Philip S. Alexander, "Incantations and Books of Magic," in *The History of the Jewish People in the Age of Jesus Christ (175 B.C.–A.D. 135) by Emil Schürer, (Revised Version)*, volume 3, part 1, ed. Geza Vermes, Fergus Millar, and Martin Goodman (Edinburgh: T. & T. Clark, 1986), 342–79.

89. See, for example, *M. Shabbat* 8:3 and *M. Miqva'ot* 10:2; and cf. Julius Preuss, *Biblical and Talmudic Medicine*, trans. Fred Rosner (New York: Sanhedrin, 1978), 146–47.

90. See *M. Shabbat* 6:2; *M. Shabbat* 8:3; *M. Shekalim* 3:2; *M. Kelim* 23:1; *M. Mikva'ot* 10:2; *T. Kelim Bava Batra* 2:6, in all of which *tefillin* and *qame'a* are mentioned in the same clause and share the same ruling.

91. See *T. Shabbat* 4:9. The word *qame'a* was ultimately transformed into English as "cameo."

92. See chap. 4 for further discussion of *tefillin* on Shabbat.

cal role for *tefillin*—in the absence of such a function there was every reason to ban carrying them out of the house on Shabbat, much as the performance of other *mitsvot*, such as *shofar, lulav* and *aravah*, did not override the important Shabbat rules governing the transport of such objects.[93]

Against Which Dangers Did *Tefillin* Protect?

Tefillin and *mezuzah* seem to have protected their adherents from a variety of dangers, but no one appears to have addressed these directly. A connection to long life was made in chapter 3, but such an outcome could have been impeded by any number of dangers. Accordingly, it seems best to imagine these items as general-purpose *phylakteria*, whose role would have included protection against the demonic realm.[94] No doubt Jews did believe in demons, with some seeing them as agents of God and others as separate from God, whether in well-defined ways or otherwise.[95] Then, as now, people could readily believe in bad luck without giving much thought to the powers that caused it.

The Significance of When, Where, and by Whom *Tefillin* Were Worn

For the purposes of justifying their halakot regarding the captioned issues, the Mekhiltot employ the verb *nhg* in comparing and contrasting *tefillin* practice with *mezuzah* practice.[96] The usage may be telling, as the word is sometimes best understood, in contexts of ritual power, as connoting effectiveness. Thus, in *Mekhilta Derabbi Shimon bar Yohai*: "If a curse, which is not effective against everyone (*noheget bakol*) . . . then (how much more so) a physical blow, which is effective against everyone."[97] In like manner, a midrashic discussion that connected the effectiveness of the *mezuzah* to the names of God it contained (to be discussed below in further detail) categorized the practice as "*noheget* for day and night and for all generations."

93. See *M. Rosh Hashanah* 4:1; *M. Sukkah* 3:13–14; *M. Sukkah* 4:4–6; and, in addition, *M. Megillah* 1:2.

94. One agent of danger mentioned in the *Mekhilta,* albeit in connection with *mezuzah,* is the destroyer/*mash'hit,* although the reference is to a biblical verse describing the exodus. See H-R p. 39 lines 8–13 (to Exod 12:23).

95. See *M. Sanhedrin* 4:5, which refers to heretics who believe there are multiple powers in heaven.

96. H-R p. 68 line 1–p. 69 line 4 (to Exod 13:9–10); E-M p. 41 line 16–p. 42 line 5 (to Exod 13:10).

97. E-M p. 172 line 2 (to Exod 21:15).

Presuming the shade of meaning suggested by these examples, the implication of the use of *nhg*, in the contrasts made between *mezuzah* and *tefillin* in the Mekhiltot, can be highlighted in tabular form as follows:

Mezuzah alone effective	*Tefillin and Mezuzah effective*	*Tefillin alone effective*
for women (and girls?)	for men	
for infants[98]	for older children	
by night	by day	
		for those at sea/in desert
on festivals and Shabbat		

The last line is anomalous, and will be discussed separately, but the structure of the rest of the table is striking. *Mezuzah* alone was effective for those primarily associated with the home, as well as at nighttime, when people in general were most likely to be found inside the home. (It is noteworthy that both Yerushalmi and Bavli characterize the onset of night, with regard to not wearing *tefillin* then, as the time when footfall ceases at the marketplace.[99]) *Tefillin* were additionally effective, although only by day, for those most likely to be outside the home at that time, namely men and older children. For those at sea or in the desert, who did not have access to a home, *tefillin* alone were effective.

Here it is to be noted that *mezuzot* (as well as *tefillin* and *tsitsit*) were thought of as "surrounding" Israel.[100] One might surmise that women and infants, as well as males and older children (once night fell), would have been considered within the domain of the *mezuzah* more often than not, where there would have been no need for the protective function of *tefillin*. Perhaps for this reason, women and infants typically did not wear them, nor were they typically worn at night; and the rabbis' conceptual framework was simply a schematic mapping of standard practice. Cynthia Baker has observed that "'woman' and 'house' . . . intersect continually and in all manner of configurations in ancient Mediterranean discourses. . . . Even though such stark gender-space dichotomies as those prescribed by Xenophon and Philo—namely, that women belong inside houses and men outside—are strikingly absent from earliest rabbinic discourse, the early Palestinian rabbinic traditions are very much a part of these same cultural and intercultural articulations."[101] She also comments that "the rabbinically imagined woman/wife . . . is not confined *to* the house, but identified and inscribed with it in such a manner that she is

---

98. Defined as a child who does not yet know how to look after *tefillin*.

99. *Y. Eruvin* 10:1 (26a), and *B. Menahot* 36a (the latter is a *baraita*).

100. *T. Shabbat* 6:25 and *Sifre Devarim* to Deut 6:9, discussed earlier.

101. Cynthia Baker, *Rebuilding the House of Israel: Architecture of Gender in Jewish Antiquity* (Stanford: Stanford University Press, 2002), 48–51.

rendered inextricable from it *regardless of where she stands* at any point in time or space."[102]

The blanket exclusion of Shabbat *tefillin* practice can be explained in similar fashion.[103] When at home, surrounded by the *mezuzah*, there would have been little reason for people to wear *tefillin*. Upon leaving the home, however, there would have been an immediate conflict with Shabbat rules, and so the rabbis elected to ban *tefillin* wearing on Shabbat. How, though, could one be sure of God's protection when leaving the domain of the *mezuzah* for the potentially dangerous outdoors (without wearing *tefillin*)?[104] The tanna'im in the Mekhiltot reassuringly explained that Shabbat is an *ot*.[105] The scriptural *ot*, after all, was known to be protective; not only were *tefillin* themselves referred to as an *ot*,[106] but the learned would also have known that the mark of Cain (Gen 4:15) and the rainbow (Gen 9:11–17) had both been characterized explicitly as protective *otot*. R. Yitzhaq observed that unlike *tefillin* Shabbat was not merely an *ot* but also a *brit*.[107] So too, one might have noted, was the rainbow. Not only is Shabbat an *ot*, stated R. Aqiva, but so too are festivals, to which the Shabbat exclusion had been extended.[108]

A New Source for the Magic of *Tefillin*?

A connection between *tefillin* and the promise of long life in Deut 11:21, argued in chapter 3, is absent in the literature under consideration here, but does resurface in amora'ic discussions.[109] It is quite possible, in view of the evidence for this connection both before and after the tanna'itic period, that there was continuity in this regard. Equally, however, it needs to be borne in mind that tanna'itic literature came together in the aftermath of the dislocation engendered by the failure of the Bar Kokhba revolt. Under such circumstances, the promise of the above verse—of long life on the

---

102. Ibid., 76. The italics are hers.

103. See chap. 4 for an earlier discussion of this issue (as well as the exclusion on festivals), which did not, however, address the issue of protection.

104. See *T. Berakhot* 6:16–17 for blessings that included a wish to return home safely, to be recited in a situation where one was away from home.

105. Presumably a reference to Exod 31:13 and/or 31:17. See H-R p. 69 lines 5–10, and E-M p. 41 line 25—p. 42 line 5 (to Exod 13:10).

106. In the understanding that Exod 13:9 and 16 and Deut 6:8 and 11:18 all referred to *tefillin*.

107. Presumably a reference to Exod 31:16. See H-R p. 69 lines 5–7 (to Exod 13:10).

108. E-M p. 42 line 5 (to Exod 13:10).

109. See *B. Menahot* 44a and *B. Ta'anit* 20b (the latter is paralleled in *B. Megillah* 28a).

land pledged to the patriarchs—might have rung hollow, and the magical aspect of *tefillin* may have undergone some transformation.

Mekhilta Derabbi Yishma'el provides an entirely different rationale for the anticipated efficacy. Although the reference deals with *mezuzah*, a link between any magical function for the two objects seems likely a priori, as pointed out earlier, and was confirmed by texts adduced above. It is additionally reinforced by the nature of this novel source for the magic of *mezuzah*, for which the relevant text is as follows:[110]

> "And the Lord will pass over the door" [Exod 12:23]. Behold, by using the method of *qal vahomer*[111] we can reason as follows: With respect to the performance of the blood of the paschal sacrifice in Egypt, the less important—since it was only for the time being, was not effective both by day and by night, and was not effective in subsequent generations—it is said "And he will not suffer the destroyer to come in" [Exod 12:23].

> The *mezuzah*, the more important—since it contains the name of God ten times and is effective for day and night and for all generations—should all the more be the cause of God's not suffering the destroyer to come into our houses.

> But what caused it to be otherwise? Our sins. As it is said: "Our iniquities have turned away these things."[112] And it is also written: "But your iniquities have separated between you and your God, and your sins have hid his face from you, that he will not hear" [Isa 59:2].

Here the *Mekhilta* associates the protective function of the *mezuzah* with the ten names of God that it contains. Had it not been for sin, protection by the *mezuzah* would have been assured, and fully equal, against the (Roman?) "destroyer," to the protection afforded by blood in the biblical narrative.[113] (Although the limits of the *mezuzah* texts are nowhere delineated by the tanna'im, reference is made in *M. Menahot* 3:7 to the two text-sections of the *mezuzah*. There can be little doubt that these refer to Deut 6:4–9 and Deut 11:13–21, the MT passages that contain the instruction to write on the doorpost. There are five names of God in each of these pas-

---

110. The text is to be found in H-R p. 39 lines 8–13 (to Exod 12:23). The translation is based on Lauterbach, *Mekilta De-Rabbi Ishmael*, 1:88–89. I have, however, departed from Lauterbach on the rendering of the verb *nhg*, because, in this context, "to be effective" is superior to his "to be observed/prescribed." The text, after all, is about effectiveness.

111. *A majori ad minus* reasoning.

112. A play on Jer 5:25, which actually states this in the second person, and continues, "and your sins have held back the good from you."

113. See Eva-Maria Jansson, *The Message of a Mitsvah: The Mezuzah in Rabbinic Literature* (Lund: 1999), 45–47.

sages, if one includes both the Tetragrammaton and derivations of the word *elohim*, excluding the one in 11:16 that refers to other gods.)

The power of the name of the Jewish God in this period, even among non-Jews, is well known from the magical papyri and elsewhere.[114] For Jews it would have been at least as significant, reinforced by scriptural references.[115] As *tefillin* contain the same names of God as the *mezuzah*, as well as additional ones from Exod 13:1–16, there is every reason to imagine that they derived similar power from their contained names, arising in particular from these being worn on the body.[116] As far as the tanna'im were concerned, any such power was likely contingent on the absence of sin, for *tefillin* no less than *mezuzah*. It is noteworthy that in *T. Berakhot* 6:25 *tefillin* (as well as other "encompassing" commandments mentioned, including *mezuzah*) resemble a rescuing angel *for those who fear him*. God's protection was considered necessary for dealing with a dangerous world, and might be achieved through some combination of amuletic ritual and righteousness.[117]

114. See Alexander, "Incantations and Books of Magic," 357–61; Betz, *The Greek Magical Papyri in Translation*.

115. For classical treatments, see Ludwig Blau, *Das altjüdische Zauberwesen* (Budapest, 1898), 117–37; E. E. Urbach, *The Sages* (Cambridge Mass.: Harvard University Press, 1975; reprint, 1987), 124–34. For scriptural references, see Jer 10:6; Ps 20:8; Deut 28:10. For more recent studies of the significance of the divine name, see Michael D. Swartz, *Scholastic Magic* (Princeton: Princeton University Press, 1996), 20; Hans-Jürgen Becker, "The Magic of the Name and Palestinian Rabbinic Literature," in *The Talmud Yerushalmi and Graeco-Roman Culture*, vol. 3, ed. Peter Schaefer (Tübingen: Mohr Siebeck, 2002); Naomi Janowitz, *Icons of Power: Ritual Practices in Late Antiquity* (University Park: Pennsylvania State University Press, 2002). The employment of the name was also on occasion disdained by the rabbis; see Samuel Solomon Cohon, "The Name of God, a Study in Rabbinic Theology," *Hebrew Union College Annual* 23,1 (1950–51): 592–98.

116. A citation to this effect appears six times in the Bavli, always as a *baraita* in the name of R. Eli'ezer the Great, an early-second-century figure. The verse from which he derives the power of the name in *tefillin* is Deut 28:10, "And all the nations of the earth shall see that the name of God is read upon you, and they will fear you."

117. There is a possible parallel in the decidedly nonrabbinic Odes of Solomon, one of which includes a description of the dangers of raging rivers, and continues:

> 39:5 But those who cross them in faith shall not be disturbed
>
> . . .
>
> 39:8 Therefore, put on the name of the Most High and know him, and you shall cross without danger; because the rivers shall be obedient to you.

Here, wearing the name seems to be a synonym for having faith, and leads to God's protection. (In Syriac the expression is "wear the name" rather than "put on the name"; see G. Scholem, *Major Trends in Jewish Mysticism* [New York: Schocken, 1946], 368. Syriac is generally believed to be the original language of the *Odes*; see James H. Charlesworth, *Critical Reflections on the Odes of Solomon* [Sheffield: Sheffield Academic Press, 1998], 135.) The reference to protection achieved by wearing God's name, against dangerous waters, is also to be compared to the description of *tefillin* as worn by those who "go to the seas and go to

The ritual power of *mezuzah* and *tefillin*, by the end of our period, thus seems to have inhered in the names of God inscribed on their parchments, in a development that serves as a bridge to one of the most prominent aspects of Jewish magic in late antiquity. As Naomi Janowitz has observed, in the context of other Jewish amuletic practice "Wearing a divine name on one's body both instantiates the divine presence and brings it in direct spatio-temporal contact with the wearer . . . it directly represents the divine presence in a specific location (on a person, in a house)."[118] The destruction of the Temple and the inaccessibility of Jerusalem after the Bar Kokhba revolt could only have augmented the importance of this feature of *tefillin* (and *mezuzah*) ritual, without detracting from its religious significance as biblically ordained *mitsvah*.

---

the deserts" in the *Mekhilta Derabbi Shimon bar Yohai*, as well as to the protective function of *tefillin* at the Sea of Reeds (see above).

The *Odes of Solomon* has been given dates ranging from the late first to the late second century, and its references to gentiles suggest a product of Jewish-Christian circles; see James H. Charlesworth, "Odes of Solomon," in *The Old Testament Pseudepigrapha* (1985), 725–27; Sebastian Brock, "The Odes of Solomon," in *The History of the Jewish People in the Age of Jesus Christ (175 B.C.–A.D. 135) by Emil Schürer, (Revised Version),* volume 3, part 2 (Edinburgh: T. & T. Clark, 1987), 787–89; Michael Lattke, *Die Oden Salomos in ihrer Bedeutung für neues Testament und Gnosis,* vol. 4 (Freiburg: Universitätsverlag Freiburg Schweitz, 1998), 129. The above rendering is taken from Charlesworth, "Odes of Solomon," 768.

118. Janowitz, *Icons of Power,* 102.

Bibliography

Aarne, A., and S. Thompson. *The Types of the Folktale: A Classification and Bibliography.* Helsinki: Suomalainen Tiedeakatemia, 1961.

Abusch, Ra'anan. "Negotiating Difference: Genital Mutilation in Roman Slave Law and the History of the Bar Kokhba Revolt." In *The Bar Kokhba War Reconsidered.* Edited by Peter Schaefer, 71–91. Tübingen: Mohr Siebeck, 2003.

Ackroyd, P. R. "Yad." In *Theological Dictionary of the Old Testament.* Edited by G. J. Botterweck et al. Translated D. E. Green et al. Grand Rapids: Eerdmans, 1986.

Adler, Yonatan. "Identifying Sectarian Characteristics in the Phylacteries from Qumran." *Revue de Qumran* 23, no. 1 (2007): 79–92.

Aharoni, Y. "The Expedition to the Judean Desert, 1960, Expedition B." *Israel Exploration Journal* 11 (1961): 11–24.

Albeck, Hanokh. *Shishah Sidrei Mishnah, Seder Mo'ed.* Jerusalem: Mosad Bi'alik and D'vir, 1958.

———. *Shishah Sidrei Mishnah, Seder Nashim.* Jerusalem: Mosad Bi'alik and D'vir, 1958.

———. *Shishah Sidrei Mishnah, Seder Qodashim.* Jerusalem: Mosad Bi'alik and D'vir, 1959.

Albright, W. F. "A Biblical Fragment from the Maccabaean Age: The Nash Papyrus." *Journal of Biblical Literature* 56 (1937): 145–76.

Alexander, Elizabeth Shanks. "From Whence the Phrase 'Timebound, Positive Commandments'?" *Jewish Quarterly Review* 97, no. 3 (2007): 317–46.

Alexander, Philip S. "Review of *Jesus and Judaism*, by E. P. Sanders." *Journal of Jewish Studies* 37 (1986): 103-6.

———. "Incantations and Books of Magic." In *The History of the Jewish People in the Age of Jesus Christ (175 B.C.–A.D. 135) by Emil Schürer, (Revised Version).* Volume 3, part 1. Edited by Geza Vermes, Fergus Millar, and Martin Goodman, 342–79. Edinburgh: T. & T. Clark, 1986.

———. "Magic and Magical Texts." In *Encyclopedia of the Dead Sea Scrolls.* Edited by Lawrence H. Schiffman and James C. VanderKam. Oxford and New York: Oxford University Press, 2000.

Allison, Dale C. "Matthew." In *The Oxford Bible Commentary.* Edited by John Barton and John Muddiman, 844–86. Oxford: Oxford University Press, 2001.

——— *Matthew.* London: T. & T. Clark, 2004.

Alter, Robert. *The Five Books of Moses.* New York: W. W. Norton, 2004.

Altshuler, David. "On the Classification of Judaic Laws in the Antiquities of Josephus and the Temple Scroll of Qumran." *AJS Review* 7/8 (1982–1983): 1–14.

Assman, Jan. "Magic and Theology in Ancient Egypt." In *Envisioning Magic: A Princeton Seminar and Symposium.* Edited by Peter Schaefer and Hans G. Kippenberg. Leiden: Brill, 1997.

Avigad, N. "The Palaeography of the Dead Sea Scrolls and Related Documents." In *Scripta Hierosolymitana.* Vol. 4. Edited by Chaim Rabin and Yigael Yadin, 58–67. Jerusalem: Magnes Press, Hebrew University, 1958.

Bacher, Wilhelm. *Die exegetische Terminologie der jüdischen Traditionsliteratur,* 1899. Reprint, Darmstadt: Wissenschaftliche Buchgesellschaft, 1965.

———. *Tradition und Tradenten in Schulen Palaestinas und Babyloniens.* Leipzig, 1914.

Baillet, M. "Grotte 8: Phylactère, Mezouza." In *Discoveries in the Judaean Desert of Jordan.* Vol. 3* *(Textes),* 149–61. Oxford: Oxford University Press, 1962.

———. "Nouveaux phylactères de Qumran (XQPhyl 1–4). A propos d'une édition récente." *Revue de Qumran* 7, no. 27 (1970): 403–15.

Baker, Cynthia. *Rebuilding the House of Israel: Architecture of Gender in Jewish Antiquity.* Stanford: Stanford University Press, 2002.

Barb, A. A. "The Survival of Magic Arts." In *The Conflict between Paganism and Christianity in the Fourth Century.* Edited by Arnaldo Momigliano, 100–25. Oxford: Clarendon, 1963.

Barclay, John M. G. *Jews in the Mediterranean Diaspora from Alexander to Trajan.* Edinburgh: T. & T. Clark, 1996.

Bar-Ilan, M. "So Are They to Put My Name Upon the Children of Israel." *Hebrew Union College Annual* 60 (1989): 19–31 (in Hebrew).

Barkay, G. "The Priestly Benediction on Silver Plaques from Ketef Hinnom in Jerusalem." *Tel Aviv* 19 (1992): 139–94.

———. "The Priestly Benediction on the Ketef Hinnom Plaques." *Cathedra* 52 (1989): 37–76 (in Hebrew).

Barkay, G., M. Lundberg, A. Vaughn, and B. Zuckerman. "The Amulets from Ketef Hinnom: A New Edition and Evaluation." *Bulletin of the American Schools of Oriental Research* 334 (2004): 41–71.

Bar-Levav, Avriel. "Death and the (Blurred) Boundaries of Magic: Strategies of Coexistence." *Kabbalah: Journal for the Study of Jewish Mystical Texts* 7 (2002): 51–64.

Barr, James. *Holy Scripture: Canon, Authority, Criticism.* Philadelphia: Westminster, 1983.

Barthélemy, D. "Textes Bibliques, Phylactère." In *Discoveries in the Judaean Desert.* Vol. 1, 72–76. Oxford: Oxford University Press, 1955.

Baumgarten, Albert. "Invented Traditions of the Maccabean Era." In *Geschichte— Tradition—Reflexion.* Vol. 1. *Judentum.* Edited by Peter Schaefer, 197–210. Tübingen: Mohr Siebeck, 1996.

———. "Literacy and the Polemic Concerning Biblical Hermeneutics in the Second Temple Era." In *Education and History: Cultural and Political Contexts.* Edited by Rivka Feldhay and Immanuel Etkes, 33–45. Jerusalem: Zalman Shazar Center for Jewish History, 1999 (in Hebrew).

Becker, Andrea. "Phylakterion." In *Brill's New Pauly (Encyclopedia of the Ancient World).* Leiden: Brill, 2007.

Becker, Hans-Jürgen. "The Magic of the Name and Palestinian Rabbinic Literature." In *The Talmud Yerushalmi and Graeco-Roman Culture*. Vol. 3. Edited by Peter Schaefer, 391–407. Tübingen: Mohr Siebeck, 2002.

Betz, Hans Dieter. *The Greek Magical Papyri in Translation, Including the Demotic Spells*. 2nd ed. Chicago: University of Chicago Press, 1992.

Biblia Hebraica Stuttgartensia. Stuttgart: Deutsche Bibelgesellschaft, 1984.

Bickerman, E. J. *Der Gott der Makkabäer*. Berlin: Schocken, 1937.

Blau, Ludwig. *Das altjüdische Zauberwesen*. Budapest, 1898.

———. "Phylacteries—Historical View." In *The Jewish Encyclopedia*. Vol. 10, 26–28. New York and London: Funk & Wagnalls, 1905.

Boccaccini, Gabriele. *Middle Judaism*. Minneapolis: Fortress, 1991.

Bohak, Gideon. "Hebrew, Hebrew Everywhere?" In *Prayer, Magic and the Stars in the Ancient and Late Antique World*. Edited by S. Noegel, J. Walker, and B. Wheeler, 69–82. University Park: Pennsylvania State University Press, 2003.

———. "A Jewish Myth in Pagan Magic in Late Antiquity." In *Myths in Judaism*. Edited by Ithamar Gruenwald and Moshe Idel, 97–122. Jerusalem: Zalman Shazar Center for Jewish History, 2004 (in Hebrew).

Bonner, Campbell. *Studies in Magical Amulets, Chiefly Graeco-Egyptian*. Ann Arbor: University of Michigan Press, 1950.

Bourriau, J. D., and J. D. Ray. "Brief Communications." *The Journal of Egyptian Archaeology* 61 (1975): 257–58.

Bowman, John. "The History of the Samaritans." *Abr-Nahrain* 18 (1978/79): 101–15.

Braarvig, Jens. "Magic: Reconsidering the Grand Dichotomy." In *The World of Ancient Magic*. Edited by David R. Jordan, Hugo Montgomery, and Einar Thomassen, 21–54. Athens: Norwegian Institute at Athens, 1999.

Brock, Sebastian. "The Odes of Solomon." In *The History of the Jewish People in the Age of Jesus Christ (175 B.C.–A.D. 135) by Emil Schürer, (Revised Version)*. Volume 3, part 2, 787–89. Edinburgh: T. & T. Clark, 1987.

———. "Some Syriac Accounts of the Jewish Sects." In *A Tribute to Arthur Voobus*. Edited by R. H. Fischer, 265–76. Chicago: Lutheran School of Theology at Chicago, 1977.

Brock, Sebastian, and David G. K. Taylor. *The Hidden Pearl: The Syrian Orthodox Church and Its Ancient Aramaic Heritage*. Vol. 3. Rome: Trans World Film, 2001.

Brody, Robert. *The Geonim of Babylonia and the Shaping of Medieval Jewish Culture*. New Haven and London: Yale University Press, 1998.

Brooke, George J. "Deuteronomy 5–6 in the Phylacteries from Qumran Cave 4." In *Emanuel: Studies in Hebrew Bible, Septuagint, and Dead Sea Scrolls in Honor of Emanuel Tov*. Edited by Shalom M. Paul, Robert A. Kraft, Lawrence H. Schiffman, and Weston W. Fields, 57–70. Leiden: Brill, 2003.

———. *Exegesis at Qumran: 4QFlorilegium in Its Jewish Context*. Sheffield: JSOT Press, 1985.

Brown, Peter. *The Body and Society: Men, Women and Sexual Renunciation in Early Christianity*. New York: Columbia University Press, 1988.

———. *The Cult of the Saints: Its Rise and Function in Latin Christianity*. Chicago: University of Chicago Press, 1981.

———. "Sorcery, Demons and the Rise of Christianity: From Late Antiquity into the Middle Ages." In *Witchcraft Confessions and Accusations*. Edited by Mary Douglas, 17–45. London: Tavistock, 1970.

Buckley, J. J. "The Mandaean Appropriation of Jesus' Mother Miriai." *Novum Testamentum* 35, no. 2 (1993): 181–95.

Budge, E. A. W. *Amulets and Talismans*. New Hyde Park: University Books, 1930. Reprint, 1961.

Buechler, A. *Der galilaeische 'Am-ha'Ares des zweiten Jahrhunderts*. Vienna, 1906.

Bultmann, Christoph. "Deuteronomy." In *The Oxford Bible Commentary*. Edited by John Barton and John Muddiman. Oxford: Oxford University Press, 2001.

Burkitt, Francis Crawford, ed. *Evangelion Da-Mepharreshe: The Curetonian Version of the Four Gospels, with the Readings of the Sinai Palimpsest*. Cambridge: Cambridge University Press, 1904.

Caloz, M. "Exode, xiii, 3–16 et son rapport au Deutéronome." *Revue Biblique* 75 (1968): 5–62.

The Cambridge Annotated Study Bible: N.R.S.V. Cambridge: Cambridge University Press, 1993.

Charlesworth, James H. *Critical Reflections on the Odes of Solomon*. Sheffield: Sheffield Academic Press, 1998.

———. "Odes of Solomon." In *The Old Testament Pseudepigrapha*. Volume 2. Edited by James H. Charlesworth, 725–71. Garden City: Doubleday, 1985.

Childs, Brevard S. *Exodus*. London: SCM, 1974.

Christensen, Duane L. *Deuteronomy 1:1–21:9*. Nashville: Thomas Nelson, 2001.

Cohen, Naomi G. "The Elucidation of Philo's Spec. Leg. 4 137–8: 'Stamped Too with Genuine Seals.'" In *Classical Studies in Honor of David Sohlberg*. Edited by R. Katzoff, 153–66. Ramat Gan: Bar-Ilan University Press, 1996.

———. "The Jewish Dimension of Philo's Judaism—An Elucidation of De Spec. Leg. 4 132–150." *Journal of Jewish Studies* 38, no. 2 (1987): 165–86.

———. *Philo Judaeus: His Universe of Discourse*. Frankfurt am Main: Peter Lang, 1995.

Cohen, Shaye J. D. *The Beginnings of Jewishness*. Berkeley: University of California Press, 1999.

———. "The Rabbi in Second-Century Jewish Society." In *Cambridge History of Judaism*, 922–90. Cambridge: Cambridge University Press, 1999.

———. "The Place of the Rabbi in Jewish Society." In *The Galilee in Late Antiquity*. Edited by Lee I. Levine, 157–73. New York: Jewish Theological Seminary of America, 1992.

Cohn, Yehudah. "Rabbenu Tam's Tefillin: An Ancient Tradition or the Product of Medieval Exegesis?" *Jewish Studies Quarterly* 14, no. 4 (2007): 319–27.

Cohon, Samuel Solomon. "The Name of God, a Study in Rabbinic Theology." *Hebrew Union College Annual* 23, no. 1 (1950–51): 579–604.

Collins, John J. "Cult and Culture: The Limits of Hellenization in Judea." In *Hellenism in the Land of Israel*. Edited by John J. Collins and Gregory E. Sterling, 38–61. Notre Dame, Ind.: University of Notre Dame, 2001.

Cook, Stanley A. "A Pre-Masoretic Biblical Papyrus." *Proceedings of the Society of Biblical Archaeology* 25 (1903): 34–56.

Cotton, H. M. "The Rabbis and the Documents." In *Jews in a Graeco-Roman World*. Edited by Martin Goodman, 167–79. Oxford: Clarendon, 1998.

———, and A. Yardeni. "General Introduction." In *Discoveries in the Judaean Desert*. Vol. 27, 1–6. Oxford: Oxford University Press, 1997.

Couroyer, B. "La Tablette du Coeur." *Revue Biblique* 90 (1983): 416–34.

Cowley, A. *Aramaic Papyri of the 5th Century B.C.* Oxford: Clarendon, 1923.

Crawford, Sidnie White. "4QDeut^c." In *Discoveries in the Judaean Desert*. Vol. 14, 15–34. Oxford: Clarendon, 1995.

———. "4QDeut^n." In *Discoveries in the Judaean Desert*. Vol. 14, 117–28. Oxford: Clarendon, 1995.

———. "4QDeut^p." In *Discoveries in the Judaean Desert*. Vol. 14, 135–36. Oxford: Clarendon, 1995.

Crosman, Robert. "Do Readers Make Meaning?" In *The Reader in the Text*. Edited by Susan R. Suleiman and Inge Crosman, 149–64. Princeton: Princeton University Press, 1980.

Daniel-Nataf, Suzanne. "De Specialibus Legibus, Book 4." In *Philo of Alexandria, Writings, Exposition of the Law (Part 2)*. Edited by Suzanne Daniel-Nataf, 127–81. Jerusalem: Bialik Institute, 2000 (in Hebrew).

Darnton, Robert. *The Great Cat Massacre and Other Episodes in French Cultural History*. New York: Vintage Books, 1985.

Davies, W. D., and Dale C. Allison. *The Gospel According to Saint Matthew*. Vol. 1. International Critical Commentary. Edinburgh: T. & T. Clark, 1988.

Day, John. "Foreign Semitic Influence on the Wisdom of Israel and Its Appropriation in the Book of Proverbs." In *Wisdom in Ancient Israel: Essays in Honour of J. A. Emerton*. Edited by John Day, R. P. Gordon, and H. G. M. Williamson. Cambridge: Cambridge University Press, 1995.

de Vaux, R. "Archéologie: historique des découvertes." In *Discoveries in the Judaean Desert*. Vol. 2* (Texte), 3–8. Oxford: Oxford University Press, 1961.

———. "Archéologie: la période Romaine." In *Discoveries in the Judaean Desert*. Vol. 2* (Texte), 29–48. Oxford: Oxford University Press, 1961.

———. "Archéologie: les grottes 7Q à 10Q." In *Discoveries in the Judaean Desert of Jordan*. Vol. 3* (Textes), 27–31. Oxford: Oxford University Press, 1962.

———. "Quelques textes hébreux de Murabba'at: une pièce du phylactère." *Revue Biblique* 60 (1953): 269.

Dein, Simon. *Religion and Healing among the Lubavitch Community in Stamford Hill, North London*. Lewiston: Edwin Mellen, 2004.

Donner, H., and W. Röllig. *Kanaanäische und aramäische Inschriften*. 2 vols. Wiesbaden: Otto Harrassowitz, 1962, 1964.

Doran, Robert. *Temple Propaganda: The Purpose and Character of 2 Maccabees*. Washington, D.C.: Catholic Biblical Association of America, 1981.

Driver, S. R. *A Critical and Exegetical Commentary on Deuteronomy*. 3rd ed. International Critical Commentary. Edinburgh: T. & T. Clark, 1895; 1965 impression.

Drower, E. S. *The Canonical Prayerbook of the Mandaeans*. Leiden: Brill, 1959.

———. *The Mandaeans of Iraq and Iran*. Leiden: Brill, 1962.

Dunbabin, Katherine. "Baiarum Grata Voluptas—Pleasures and Dangers of the Baths." *Papers of the British School at Rome* 57 (1989): 6–46.

Duncan, Julie Ann. "4QDeut^j, 4QDeut^{kl}." In *Discoveries in the Judaean Desert*. Vol. 14, 75–98. Oxford: Clarendon, 1995.

———. "Excerpted Texts of Deuteronomy at Qumran." *Revue de Qumran* 18, no. 69 (1997): 43–62.

Edwards, I. E. S. *Hieratic Papyri in the British Museum, Fourth Series: Oracular Amu-*

letic Decrees of the Late New Kingdom. Vol.1, *Text*. London: Trustees of the British Museum, 1960.

"11QApocryphal Psalms." In *Discoveries in the Judaean Desert*. Vol. 23. Edited by Florentino García Martínez, Eibert J. C. Tigchelaar, and Adam S. van der Woude, 181–205. Oxford: Clarendon, 1998.

"11QUnidentified Wads." In *Discoveries in the Judaean Desert*. Vol. 23. Edited by Florentino García Martínez, Eibert J. C. Tigchelaar, and Adam S. van der Woude, 445–46. Oxford: Clarendon, 1998.

Eliade, Mircea. *Images and Symbols: Studies in Religious Symbolism*. Translated by Philip Mairet. London: Harvill, 1961.

Eliav, Yaron Z. "The Roman Bath as a Jewish Institution." *Journal for the Study of Judaism* 31, no. 4 (2000): 416–54.

Epstein, Ya'akov Nahum Halevi. *Introduction to Tannaitic Literature*. Jerusalem: Magnes Press, Hebrew University, 1957 (in Hebrew).

Eshel, Esther. "4QDeut^n—A Text That Has Undergone Harmonistic Editing." *Hebrew Union College Annual* 62 (1991): 117–54.

———. "Demonology in Palestine During the Second Temple Period." (Ph.D. diss., Hebrew University, 1999 (in Hebrew).

Esler, Philip F. "The Madness of Saul: A Cultural Reading of 1 Samuel 8–31." In *Biblical Studies/Cultural Studies*. Edited by Cheryl J. Exum and Stephen D. Moore, 220–62. Sheffield: Sheffield Academic, 1998.

Evans-Pritchard, E. E. *Witchcraft, Oracles and Magic among the Azande*. Oxford: Clarendon, 1937.

Fagen, Ruth. "Phylacteries." In *Anchor Bible Dictionary*. Edited by David Noel Freedman. New York: Doubleday, 1992.

Falk, D. K. *Daily, Sabbath and Festival Prayers*. Leiden: Brill, 1998.

———. "Prayer in the Qumran Texts." In *The Cambridge History of Judaism*. Vol. 3. Edited by William Horbury, W. D. Davies and John Sturdy, 852–76. Cambridge: Cambridge University Press, 1999.

———. "Qumran Prayer Texts and the Temple." In *Sapiential, Liturgical and Poetical Texts from Qumran*. Edited by D. K. Falk, Florentino García Martínez and Eileen M. Schuller, 106–26. Leiden: Brill, 2000.

Falk, Z. W. "Forms of Testimony." *Vetus Testamentum* 11 (1961): 88–91.

Faraone, Christopher A. "The Agonistic Context of Early Greek Binding Spells." In *Magika Hiera: Ancient Greek Magic and Religion*. Edited by Christopher A. Faraone and Dirk Obbink, 3–32. New York: Oxford University Press, 1991.

———. *Talismans and Trojan Horses: Guardian Statues in Ancient Greek Myth and Ritual*. New York/Oxford: Oxford University Press, 1992.

Feldman, Louis H. *Jew and Gentile in the Ancient World*. Princeton: Princeton University Press, 1993.

———. *Josephus: Judean Antiquities 1–4: Translation and Commentary*. Leiden: Brill, 2000.

Fine, Steven. *Art and Judaism in the Greco-Roman World*. Cambridge: Cambridge University Press, 2005.

Fishbane, Michael. *Biblical Interpretation in Ancient Israel*. Oxford: Oxford University Press, 1985.

———. "The Biblical *Ot*." *Shnaton, An Annual for Biblical and Ancient Near Eastern Studies* 1 (1975): 213–34 (in Hebrew).

Flusser, D., and S. Safrai. "'Who Sanctified the Beloved from the Womb.'" In *Judaism of the Second Temple Period*. Edited by Serge Ruzer, 183–90. Jerusalem: Magnes, 2002 (in Hebrew).

Flusser, David. *Judaism and the Origins of Christianity*. Jerusalem: Magnes Press, Hebrew University, 1988.

Fox, Everett. *The Five Books of Moses*. New York: Schocken, 1995.

Fox, G. George. "The Matthean Misrepresentation of Tephillin." *Journal of Near Eastern Studies* 1 (1942): 373–77.

Fox, Michael V. *Proverbs 1–9*. Anchor Bible. New York: Doubleday, 2000.

———. "The Sign of the Covenant." *Revue Biblique* 81 (1974): 557–96.

Fraenkel, Yonah. *Sippur Ha'aggadah—Ahdut Shel Tokhen Vetzurah*. Tel Aviv: Hakibbutz Hameuchad, 2001 (in Hebrew).

Frankfurter, David. "The Magic of Writing and the Writing of Magic: The Power of the Word in Egyptian and Greek Traditions." *Helios* 21 (1994): 189–221.

———. "Narrating Power: The Theory and Practice of the Magical Historiola in Ritual Spells." In *Ancient Magic and Ritual Power*. Edited by Marvin Meyer and Paul Mirecki. Leiden: Brill, 1995.

Frazer, J. G. *The Golden Bough*. 1st ed. London: Macmillan, 1890.

Freud, Sigmund. "Negation." In *The Standard Edition of the Complete Psychological Works of Sigmund Freud*. Edited by James Strachey, 235–39. London: Hogarth and Institute of Psycho-Analysis, 1961. Reprint, 1995.

Friedman, Shamma. "The Holy Scriptures Defile the Hands—The Transformation of a Biblical Concept in Rabbinic Theology." In *Minhah Le-Nahum*. Edited by Marc Brettler and Michael Fishbane, 117–32. Sheffield: JSOT Press, 1993.

———. *Tosefta Atiqta*. Ramat Gan: Bar-Ilan University Press, 2002 (in Hebrew).

Gager, John G. *Curse Tablets and Binding Spells from the Ancient World*. New York/Oxford: Oxford University Press, 1992.

———. "A New Translation of Ancient Greek and Demotic Papyri, Sometimes Called Magical." *Journal of Religion* 67, no. 1 (1987): 80–86.

Gamberoni, J. "Totapot." In *Theological Dictionary of the Old Testament*. Vol. 5. Edited by H. Ringgren, 319–21. Grand Rapids: Eerdmans, 1986.

Gaster, Moses. "Charms and Amulets (Jewish)." In *Encyclopaedia of Religion and Ethics*. Edited by James Hastings, 451–55. Edinburgh: T. & T. Clark, 1908.

———. "Samaritan Phylacteries and Amulets." In *Studies and Texts*. Volume 1. Edited by Moses Gaster, 387–461. New York: Ktav, 1971 (this section first published 1915–1917).

Geertz, Clifford. *The Interpretation of Cultures*. New York: Basic Books, 1973.

Genot-Bismuth, Jacqueline. "Les Tefilim de Qumran: pour une approche anthropologique." Paper presented at the 10th World Congress of Jewish Studies 1989.

Gilat, Yitzhak. *The Halakhot of R. Eliezer Ben Hyrcanos—A Chapter in the History of the Halakha*. Jerusalem, 1965.

Ginsberg, H. L. "Aramaic Dialect Problems." *The American Journal of Semitic Languages and Literature* 52, no. 2 (1936): 95–103.

Goff, Beatrice L. "The Role of Amulets in Mesopotamian Ritual Texts." *Journal of the Warburg and Courtauld Institutes* 19, nos. 1–2 (1956): 1–39.

Golb, Norman. *Who Wrote the Dead Sea Scrolls?* New York: Scribner, 1995.

Goldberg, Abraham. *Commentary to the Mishna, Shabbat.* Jerusalem: Jewish Theological Seminary of America, 1976 (in Hebrew).

Goldin, Judah. "The Magic of Magic and Superstition." In *Aspects of Religious Propaganda in Judaism and Early Christianity.* Edited by Elisabeth Schüssler Fiorenza, 115–47. Notre Dame, Ind.: University of Notre Dame, 1976.

Goldstein, Jonathan A. *II Maccabees.* Anchor Bible 41A. New York: Doubleday, 1983.

Goode, W. J. "Magic and Religion: A Continuum." *Ethnos* 14 (1949): 172–82.

Goodenough, E. R. *Jewish Symbols in the Graeco-Roman Period.* 12 vols. Princeton: Princeton University Press, 1953–1968.

Goodman, Martin. "Epilogue." In *Hellenism in the Land of Israel.* Edited by John J. Collins and Gregory E. Sterling, 302-5. Notre Dame, Ind.: University of Notre Dame, 2001.

———. "The Function of Minim in Early Rabbinic Judaism." In *Geschichte—Tradition—Reflexion.* Volume 1. Edited by Peter Schaefer, 501–10. Tübingen: Mohr Siebeck, 1996.

———. "Jews and Judaism in the Second Temple Period." In *The Oxford Handbook of Jewish Studies.* Edited by Martin Goodman. Oxford: Oxford University Press, 2002.

———. "Jews, Greeks and Romans." In *Jews in a Graeco-Roman World.* Edited by Martin Goodman, 1–14. Oxford: Clarendon, 1998.

———. "Josephus and Variety in First-Century Judaism." *Proceedings of the Israel Academy of Sciences and Humanities* 7, no. 6 (2000): 201–13.

———. "Sacred Scripture and 'Defiling the Hands.'" *Journal of Theological Studies* n.s. 41, no. 1 (1990): 99–107.

———. *State and Society in Roman Galilee.* Totowa, N.J.: Rowman & Allanheld, 1983. Reprint, 2000.

Goren, Shlomo. "Hatefillin Mimidbar Yehudah Le'or Hahalakhah." In *Torat Hamo'adim*, 496–511. Tel Aviv: Avraham Tzi'oni, 1964 (in Hebrew).

Grabbe, Lester L. *Judaic Religion in the Second Temple Period.* London and New York: Routledge, 2000.

Graf, Fritz. *Magic in the Ancient World.* Cambridge, Mass.; London: Harvard University Press, 1997.

Greenfield, Jonas C. "The Texts from Nahal Se'elim (Wadi Seiyal)." In *The Madrid Qumran Congress.* Edited by Julio Trebolle Barrera and Luis Vegas Montaner, 661–65. Leiden: Brill, 1992.

Gruen, Erich S. *Heritage and Hellenism: The Reinvention of Jewish Tradition.* Berkeley: University of California Press, 1998.

Grünwald, Ithamar. "Hamagiyah Vehamitos—Hamehqar Vehametsi'ut Hahistorit." In *Myth in Judaism.* Edited by Havivah Pedayah, 15–28. Beer-Sheva: Ben-Gurion University of the Negev Press, 1996 (in Hebrew).

Gundry, Robert H. *Matthew: A Commentary on His Literary and Theological Art.* Grand Rapids: Eerdmans, 1982.

Habermann, A. M. "The Phylacteries in Antiquity." *Eretz Israel* 3 (1954): 174–77 (in Hebrew).

Halbertal, Moshe. *Interpretative Revolutions in the Making: Values as Interpretative Considerations in Midrashei Halakhah.* Jerusalem: Magnes Press, Hebrew University, 1997 (Hebrew).

———. *People of the Book: Canon, Meaning and Authority.* Cambridge: Harvard University Press, 1997.

Halivni, D. "Reflections on Classical Jewish Hermeneutics." *Proceedings of the American Academy for Jewish Research* 62 (1996): 19–127.

Hammer, Reuven. "What Did They Bless? A Study of Mishnah Tamid 5:1." *Jewish Quarterly Review* 81, nos. 3–4 (1991): 305–24.

Hammond, Dorothy. "Magic: A Problem in Semantics." *American Anthropologist* 72, no. 6 (1970): 1349–56.

Haran, Menahem. *The Biblical Collection.* Vol. 1. Jerusalem: Bialik Institute, 1996 (in Hebrew).

———. "The Priestly Blessing on Silver Plaques: The Significance of the Discovery at Ketef Hinnom." *Cathedra* 52 (1989): 77–89 (in Hebrew).

Harari, Yuval. "Early Jewish Magic: Methodological and Phenomenological Studies." Ph.D. diss., Hebrew University, 1998 (in Hebrew).

———. "The Sages and the Occult." In *The Literature of the Sages. Part 2.* Edited by S. Safrai, Z. Safrai, J. Schwartz, and P. J. Tomson, 521–64. Assen: Van Gorcum and Fortress, 2006.

———. "What Is a Magical Text? Methodological Reflections Aimed at Defining Early Jewish Magic." In *Officina Magica.* Edited by Shaul Shaked, 91–124. Leiden: Brill, 2005.

Harding, Lankester G. "The Archaeological Finds: Introductory. The Discovery, the Excavation, Minor Finds." In *Discoveries in the Judaean Desert.* Vol. 1, 3–7. Oxford: Oxford University Press, 1955.

Hasan-Rokem, Galit. "Narratives in Dialogue: A Folk Literary Perspective on Interreligious Contacts in the Holy Land in Rabbinic Literature of Late Antiquity." In *Sharing the Sacred: Religious Contacts and Conflicts in the Holy Land.* Edited by Arieh Kofsky and Guy G. Stroumsa, 109–29. Jerusalem: Yad Ben-Zvi, 1998.

Hauptman, Judith. *Rereading the Mishnah.* Tübingen: Mohr Siebeck, 2005.

———. *Rereading the Rabbis: A Woman's Voice.* Boulder/Oxford: Westview Press, 1998.

Heinemann, Isaak. *Philon's griechische und jüdische Bildung.* Breslau, 1932.

Helfmeyer, F. J. "Oth." In *Theological Dictionary of the Old Testament.* Edited by G. J. Botterweck et al. Translated D. E. Green et al. Grand Rapids: Eerdmans, 1977.

Hengel, Martin. *Judaism and Hellenism: Studies in Their Encounter in Palestine During the Early Hellenistic Period.* Translated by John Bowden. 1st English ed. London: SCM, 1974.

———. *Judentum und Hellenismus.* Tübingen: Mohr, 1969.

Hertz, Robert. *Death and the Right Hand.* Translated by R. and C. Needham. Aberdeen: Cohen and West, 1960.

Hezser, Catherine. *Jewish Literacy in Roman Palestine.* Tübingen: Mohr Siebeck, 2001.

———. *The Social Structure of the Rabbinic Movement in Roman Palestine.* Tübingen: Mohr Siebeck, 1997.

Hidary, Richard. "Tolerance for Diversity of Halakhic Practice in the Talmud." Ph.D. diss., New York University, 2008.

Himbaza, Innocent. "Le Décalogue du Papyrus Nash, Philon, 4Qphyl G, 8Qphyl 3 et 4Qmez A." *Revue de Qumran* 20, no. 79 (2002): 411–28.

Himmelfarb, Martha. "The Torah between Athens and Jerusalem: Jewish Difference in Antiquity." In *Ancient Judaism in Its Hellenistic Context*. Edited by Carol Bakhos, 113–29. Leiden/Boston: Brill, 2005.

Hirshman, Marc. "Polemic Literary Units in the Classical Midrashim and Justin Martyr's Dialogue with Trypho." *Jewish Quarterly Review* 83, nos. 3–4 (1993): 369–84.

Hobsbawm, Eric, and Terence Ranger, eds. *The Invention of Tradition*. Cambridge: Cambridge University Press, 1983.

Hoffman, C. A. "Fiat Magia." In *Magic and Ritual in the Ancient World*. Edited by Paul Mirecki and Marvin Meyer, 179–94. Leiden: Brill, 2002.

Hoftijzer, J., and K. Jongeling. *Dictionary of the North-West Semitic Inscriptions*. Vol. 2. Leiden: Brill, 1995.

Honigman, Sylvie. *The Septuagint and Homeric Scholarship in Alexandria: A Study in the Narrative of the Letter of Aristeas*. London: Routledge, 2003.

Horner, Timothy. *Listening to Trypho*. Leuven: Peeters, 2001.

Hoss, Stefanie. *The Culture of Bathing and the Baths and Thermae in Palestine from the Hasmoneans to the Moslem Conquest*. Oxford: BAR, 2005.

Houston, Walter. "Exodus." In *The Oxford Bible Commentary*. Edited by John Barton and John Muddiman. Oxford: Oxford University Press, 2001.

Houtman, Cornelis. *Exodus*. 2 vols. Translated by J. Rebel and S. Woudstra. Kampen: Kok, 1993, 1996.

Hyatt, J. Philip. *Exodus*. Grand Rapids: Eerdmans, 1980.

Idel, Moshe. "On Judaism, Jewish Mysticism and Magic." In *Envisioning Magic*. Edited by Peter Schaefer and Hans G. Kippenberg, 195–214. Leiden: Brill, 1997.

Ilan, Tal. *Jewish Women in Greco-Roman Palestine*. Peabody, Mass.: Hendrickson, 1996.

———. *Mine and Yours Are Hers: Retrieving Women's History from Rabbinic Literature*. Leiden: Brill, 1997.

Isaac, Benjamin. "Roman Religious Policy and the Bar Kokhba War." In *The Bar Kokhba War Reconsidered*. Edited by Peter Schaefer, 37–54. Tübingen: Mohr Siebeck, 2003.

Itzkowitz, Joel B. "Jews, Indians, Phylacteries: Jerome on Matthew 23:5." *Journal of Early Christian Studies* 15, no. 4 (2007): 563–72.

Jacobs, Louis. "Are There Fictitious Baraitot in the Babylonian Talmud?" *Hebrew Union College Annual* 42 (1971): 185–96.

———. "How Much of the Babylonian Talmud Is Pseudepigraphic?" *Journal of Jewish Studies* 28, no. 1 (1977): 45–59.

Janowitz, Naomi. *Icons of Power: Ritual Practices in Late Antiquity*. University Park: Pennsylvania State University Press, 2002.

———. *Magic in the Roman World*. London and New York: Routledge, 2001.

Jansson, Eva-Maria. *The Message of a Mitsvah: The Mezuzah in Rabbinic Literature*. Lund, 1999.

Jauss, Hans Robert. "Literary History as a Challenge to Literary Theory." *New Literary History* 2 (1970–71): 19–37.

Justin Martyr, Dialogue with Trypho the Jew. Translated by David Rokéah. Jerusalem: Hebrew University, Magnes Press, 2004 (in Hebrew).

Kaddari, M. Z. "Ot." In *A Dictionary of Biblical Hebrew.* Ramat Gan: Bar-Ilan University Press, 2006.

Kahana, Menahem. *Hamekhiltot Lepharashat Amaleq.* Jerusalem: Magnes Press, Hebrew University, 1999 (in Hebrew).

———. *Sifre Zuta on Deuteronomy.* Jerusalem: Magnes, 2002.

Keel, Othmar. "Zeichen der Verbundenheit." In *Mélanges Dominique Barthélemy.* Edited by Pierre Casetti, Othmar Keel, and Adrian Schenker, 159–240. Fribourg: Editions Universitaires, 1981.

Kennedy, A. R. S. "Phylacteries." In *A Dictionary of the Bible.* Edited by James Hastings. New York/Edinburgh: Charles Scribner's Sons/T. & T. Clark, 1903.

Kimelman, Reuven. "A Note on Weinfeld's 'Grace after Meals in Qumran.'" *Journal of Biblical Literature* 112, no. 4 (1993): 695–96.

———. "The Shema and the Amidah: Rabbinic Prayer." In *Prayer from Alexander to Constantine.* Edited by Mark Kiley, 108–20. London: Routledge, 1997.

Knibb, Michael A., and Pieter Van der Horst. *Studies on the Testament of Job.* Cambridge: Cambridge University Press, 1989.

Kock, T. *Comicorum Atticorum Fragmenta.* Leipzig: Teubner, 1880–1888.

Kotansky, Roy. *Greek Magical Amulets: The Inscribed Gold, Silver, Copper, and Bronze Lamellae:* Darmstadt: Westdeutscher Verlag, 1994.

———. "Incantations and Prayers for Salvation on Inscribed Greek Amulets." In *Magika Hiera: Ancient Greek Magic and Religion.* Edited by Christopher A. Faraone and Dirk Obbink, 107–37. New York, 1991.

Kraeling, Carl H. *The Excavations at Dura-Europos: The Synagogue.* New Haven: Yale University Press, 1959.

Krochmal, Abraham. *Iyyun Tefillah.* Lemberg, 1885 (in Hebrew).

Kugel, James. *How to Read the Bible.* New York: Free Press, 2007.

Kuhn, K. G. *Phylakterien aus Höhle 4 von Qumran.* Heidelberg: Abhandlungen der heidelberger Akademie der Wissenschaften, Phil.-Hist. Klasse 1, 1957.

Lain-Entralgo, Pedro. *The Therapy of the Word in Classical Antiquity.* Translated by L. J. Rather and John M. Sharp. New Haven and London: Yale University Press, 1970.

Langer, Georg. "Die jüdischen Gebetriemen (Phylakterien)." *Imago* 16, nos. 3–4 (1930): 435–85.

———. "Zur Funktion der jüdischen Türpfostenrolle." *Imago* 14 (1928): 457–68.

Lapin, Hayim. "Early Rabbinic Civil Law and the Literature of the Second Temple Period." *Jewish Studies Quarterly* 2 (1995): 149–83.

Lattke, Michael. *Die Oden Salomos in ihrer Bedeutung für neues Testament und Gnosis.* Vol. 4. Freiburg: Universitätsverlag Freiburg Schweitz, 1998.

Lauterbach, Jacob Z. *Mekilta De-Rabbi Ishmael.* Philadelphia: Jewish Publication Society, 1933.

Lehman, Marjorie. "The Gendered Rhetoric of Sukkah Observance." *Jewish Quarterly Review* 96, no. 3 (2006): 309–35.

Lenhardt, Andreas. "Massekhet Tefillin—Beobachtungen zur literarischen Genese eines kleinen Talmud-Traktates." In *Jewish Studies between the Disciplines.* Edited by K. Herrmann, M. Schlueter, and G. Veltri. Leiden and Boston: Brill, 2003.

Lerner, M. B. "The External Tractates." In *The Literature of the Sages.* Edited by S. Safrai, 367–403. Philadelphia: Fortress, 1987.

Levine, Baruch A. *Numbers 1–20.* Anchor Bible 4. New York: Doubleday, 1993.

Levine, Lee I. *Judaism and Hellenism in Antiquity: Conflict or Confluence.* Seattle and London: University of Washington Press, 1998.

Levy, Jacob. *Chaldäisches Wörterbuch.* Leipzig, 1881.

Lidzbarski, Mark. *Das Johannesbuch der Mandäer.* Giessen: Alfred Töpelmann, 1915.

Lieberman, Saul. *Greek in Jewish Palestine.* New York: Jewish Theological Seminary of America, 1942.

———. "Redifat Dat Yisra'el." In *Sefer Hayovel Likhvod Shalom Baron.* Edited by Saul Lieberman and Arthur Hyman, 213–45. Jerusalem: American Academy for Jewish Research, 1974 (in Hebrew).

———. *Tosefeth Rishonim, Seder Tohoroth.* New York and Jerusalem: Jewish Theological Seminary of America, 1939. Reprint, 1999.

———. *The Tosefta According to Codex Vienna, with Variants from Codices Erfurt, London, Genizah Mss. And Editio Princeps (Venice 1521).* 2nd ed. Jerusalem: Jewish Theological Seminary of America, 1992.

———. *Tosefta Ki-Fshutah.* Vol. 1. 2nd augmented ed. Jerusalem: Jewish Theological Seminary of America, 1992.

———. *Tosefta Ki-Fshutah.* Vol. 3. 2nd ed. Jerusalem: Jewish Theological Seminary of America, 1992.

———. *Tosefta Ki-Fshutah.* Vol. 5. 2nd ed. Jerusalem: Jewish Theological Seminary of America, 1992.

Lieu, Judith M. *Image and Reality: The Jews in the World of the Christians in the Second Century.* Edinburgh: T. & T. Clark, 1996.

Lohfink, N. *Das Hauptgebot. Eine Untersuchung literarischer Einleitungsfragen zu Dtn 5–11.* Rome: Pontifical Biblical Institute, 1963.

Lucian. Vol. 3: *The Lover of Lies.* Translated by A. M. Harmon. Loeb Classic Library. London: Heinemann, 1913.

Luck, Georg. *Arcana Mundi.* Baltimore: Johns Hopkins University Press, 1985.

Lupieri, Edmondo. *The Mandaeans: The Last Gnostics.* Translated by Charles Hindley. Grand Rapids: Eerdmans, 2002.

Luria, B. Z. "Differences of Opinion About the Form of Tefillin." In *The Hasmonean Kings,* 193–202. Israel: Karni, 1985 (in Hebrew).

Mann, Jacob. "Changes in the Divine Service of the Synagogue Due to Religious Persecutions." *Hebrew Union College Annual* 4 (1927): 241–310.

Manson, T. W. *The Sayings of Jesus as Recorded in the Gospels According to St. Matthew and St. Luke.* London: SCM, 1949.

Mantel, Hugo. *The Men of the Great Synagogue.* Israel: Dvir, 1983 (in Hebrew).

Mayes, A. D. H. *Deuteronomy.* Grand Rapids: Eerdmans, 1981.

McCarthy, Carmel. "Moving in from the Margins: Issues of Text and Context in Deuteronomy." In *Congress Volume Basel 2001.* Supplement to Vetus Testamentum. Vol. 92. Edited by A. Lemaire, 109–37. Leiden: Brill, 2002.

McConville, J. G. *Deuteronomy.* Leicester: Apollos, 2002.

McCown, Chester. "The Ephesia Grammata in Popular Belief." *Transactions and Proceedings of the American Philological Association* 54 (1923): 128–40.

Meier, John P. "Matthew, Gospel of." In *Anchor Bible Dictionary*. Vol. 4. Edited by David Noel Freedman, 622–41. New York: Doubleday, 1992.

Milik, J. T. "Le travail d'édition des manuscrits du désert de Juda." In Supplements to Vetus Testamentum 4 (1956): 17–26.

———. "Tefillin, Mezuzot et Targums." In *Discoveries in the Judaean Desert*. Vol. 6, 33–85. Oxford: Oxford University Press, 1977.

———. "Textes de la grotte 5Q: Phylactère." In *Discoveries in the Judaean Desert of Jordan*. Vol. 3* *(Textes)*, 178. Oxford: Oxford University Press, 1962.

———. "Textes littéraires." In *Discoveries in the Judaean Desert*. Vol. 2* *(Texte)*, 80–86. Oxford: Oxford University Press, 1961.

Milikowsky, Chaim. "Reflections on Hand-Washing, Hand-Purity and Holy Scripture in Rabbinical Literature." In *Purity and Holiness*. Edited by M. J. H. M. Poorthuis and J. Schwartz, 149–62. Leiden: Brill, 2000.

Miller, Patrick D. "Apotropaic Imagery in Proverbs 6:20–22." *Journal of Near Eastern Studies* 29 (1970): 129–30.

Miller, Stuart S. *Sages and Commoners in Late-Antique Erez Israel*. Tübingen: Mohr Siebeck, 2006.

Mishnah with the Commentary of Moses Ben Maimon (Judeo-Arabic with Hebrew Translation). Translated by Yosef Kapah. Jerusalem: Mossad Harav Kook, 1963.

Mishnah Zera'im Im Shinuyei Nusha'ot. Vol. 1. Jerusalem: Makhon Hatalmud Hayisre'eli Hashalem, 1971 (in Hebrew).

Moffatt, J. "II Maccabees." In *The Apocrypha and Pseudepigrapha of the Old Testament*. Edited by R. H. Charles. Oxford: Clarendon, 1913.

Momigliano, Arnaldo. *Essays in Ancient and Modern Historiography*. Oxford: Blackwell, 1977.

Montgomery, J. A. *The Samaritans*. Philadelphia: John C. Winston, 1907.

Morgenstern, M., and M. Segal. "XHev/SePhylactery." In *Discoveries in the Judaean Desert*. Vol. 38, 183–91. Oxford: Oxford University Press, 2000.

Morris, Jenny. "The Jewish Philosopher Philo." In *The History of the Jewish People in the Age of Jesus Christ (175 B.C.–A.D. 135) by Emil Schürer, (Revised Version)*. Volume 3, part 2. Edited by Geza Vermes, Fergus Millar, and Martin Goodman, 809–89. Edinburgh: T. & T. Clark, 1987.

Nakman, David. "The Contents and Order of the Biblical Sections in the Tefillin from Qumran and Rabbinic Halakah." *Cathedra* 112 (2004): 19–44 (in Hebrew).

Nanuam, Wassana. "Soldiers Ordered to Wear Luang Poo Jiam Talismans at All Times in Pattani." *Bangkok Post*, January 1, 2008.

Naveh, Joseph. "Script and Inscriptions in Ancient Samaria." In *The Samaritans*. Edited by Ephraim Stern and Hanan Eshel, 372–81. Jerusalem: Yad Ben-Zvi, 2002 (in Hebrew).

Naveh, Joseph, and Shaul Shaked. *Magic Spells and Formulae : Aramaic Incantations of Late Antiquity*. Jerusalem: Magnes Press, Hebrew University, 1993.

Nelson, Richard D. *Deuteronomy*. Louisville: Westminster John Knox, 2002.

Neusner, Jacob. *Development of a Legend: Studies on the Traditions Concerning Yohanan Ben Zakkai*. Leiden: Brill, 1970.

———. "Mr Sanders' Pharisees and Mine: A Response to E. P. Sanders, Jewish Law from Jesus to the Mishnah." *Scottish Journal of Theology* (1991): 73–95.

The New Brown—Driver—Briggs—Gesenius Hebrew and English Lexicon. Peabody, Mass.: Hendrickson, 1979.

Nickelsburg, G. W. E. "Epistle of Aristeas." In *Jewish Writings of the Second Temple Period*. Edited by Michael E. Stone, 75–80. Assen: Van Gorcum, 1984.

Niehoff, Maren R. *Philo on Jewish Identity and Culture*. Tübingen: Mohr Siebeck, 2001.

Nielsen, Eduard. *Deuteronomium*. Tübingen: Mohr Siebeck, 1995.

Nitzan, Bilhah. "The Use of Scriptural Passages in 'Anti-Demonic Hymns' in Qumran and in Jewish Folklore." In *Qumran Prayer and Religious Poetry*, 359–63. Leiden: Brill, 1994.

Noth, Martin. *Exodus*. Translated by J. S. Bowden. London: SCM, 1962.

Ogden, D. "Binding Spells." In *Witchcraft and Magic in Europe: Ancient Greece and Rome*. Edited by B. Ankarloo and S. Clark, 3–90. London: Athlone, 1999.

———. *Magic, Witchcraft, and Ghosts in the Greek and Roman Worlds*. Oxford: Oxford University Press, 2002.

Ong, Walter. *Orality and Literacy*. London: Methuen, 1982.

Oppenheimer, Aharon. *The 'Am Ha-Aretz*. Translated by I. H. Levine. Leiden: Brill, 1977.

Pelletier, André. *Lettre d'Aristée à Philocrate*. Paris: Les éditions du Cerf, 1962.

Peters, Melvin K. H. "Septuagint." In *Anchor Bible Dictionary*. Edited by David Noel Freedman. New York: Doubleday, 1992.

Pfann, Stephen J. "Sites in the Judean Desert Where Texts Have Been Found." In *The Dead Sea Scrolls on Microfiche: Companion Volume*. Edited by Emanuel Tov and Stephen J. Pfann, 109–19. Leiden: Brill, 1993.

Phillips, C. R. "The Sociology of Religious Knowledge in the Roman Empire to A.D. 284." In *Aufstieg und Niedergang der römischen Welt*, 2.16.3. Berlin: de Gruyter, 1986.

Philo. Vol. 8. Translated by F. H. Colson. Loeb Classical Library. London: Heinemann, 1939.

Pope, Marvin H., and Jeffrey H. Tigay. "A Description of Baal, Part 4." *Ugarit-Forschungen* 3 (1971): 124–27.

Porten, Bezalel, and Ada Yardeni. *Textbook of Aramaic Documents from Ancient Egypt*. Vol. 3: *Literature, Accounts, Lists*. Jerusalem: Hebrew University, 1993.

"Prayer Shawls and Phylacteries." In *Pagan Rites in Judaism*. Edited by Theodor Reik. New York: Farrar, Straus, 1964.

Preuss, Julius. *Biblical and Talmudic Medicine*. Translated by Fred Rosner. New York: Sanhedrin, 1978.

Propp, William H. C. *Exodus 1–18*. Anchor Bible 2. New York: Doubleday, 1999.

Purvis, James D. *The Samaritan Pentateuch and the Origin of the Samaritan Sect*. Cambridge, Mass.: Harvard University Press, 1968.

Rabinowitz, Isaac. *A Witness Forever*. Bethesda: CDL, 1993.

Rabinowitz, Louis. "Tefillin." In *Encyclopaedia Judaica*. Jerusalem: Keter, 1972.

Ray, John. "Two Inscribed Objects in the Fitzwilliam Museum, Cambridge." *The Journal of Egyptian Archaeology* 58 (1972): 251–53.

Regev, Eyal. "Non-Priestly Purity and Its Religious Aspects." In *Purity and Holiness*. Edited by M. J. H. M. Poorthuis and J. Schwartz, 223–44. Leiden: Brill, 2000.

Reik, Theodor. "Gebetmantel und Gebetriemen der Juden." *Imago* 16, nos. 3–4 (1930): 389–434.

Reiner, E. "Magic Figurines, Amulets and Talismans." In *Monsters and Demons in the Ancient and Medieval Worlds.* Edited by A. E. Farkas, P. O. Harper, and E. B. Harrison, 27–36. Mainz on Rhine: Philipp von Zabern, 1987.

———. "Plague Amulets and House Blessings." *Journal of Near Eastern Studies* 19 (1960): 148–55.

Rodkinson, Michael L. *History of Amulets, Charms and Talismans.* New York, 1893.

———. *Tefillah Lemosheh.* Pressburg, 1883 (in Hebrew).

Rofé, Alexander. "Deuteronomy 5:28–6:1, Composition and Text in the Light of Deuteronomic Style and Three Tefillin from Qumran." *Henoch* 7 (1985): 1–14.

Rothstein, David. "From Bible to Murabba'at: Studies in the Literary, Textual and Scribal Features of Phylacteries and Mezuzot in Ancient Israel and Early Judaism." Ph.D. diss., UCLA, 1992.

Rovner, Jay. "Rhetorical Strategy and Dialectical Necessity in the Babylonian Talmud: The Case of Kiddushin 34a–35a." *Hebrew Union College Annual* 65 (1994): 177–231.

Rubin, Nisan. "The Stretching of the Foreskin and the Enactment of 'Peri'ah.'" *Zion* 54 (1989): 105–17 (in Hebrew).

Rudolph, Kurt. *Mandaeism.* Leiden: Brill, 1978.

Sadaqa, Avraham and Ratson Sadaqa. *Jewish and Samaritan Version of the Pentateuch.* Israel: Rubin Mass, 1961–64.

Safrai, S. "The Mitzva Obligation of Women in Tannaitic Thought." *Annual of Bar-Ilan University. Studies in Judaica and the Humanities* 26/27 (1995): 227–36 (in Hebrew).

Saldarini, Anthony J. *Matthew's Christian-Jewish Community.* Chicago: University of Chicago Press, 1994.

Sanders, E. P. *Judaism: Practice and Belief 63 B.C.E.–66 C.E.* London: SCM, 1992.

———. *Paul and Palestinian Judaism.* Philadelphia: Fortress, 1977.

Sanders, J. A. *Discoveries in the Judaean Desert of Jordan.* Vol. 4: *The Psalms Scroll of Qumran Cave 11.* Oxford: Clarendon, 1965.

Sanderson, Judith E. "4QExod^d." In *Discoveries in the Judaean Desert.* Vol. 12, 127–28. Oxford: Clarendon, 1994.

———. "4QExod^e." In *Discoveries in the Judaean Desert.* Vol. 12, 129–31. Oxford: Clarendon, 1994.

Sarfatti, G. "Semantics of Mishnaic Hebrew and Interpretation of the Bible by the Tanna'im." *Lesonenu* 30 (1965–66): 29–40.

Sarna, Nahum M. "Exodus, Book of." In *The Anchor Bible Dictionary.* New York: Doubleday, 1992.

Satlow, Michael. "Fictional Women: A Study in Stereotypes." In *The Talmud Yerushalmi and Graeco-Roman Culture.* Vol. 3. Edited by Peter Schaefer, 225–43. Tübingen: Mohr Siebeck, 2002.

———. "Jewish Constructions of Nakedness in Late Antiquity." *Journal of Biblical Literature* 116, no. 3 (1997): 429–54.

Sayce, H., and A. Cowley. "An Aramaic Papyrus of the Ptolemaic Age from Egypt." *Proceedings of the Society of Biblical Archaeology* 29 (1907): 260–72.

Schaefer, Peter. *Der Bar Kokhba-Aufstand: Studien zum zweiten jüdischen Krieg gegen Rom.* Tübingen: Mohr Siebeck, 1981.

———. "Magic and Religion in Ancient Judaism." In *Envisioning Magic*. Edited by Peter Schaefer and Hans G. Kippenberg, 19–43. Leiden: Brill, 1997.

Schaller, B. *Das Testament Hiob*. Gütersloh: Gerd Mohn, 1979.

Schienerl, Peter W. "Der Ursprung und die Entwicklung von Amulettbehaeltnissen in der antiken Welt." *Antike Welt* (1984): 45–54.

———. "A Historical Survey of Tubular Charm-Cases up to the 7th Century A.D." *Ornament* 4, no. 4 (1980): 10–14.

Schiffman, Lawrence H. *The Halakhah at Qumran*. Leiden: Brill, 1975.

———. *Journal of the American Oriental Society* 100, no. 2 (1980): 170–72.

———. "Phylacteries and Mezuzot." In *Encyclopedia of the Dead Sea Scrolls*. Edited by Lawrence H. Schiffman and James C. VanderKam, 675–77. Oxford and New York: Oxford University Press, 2000.

———. *Reclaiming the Dead Sea Scrolls*. Philadelphia: Jewish Publication Society, 1994.

Schneider, Heinrich. "Der Dekalog in den Phylakterien von Qumran." *Biblische Zeitschrift* 3 (1959): 18–31.

Schniedewind, William M. *How the Bible Became a Book*. Cambridge: Cambridge University Press, 2004.

———. *Society and the Promise to David*. New York: Oxford University Press, 1999.

Scholem, G. *Jewish Gnosticism, Merkabah Mysticism and Talmudic Tradition*. New York: Jewish Theological Seminary of America, 1960.

———. *Major Trends in Jewish Mysticism*. New York: Schocken, 1946.

Schorr, Y. H. "Tefillin." *Hehaluts* 5 (1860): 11–26 (in Hebrew).

Schremer, Adiel. "'[T]He[Y] Did Not Read in the Sealed Book': Qumran Halakhic Revolution and the Emergence of Torah Study in Second Temple Judaism." In *Historical Perspectives: From the Hasmoneans to Bar Kokhba in Light of the Dead Sea Scrolls*. Edited by D. Goodblatt, A. Pinnick, and D. R. Schwartz, 105–26. Leiden: Brill, 2001.

Schürer, Emil. *Geschichte des jüdischen Volkes im Zeitalter Jesu Christi*. 4th ed. Leipzig, 1901–1909.

Schwartz, D. R. *The Second Book of Maccabees*. Jerusalem: Yad Ben-Zvi, 2004.

Schwartz, Seth. "Historiography on the 'Talmudic Period'." In *The Oxford Handbook of Jewish Studies*. Edited by Martin Goodman, 79–114. Oxford: Oxford University Press, 2002.

———. *Imperialism and Jewish Society, 200 B.C.E.–640 C.E.* Princeton: Princeton University Press, 2001.

Schwarzbaum, Haim. "Female Fickleness in Jewish Folklore." In *Jewish Folklore between East and West*. Edited by Eli Yassif, 173–96. Beer-Sheva: Ben-Gurion University of the Negev Press, 1989.

———. "International Folklore Motifs in Joseph Ibn Zabara's 'Sepher Sha'shu'im.'" In *Studies in Aggadah and Jewish Folklore*. Vol. 7. Edited by Issachar Ben-Ami and Joseph Dan, 55–81. Jerusalem: Magnes Press, Hebrew University, 1983.

Segal, Alan F. "Hellenistic Magic—Some Questions of Definition." In *Studies in Gnosticism and Hellenistic Religions*. Edited by R. Van den Broek and M. J. Vermaseren, 349–75. Leiden: Brill, 1981.

Seidel, Jonathan Lee. "Studies in Ancient Jewish Magic." Ph.D. diss., University of California at Berkeley, 1996.

Shaked, Shaul. "Form and Purpose in Aramaic Spells: Some Jewish Themes." In *Officina Magica*. Edited by Shaul Shaked, 1–30. Leiden: Brill, 2005.

Shochat, Azriel. "Haskalah." In *Encyclopaedia Judaica*. Jerusalem: Keter, 1972.

Shutt, R. J. H. "Letter of Aristeas." In *The Old Testament Pseudepigrapha.* Volume 2. Edited by James H. Charlesworth, 7–34. Garden City: Doubleday, 1985.

Sigal, Phillip. "An Inquiry into Aspects of Judaism in Justin's Dialogue with Trypho." *Abr-Nahrain* 18 (1978/79): 74–100.

Sirat, Colette. *Les papyrus en caractères hébraïques trouvés en Égypte.* Paris: Centre National de la Récherche Scientifique, 1985.

Skehan, Patrick W., and Eugene Ulrich. "4QDeut[q]." In *Discoveries in the Judaean Desert.* Vol. 14, 137–42. Oxford: Clarendon, 1995.

Smith, Jonathan Z. "Birth Upside Down or Right Side Up?" *History of Religions* 9 (1970): 281–303.

———. "Here, There and Anywhere." In *Relating Religion,* 323–39. Chicago: University of Chicago Press, 2004.

———. "Towards Interpreting Demonic Powers in Hellenistic and Roman Antiquity." In *Aufstieg und Niedergang der römischen Welt,* 425–39. Berlin: Gruyter, 1978.

Sodano, A. R., ed. *Porphry, Epistula ad Anebonem.* Naples, 1958.

Sonnet, Jean-Pierre. *The Book within the Book: Writing in Deuteronomy.* Leiden: Brill, 1997.

Speiser, E. A. "Palil and Congeners: A Sampling of Apotropaic Symbols." In *Studies in Honor of Benno Landsberger,* 389–93. Chicago: University of Chicago Press, 1965.

———. "TWTPT." *Jewish Quarterly Review* 48 (1957–58): 208–17.

Sperber, Daniel. *Material Culture in Eretz-Israel During the Talmudic Period.* Jerusalem: Yad Izhak Ben-Zvi Press/Bar-Ilan University Press, 1993 (in Hebrew).

Spiro, Solomon J. "Who Was the Haber?" *Journal for the Study of Judaism* 11, no. 2 (1980): 186–216.

Spittler, R. P. "The Testament of Job: A History of Research and Interpretation." In *Studies on the Testament of Job.* Edited by Pieter Van der Horst, 7–32. Cambridge: Cambridge University Press, 1989.

Stander, H. F. "Amulets and the Church Fathers." *Ekklesiastikos Pharos* 75, no. 2 (1993): 55–66.

Stegemann, Hartmut. "Hinweis auf eine uneditierte Handschrift aus Höhle 4Q mit Exzerpten aus dem Deuteronomium." *Revue de Qumran* 6, no. 22 (1967): 217–27.

———, and Jürgen Becker. "Zum Text von Fragment 5 aus Wadi Murabba'at." *Revue de Qumran* 3, no. 11 (1961): 443–48.

Stern, Sacha. "Attribution and Authorship in the Babylonian Talmud." *Journal of Jewish Studies* 45 (1994): 28–51.

Strack, H. L., and Günter Stemberger. *Introduction to the Talmud and Midrash.* Translated by Marcus Bockmuehl. Minneapolis: Fortress, 1996.

Strack, Hermann L., and Paul Billerbeck. "Die Tephillin (Gebetsriemen)." In *Kommentar zum neuen Testament aus Talmud und Midrasch.* Vol. 4, part 1, 250–76. Munich: C. H. Beck'sche, 1928.

Styers, R. *Making Magic: Religion, Magic and Science in the Modern World.* Oxford: Oxford University Press, 2004.

Suleiman, Susan R. "Introduction: Varieties of Audience-Oriented Criticism." In *The Reader in the Text.* Edited by Susan R. Suleiman and Inge Crosman, 3–45. Princeton: Princeton University Press, 1980.

Sussmann, Yaakov. "The History of Halakha and the Dead Sea Scrolls—Preliminary Observations on Miqsat Ma'se Ha-Torah (4qmmt)." *Tarbiz* 59, nos. 1–2 (1989/90): 11–76 (in Hebrew).

———. "Torah Shebe'al Peh, Peshutah Kemashma'ah." In *Mehqerei Talmud*. Vol. 3, *part 1*. Edited by Yaakov Sussmann and David Rosenthal, 209–384. Jerusalem: Hebrew University, Magnes Press, 2005 (in Hebrew).

Swartz, Michael D. *Scholastic Magic*. Princeton: Princeton University Press, 1996.

Tal, Abraham. *The Samaritan Pentateuch*. Tel Aviv: Tel Aviv University, 1994.

Talmon, S. "The 'Manual of Benedictions; of the Sect of the Judaean Desert." *Revue de Qumran* 2, no. 8 (1960): 475–500.

Tambiah, S. J. "Form and Meaning of Magical Acts: A Point of View." In *Modes of Thought; Essays on Thinking in Western and Non-Western Societies*. Edited by edited by Robin Horton and Ruth Finnegan., 199–229. London: Faber, 1973.

Tanakh: A New Translation. Philadelphia and Jerusalem: Jewish Publication Society, 1985.

Tcherikover, Victor. *Hellenistic Civilization and the Jews*. Philadelphia/Jerusalem: Jewish Publication Society of America/Magnes Press, 1959.

Thorndike, L. *History of Magic and Experimental Science*. Vol. 1. New York: Macmillan, 1923.

Thornhill, R. "The Testament of Job." In *The Apocryphal Old Testament*. Edited by H. F. D. Sparks, 617–48. Oxford: Clarendon, 1984.

Tigay, Jeffrey H. *The JPS Torah Commentary: Deuteronomy*. Philadelphia: Jewish Publication Society, 1996.

———. "On the Meaning of T(W)TPT." *Journal of Biblical Literature* 101 (1982): 321–31.

———. "On the Term Phylacteries (Matt 23:5)." *Harvard Theological Review* 72, nos. 1–2 (1979): 45–53.

———. "Tefillin." In *Encyclopaedia Biblica*. Vol. 8, 883–95. Jerusalem: Mosad Bi'alik, 1982 (in Hebrew).

Tov, Emanuel. "Categorized List of the 'Biblical Texts': Appendix—Phylacteries (Tefillin) and Mezuzot." In *Discoveries in the Judaean Desert*. Vol. 39, 182–83. Oxford: Oxford University Press, 2002.

———. *Scribal Practices and Approaches Reflected in the Texts Found in the Judaean Desert*. Leiden: Brill, 2004.

———. "Tefillin of Different Origin from Qumran?" In *A Light for Jacob: Studies in the Bible and the Dead Sea Scrolls in Memory of Jacob Shalom Licht*. Edited by Y. Hoffman and F. H. Polak, 44–54. Jerusalem: Bialik Institute and Tel Aviv University, 1997.

Trevor-Roper, Hugh. "The Invention of Tradition: The Highland Tradition of Scotland." In *The Invention of Tradition*. Edited by Eric Hobsbawm and Terence Ranger, 15–41. Cambridge: Cambridge University Press, 1983.

Tur-Sinai, N. H. "*Otot* in the Bible and in the Lachish Letters." In *J. N. Epstein Jubilee Volume*, 49–57. Jerusalem: Magnes Press, Hebrew University, 1950 (in Hebrew).

Ullmann-Margalit, Edna. *Out of the Cave: A Philosophical Inquiry into the Dead Sea Scrolls Research*. Cambridge: Harvard University Press, 2006.

Urbach, E. E. "The Role of the Ten Commandments in Jewish Worship." In *The Ten Commandments in History and Tradition*. Edited by Ben-Zion Segal and Gershon Levi, 161–89. Jerusalem: Magnes Press, Hebrew University, 1985.

———. *The Sages.* Cambridge Mass.: Harvard University Press, 1975. Reprint, 1987.

Van der Horst, Pieter. "Images of Women in the Testament of Job." In *Studies on the Testament of Job.* Edited by Michael A. Knibb and Pieter Van der Horst, 93–116. Cambridge: Cambridge University Press, 1989.

van der Toorn, Karel. *Family Religion in Babylonia, Syria and Israel.* Leiden: Brill, 1996.

van der Woude, Adam S. "Fifty Years of Qumran Research." In *The Dead Sea Scrolls after Fifty Years.* Vol. 1. Edited by Peter W. Flint and James C. VanderKam, 1–45. Leiden: Brill, 1998.

Veltri, Giuseppe. "Defining Forbidden Foreign Customs: Some Remarks on the Rabbinic Halakhah of Magic." Paper presented at the Eleventh World Congress of Jewish Studies, Jerusalem 1994.

———. *Magie und Halakha.* Tübingen: Mohr, 1997.

———. "The "Other" Physicians: The Amorites of the Rabbis and the Magi of Pliny." *Korot* 13 (1998–99): 37–54.

———. "The Rabbis and Pliny the Elder: Jewish and Greco Roman Attitudes toward Magic and Empirical Knowledge." *Poetics Today* 19, no. 1 (1998): 63–89.

Vermes, Geza. "Pre-Mishnaic Jewish Worship and the Phylacteries from the Dead Sea." *Vetus Testamentum* 9 (1959): 65–72.

———, and Fergus Millar. *The History of the Jewish People in the Age of Jesus Christ (175 B.C.–A.D. 135) by Emil Schürer, (Revised Version). Volume 1.* Edinburgh: T. & T. Clark, 1973.

———, and Fergus Millar. *The History of the Jewish People in the Age of Jesus Christ (175 B.C.–A.D. 135) by Emil Schürer, (Revised Version). Volume 2.* Edinburgh: T. & T. Clark, 1979.

———, Fergus Millar, and Martin Goodman, eds. *The History of the Jewish People in the Age of Jesus Christ (175 B.C.–A.D. 135) by Emil Schürer, (Revised Version). Volume 3, part 1.* Edinburgh: T. & T. Clark, 1986.

Versnel, Henk S. "Some Reflections on the Relationship Magic-Religion." *Numen* 38, no. 2 (1991): 177–97.

Von Gall, A. F. *Der hebräische Pentateuch der Samaritaner.* Giessen: Alfred Töpelmann, 1918.

Weinfeld, Moshe. *The Decalogue and the Recitation of "Shema": The Development of the Confessions.* Tel Aviv: Hakibbutz Hameuchad, 2001 (in Hebrew).

———. *Deuteronomy 1–11.* Anchor Bible 5. New York: Doubleday, 1991.

———. *Deuteronomy and the Deuteronomic School.* Oxford: Oxford University Press, 1972.

———. "Grace after Meals in Qumran." *Journal of Biblical Literature* 111, no. 3 (1992): 427–40.

———. "Deuteronomy, Book of." In *The Anchor Bible Dictionary.* New York: Doubleday, 1992.

Weis, P. R. "Some Samaritanisms of Justin Martyr." *Journal of Theological Studies* 45 (1944): 199–205.

Wevers, J. W. *Notes on the Greek Text of Deuteronomy.* Atlanta: Scholars Press, 1995.

———. *Notes on the Greek Text of Exodus.* Atlanta: Scholars Press, 1990.

———. *Septuaginta, Deuteronomium.* Göttingen: Vandenhoeck & Ruprecht, 1977.

———. *Septuaginta, Exodus.* Göttingen: Vandenhoeck & Ruprecht, 1991.

Williams, A. Lukyn. *Justin Martyr: The Dialogue with Trypho*. London: Macmillan, 1930.

Wittgenstein, Ludwig. *Philosophical Investigations. Part 1*. Translated by G. E. M. Anscombe. Oxford: Basil Blackwell, 1953.

Wuensch, R. *Defixionum Tabellae Atticae*. Berlin, 1897.

Würthwein, Ernst. *The Text of the Old Testament: An Introduction to the Biblia Hebraica*. 2nd ed. Grand Rapids: Eerdmans, 1995.

Yadin, Azzan. "A Greek Witness to the Semantic Shift "Lqh"—"Buy."" *Hebrew Studies* 43 (2002): 31–37.

Yadin, Yigael. "Tefillin (Phylacteries) from Qumran (XQPhyl 1–4)." *Eretz Israel* 9 (1969): 60–83 (in Hebrew).

———. *Tefillin from Qumran (XQPhyl 1–4)*. Jerusalem: Israel Exploration Society and Shrine of the Book, 1970.

Yardeni, Ada. "Remarks on the Priestly Blessing on Two Ancient Amulets from Jerusalem." *Vetus Testamentum* 41 (1991): 176–85.

Zahavy, Tzvee. "Political and Social Dimensions in the Formation of Early Jewish Prayer: The Case of the Shema." Paper presented at the Tenth World Conference of Jewish Studies, Jerusalem 1989.

Zahn, Molly M. "Remember This Day : Grounding Law in Narrative through Redactional Composition (Exod 13:1–16)." M.Phil. diss., University of Oxford, 2003.

Zakovitch, Yair. *And You Shall Tell Your Son. . . .* Jerusalem: Magnes Press, Hebrew University, 1991.

Index of Passages

Index of Subjects